SHEILA

Portrait of an Unknown Artist through the Eyes of her Daughter

A Memoir by

TERESA THORNHILL

Published by Dornberger Books 2026,
www.teresathornhill.com

A catalogue record of this book is available
from the British Library.
ISBN 978-1-0369-6723-9

A selection of Sheila Denning's art work
can be seen at www.sheiladenning.com
Images of Sheila Denning's work are reproduced
from photographs by Nigel Noyes.

Book design by Erica Smith, wordsmithdesign.co.uk
Printed and bound in Britain by Scan-Tech, scantechprint.co.uk

In memory
of Sheila

Contents

List of art works & photographs

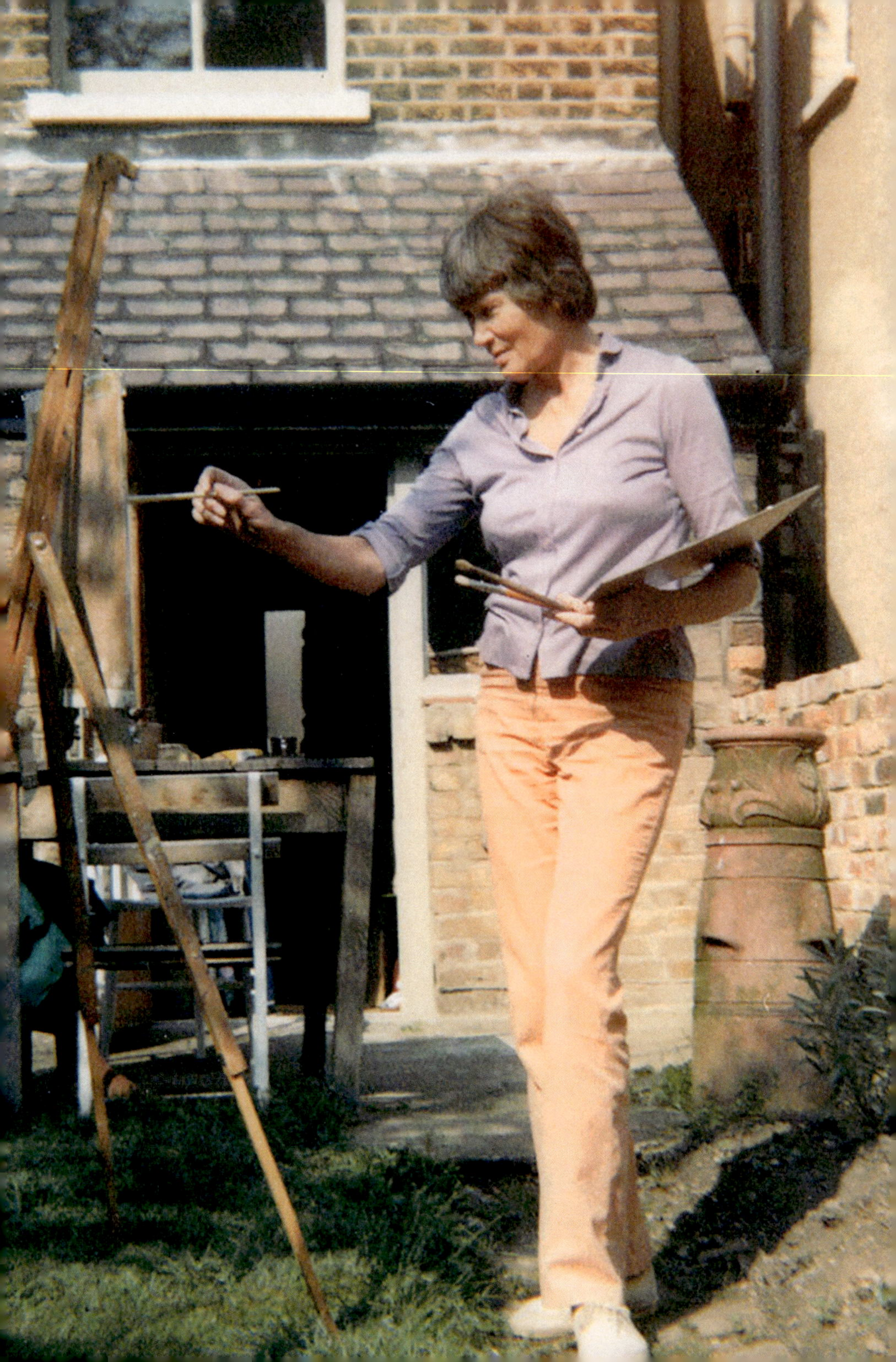

Introduction

SHEILA DENNING (1920–2015), my mother, was one of many twentieth century women artists whose work wasn't recognised by the British art establishment. Some were eclipsed by the limelight shone on the work of their artist husbands by an establishment which saw art as a male preserve. Others, after several productive years at art school, became overwhelmed by the demands of marriage and motherhood. Yet other women worked away doggedly but were insufficiently confident, or insufficiently pushy, to demand the attention they deserved.

Sheila falls into the latter two categories. The grief she carried from her wartime experiences drove her into an unhappy marriage which would overshadow her life for two decades. My sculptor father pursued his creative work with such single-mindedness that most domestic tasks and most parenting fell to Sheila. After many years of barely painting at all, Sheila left him, set up her easel and produced her most powerful portraits; but she wasn't successful in getting her work exhibited in London. I too am a painter and it was the strength of those portraits that motivated me to write this book.

When Sheila and I discussed the idea of my writing about her, two years before her death, she was clear she didn't want me to write about her marriage. The subject still caused her pain and she was unable to shake off a sense of shame that she hadn't been able to 'make things work'. I agreed to Sheila's terms; but five years later, when I started writing, I discovered that I couldn't disentangle the story of my mother's life as a painter from the story of her personal life, beginning with her childhood, the war years, marriage and motherhood.

As to my presence in the narrative, I didn't think about it during those early conversations with Sheila; but once I began writing, it became clear that I wasn't going to produce a conventional, third person biography. The book is best described as a memoir, in which the focus switches between Sheila the painter, Sheila the woman carrying deep wounds from her war-time losses, Sheila's struggle to leave a toxic marriage *and* the intense mother-daughter relationship which formed between the two of us. I narrate childhood memories of struggling to support the mother I adored, and whose collapse I feared. I don't hide the rage I often felt towards my father for what I perceived as his ill-treatment of her; and I reveal the views I formed as an adult, through the latter years of my parents' lives.

PART ONE

MAY 2015

I was sitting beside Dad's hospital bed, on an uncomfortable office chair with castors. The bed stood like a throne in the centre of his former studio at Ivy Cottage, with the headrest raised to maximum height. Afternoon light streamed in from the garden, filtered through foliage at the five windows set into the thick stone walls; a fire smouldered in the grate, under the marble mantelpiece. If you have the misfortune to be bed-ridden, there could be no lovelier setting in which to pass your time.

Propped on pillows, Dad was gazing at a painting which hung on the wall beside the door. At 93 he still had a strong, angular bone structure, accentuated by the Afghan wool hat he wore to help retain his fragile body heat. The painting was of a copper mug containing shocking-pink dahlias, positioned in the centre of an old pine table. A shaft of light fell across the uneven boards, giving them a rust-coloured tinge.

'Isn't it ravishing?' Dad murmured, his voice aquiver.

Taken aback, I glanced from the bumpy line of his Roman nose to the painting. I wasn't used to hearing Dad say nice things about my mother's work. 'Yes,' I replied. I preferred her portraits to her still life work, but I wasn't going to argue with an unexpected compliment. Less than three months had elapsed since her death and it surprised me that some of Mum's work had already found its way onto Dad's wall. That must be down to my sister Anna. Had Dad asked for the painting, or had she simply brought it over and hung it up?

'Sheila was such a great painter,' he went on. 'Don't you think so?' He threw me one of his challenging glances, although the fire in his eyes was cooler than the furnace I remembered from his younger days, which stirred both love and fear in those around him. The look meant

something like 'Disagree with me if you dare, but you'll need a damn good reason!'

I returned his gaze, wondering what had prompted this sudden re-appraisal of Mum's talent and skill. 'Of course she was,' I replied. Anna and I had spent the past fortnight going through a hundred of her paintings, one by one. In addition to the work we knew, we'd found paintings we'd never seen before: landscapes, portraits of strangers and self portraits made at art school in the late 1940s, from which a younger version of the woman we'd loved gazed at the viewer with a look of raw uncertainty. Mum's height and good looks were no surprise: her beauty had lasted well into her eighties. We knew she'd worked as a fashion model to pay her art school fees: we'd seen the photos of her in chic dresses with shoulder pads and pinched waist, hair permed, skin pale, lips red. But the vulnerability apparent in the early self portraits was something new. I'd always thought her rough times had begun later, after she met and married Dad.

Dad's gaze had returned to the dahlias. 'Look at the way she's got the light falling across the brass mug, onto the table!' He lifted his gnarled white fingers from the blanket which covered his chest and interlaced them with characteristic force. His muscles were wasting as he lay in bed and his clayworker's hands were shrinking, but the gesture was an old, familiar one. He let out a sigh. 'She was a much greater artist than I ever was.'

Astonished, I wondered if I'd heard him right. Acknowledgement of Mum's worth as an artist was something Dad had never managed, much as he'd rarely acknowledged her worth as a human being. I'd heard him admit that she'd been a good mother, but that was a realm where he hadn't sought to compete. 'Is that really what you think?' I said at last.

'Oh yes,' he replied, without hesitation. 'She was a fine painter, a very, very fine painter'.

I reeled for days after that conversation. I felt triumphant that at last Dad had recognised Mum's ability, but at the same time I was outraged that he'd waited till after her death to do so. His admiration would have meant a lot to Mum, and he must have known it. I wanted to phone her up and tell her what he'd said; I wanted to sit beside her on her old white sofa, with a cup of tea apiece, and recount how the conversation had come about. I would have so loved to see the look on her face.

For lengthy tranches of my adult life, I'd felt unsafe in Dad's presence and chosen not to see him, whereas Mum and I had always been close. It was only because I missed her that I was visiting him now: he was one of very few people still alive who'd known her well enough that we could have a meaningful conversation about her. That was partly due to the fact that, after she left London, Mum had lived an increasingly reclusive life; but also because, by the time she died, aged 95, most of her close friends had already departed.

Even now I didn't find it easy to sit with Dad: being in his presence triggered feelings and memories I'd rather shut out.

Throughout my childhood, Dad had prioritized his creative life over everything else: wife, children, money, home. Even before they separated, Mum's life had been that of a lone parent: Dad was so preoccupied with his career as a sculptor that everything else had fallen to her. Perhaps if she hadn't been an artist, too, it would have seemed less unfair. And perhaps if he'd made money from his work and treated Mum with love and respect, I'd have felt more forgiving. But Dad's work didn't sell and his affairs made her life hell. We lived precariously in the shadow of Mum's grief, dressed in cast-offs from Dad's affluent Oxford friends, driving around in a Hillman van that was barely road-worthy and eating more than our share of potatoes.

Pleased though I was with Dad's admission that Mum had been a better artist than him, I told myself that his judgment of her didn't make any difference to mine. I knew she'd been a fine painter. I'd been with her all along, watching her struggle to get her work shown. I'd sat with her at the kitchen table when I was as young as seven, watching her submit work to group exhibitions: The Royal Society of Portrait Painters, The Contemporary Portrait Society, the Royal Academy Summer Exhibition… Occasionally a painting was accepted, but most of the time the response was a rejection slip and a curt note asking her to collect her work. Every time it happened, I witnessed how the experience knocked her confidence. She could have done with another adult to tell her to keep going, to suggest that the selection panel were biased towards men, or artists they knew personally – or simply blind; but all she had was me, her mother and a small group of friends.

About two years before her death, when Mum was already thin and frail, we sat down together and went through an album of photos of her portraits. I'd not looked at her work in years and the quality of some of it astonished me. These were brave, honest paintings, in which you felt she'd looked deeply into the face of the sitter. The result was unsentimental, often unsmiling. She had a knack of depicting the tension between a person's inner world and their outer persona. And the quality of the paint itself was rich, oily and generous, so that gazing at a portrait was like eating a delicious meal.

As I looked through the album, it dawned on me that even I had failed to give Mum's work the appreciation it was due. Perhaps, unwittingly, I'd absorbed the indifference of the art establishment, which even in the nineteen sixties and seventies had little time for women painters. Probably, although I hated to admit it, I'd been influenced by Dad's lack of interest in what Mum did.

The next time we met I suggested that, one day in the future, after she was gone, I might write about her life as a painter. Mum stared at me with a look of suppressed pleasure, even as she asked me how I'd ever find the time. 'Don't burden yourself, T,' she murmured. 'You've got enough to do without taking that on.'

She was right, of course: I was a lone mum, a part time lawyer and a writer. But the idea took hold in me. Over the next few weeks, I engineered some long conversations about her experiences at school and art college, and made detailed notes. It might be years before I had the time to use them, but I knew I'd kick myself if I hadn't asked the questions while I had the chance.

Mum died in 2015. In the months that followed, I was too upset to write more than small fragments about her. Three years went by until, in the autumn of 2018, I felt the time was right. My son had just left home for a gap year adventure, leaving me bereft but with the time and space I needed to embark on a new project. Dad was ninety six by now, still in his own home, attended by a posse of devoted live-in carers. I'd recently cut my legal work to a bare two days a week, which meant less money but plenty of time. It was late September and the leaves on the trees in the woods near my home were curling up like aged, arthritic hands and turning gold. The days were sunny but the nights were cold. On my first free morning, I lit the woodburner in my writing shed at the bottom of the garden, propped one of Mum's larger paintings on the desk and stood back to study it.

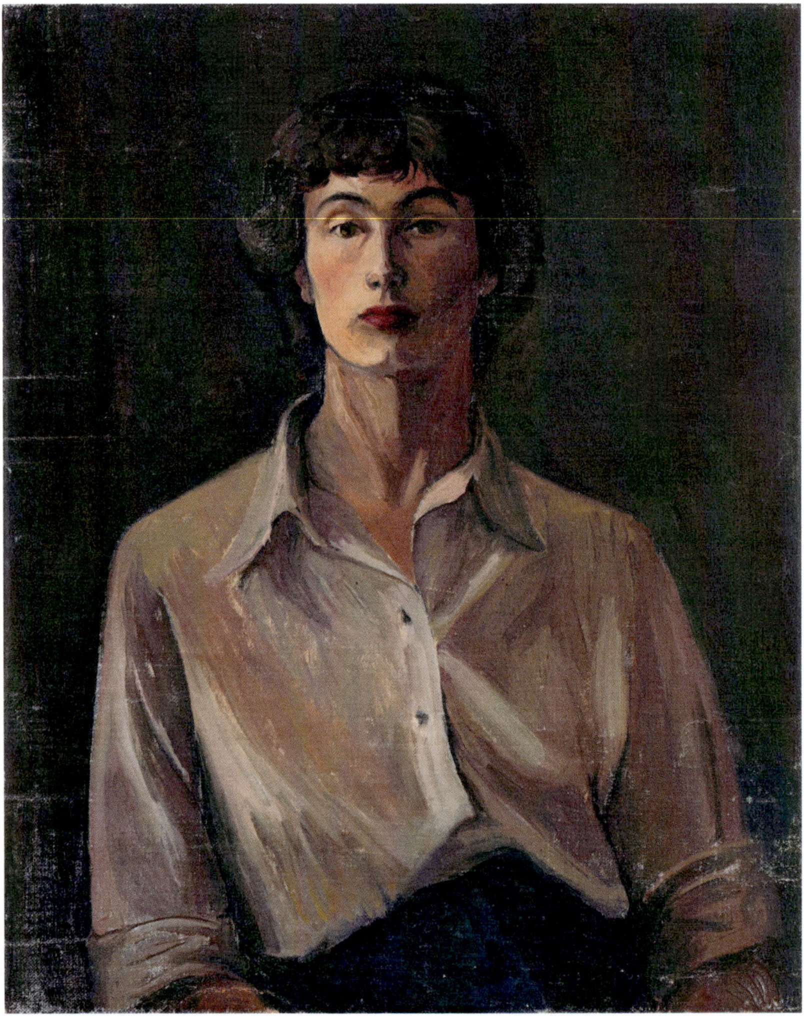

Self Portrait in Browns, c. 1946

CHAPTER 1
Self Portrait in Browns

THE WORK I WAS LOOKING AT was a near life size figure painting which Mum had never shown to us when she was alive. Here was a young woman – head, shoulders and torso to the hips – standing tall and upright against a drab, green-brown wall. Much of her form was in shadow; the small amount of light entering the penumbra lit only the right side of her hair, face and neck. The dark wall behind the figure, the shadow on the left side of the face and a shapeless man's shirt over an even darker skirt combined to give the painting a sombre feel.

The likeness to Mum was unmistakable. Here were her high cheekbones, arched eyebrows, amber eyes, small nose and pretty mouth – coloured with a lavish quantity of dark red lipstick.

I examined the painting closely, sensing it had a lot to tell me. Mum stood very straight against the wall, her shoulders squared, head pulled back, staring out at the world. Her gaze was confident, almost to the point of defiance, but the deadpan look in her eyes disturbed me.

She cast her gaze towards the viewer and her eyes almost met mine. But at the last moment, she threw up a wall, so that for all the boldness of her stance, her impressive height and remarkable beauty, it was apparent that the inner woman was far away, remote, unwilling to reveal herself. Initially I read her expression as one of disillusion, bordering on disgust with life; but as I looked more closely, I glimpsed profound sorrow; and a sorrow that must be kept under wraps, hence the straight back and square shoulders.

Sheila must have made this portrait in the aftermath of World War II. The year was perhaps 1947, when she was 27 years old –

very much younger than the mother I loved, who was 37 when I was born. But despite her unfamiliar youthfulness, I knew I was looking at the big, strong person I'd depended on for so many years. I chided her silently for the way she'd painted her neck, making it too wide and muscly. The shoulders were also an inch too broad, and reminded me of her bizarre conviction that her real life shoulders were square and 'mannish'. Sheila was six foot tall, but her shoulders were shapely and in proportion to the rest of her. The breadth they appeared to have in the painting was due in part to the voluminous shirt, with its stiff collar open at the neck and its loose sleeves rolled up to the elbow. Why did she dress like that to paint herself, I wondered? To keep the oil paint off her real clothes, which were underneath? Although, from the way it draped and folded, the beige fabric of the shirt could be silk. I liked the way she'd caught the pale tones where the light fell on the collar and the dark shadows where her arms rested against the sides of her body. And she hadn't tried to hide the fact that under that shapeless shirt she had a large, womanly bosom. As a small child my moments of deepest comfort were when she wrapped her long arms around me and I nestled my head against her.

Now my eyes returned to the face; and for the second time I was struck by the sadness in Sheila's guarded gaze. What produced that, I asked myself, in 1947? Several years would pass before she met my father; and she'd always described her childhood as happy. What had happened, by her mid-twenties, to cause her so much pain?

My thoughts drifted to the hot day in June 1981 which Mum and I spent in Sparta in Greece. After decades of financial stricture, when travel had been out of the question, Mum had inherited some money and taken me and my sister on a fortnight's holiday. We flew to Athens, accompanied by Mum's friend Veronica, and stayed in a rented apartment on the coast, near Nafplion. I was 24 and had just done my finals.

On the day we went to Sparta, Mum and I got up early and tiptoed out, leaving Anna and Veronica to sleep. On the first bus we found seats, but when we changed to a second, it was crowded with middle aged Greeks with bags of shopping and we had to stand, clinging to an overhead rail. At nine in the morning the silver was already touching twenty six degrees. Sweat ran down between my shoulder blades as I stood in my shorts, braced against the rail, watching Mum closely for signs of heat fatigue.

When the driver tackled a series of sharp bends at the entrance to a village, our hips lurched against the shoulders of the seated passengers. Given what I saw as Mum's venerable age of 61, I thought somebody should offer her a seat; but she looked ten years younger than she was, and nobody did. Her cheeks were turning pink and beads of perspiration appeared on her forehead; for all that, I'd never seen her looking better than she did today. With her height, fine cheekbones and dark hair, she was something of a goddess.

She was wearing a full-length sundress she'd made for the holiday from a length of patterned cotton. It was little more than a sack and my sister and I, both competent dressmakers, had winced when we first saw it laid out on her bed. We were mildly appalled at the way she'd used a length of red ribbon to gather the sack at one end and suspend it from her shoulders; but when she put it on, we had to admit that the fabric's miniature orange and red flowers looked good against her swiftly bronzing neck and shoulders. We could see Mum was pleased with her handiwork and we loved her too much to do other than congratulate her, exchanging knowing glances as we did so.

For several years now, Mum had studied modern Greek at evening classes and read her way through the ancient Greek playwrights in translation. Her excitement at being in the Peleponnese, with her daughters, her friend and enough money to wander where she chose, was a pleasure to witness; especially for me, who'd seen her struggling with poverty, intellectual frustration and social isolation for much of my life. She loved the sun; she loved the snatches of conversation she was exchanging hourly with friendly strangers; and the ancient sites fascinated her.

After a particularly sharp bend, Mum struggled to right herself and I reached out my hand to steady her. Through the window I glimpsed a dazzling white light which bounced off the walls of the village houses, turning the surface of the road to silver.

'I'm fine,' she insisted, tightening her grip on the overhead rail and fanning herself with the bus timetable. 'We'll be there soon. How about *you*?'

That was typical: if anyone expressed concern for her, she would immediately turn it back on them.

'I'm fine too,' I lied. If I didn't drink some water soon I was likely to pass out; but I wasn't going to tell her.

'There's not a huge amount to see in Sparta,' Mum remarked a moment later. 'Much of the ancient city was destroyed...'

'Good,' I replied. 'It's too hot for a gigantic site.' We'd been to Epidavros a few days earlier, with my sister. After a couple of hours exploring the amphitheatre I'd felt desperate to get back to Nafplion and plunge into the sea. My offer to accompany Mum to Sparta today had been motivated less by a desire to see more ruins, than by a wish to have her to myself for a few hours.

Now I watched as her gaze wandered to the face of an old man seated on the far side of the bus. Her glances were subtle, not long enough for him to feel intruded upon; but I knew what she was doing. As far as I could tell, the man was alone; he sat with heavily veined hands neatly folded over the top of a wooden staff, which rested on the floor between his feet. The prominent, ball-like shape of his skull was visible through his fine, translucent skin. Thick white eyebrows contrasted with the mottled browns, pinks and blues of his forehead. He had a large, weathered nose; pale, watery eyes and sagging cheeks. A look of doubt played about his mouth, as if he felt vulnerable riding on a bus towards a city.

Mum looked away and caught my eye. A moment later, very slowly, she delivered one of her subtle but insistent winks. There was no need for words. I, too, would have liked to draw the old man.

At last we were in Sparta. A wall of warm air hit us as we climbed out of the bus and walked slowly across the city street, blinking in the bright light of mid morning. Diesel fumes mixed with cigarette smoke and the smell of rotting meat.

'A cold drink?' Mum asked. 'You're very pale.'

I nodded weakly, wondering if I was about to get one of those thumping headaches which are my body's usual reaction to an excess of heat. Mum was much better in the sun than I was. I slung my little backpack over my shoulder and slipped my arm through hers.

After we'd drunk a bottle of Fanta each in a café and a glass of cold water, Mum asked the man behind the bar for directions to the ruins. He was short and broad-shouldered, with dark, wiry hair and an angular jaw. I watched as he rested his smouldering cigarette in an ashtray and listened to Mum's Greek with a look of approval. Then he picked up a scrap of paper and drew a little map with a pencil. Finally he beckoned to her to follow him to the door and pointed down the street, reeling off a series of instructions.

'*Endaxi*?' (Okay?) he asked at last.

'*Endaxi*!' She replied, smiling in delight. '*Evaristo poli!*'

It was noon by the time we reached the site, after stopping to buy bread, feta and olives.

We made our way into a grassy area where leafy saplings grew in gaps between giant blocks of rock. Unlike at Epidavros there was no fence, no ticket kiosk, and only two other tourists. We moved slowly, aware of the sun scorching the backs of our necks through the brims of our sunhats. Mum made for a place where several boulders formed a line. A fig tree spread its branches over the highest one, creating a patch of shade just large enough for the two of us to sit side by side.

We ate the whole loaf of bread between us, perched on the mercifully cold stone, our legs dangling over the edge, tearing off the sesame-coated segments, ripping them open and stuffing the soft centre with lumps of feta. As we chewed, our eyes wandered from the green-glazed fingers of the fig leaves to the intense cobalt of the sky, the ancient grey-green blocks and broken archways and the cadmium yellow wildflowers. Crickets whirred in the long grass all around us; a lizard darted out of a hole, quivered and vanished; the blinding sun hung static in the midday sky and in the distance the city traffic rumbled on. When the bread was gone we started on the little bag of wrinkled black olives, sucking the oil off our fingers and hurling the stones into the buttercups.

'I dreamt about Gaga last night,' I told Mum. It was nearly three years since my grandmother had died and I'd lost count of how many times she'd appeared to me in the night. 'I went to her house and she was there, just like before.'

Mum glanced at me. 'Was it nice to see her?'

'Kind of. I felt bad, because we all thought she was dead, but actually she wasn't.'

'Mm. I've had one or two dreams like that; they say it's a normal part of grieving.'

We sat in silence for a while. Then I asked, 'Do you miss her?'

Mum's gaze rested on a clump of tiny blue anemones. 'Yes, and no. Of course I do, at times; it's hard to lose your last surviving parent.' She shook the crumbs from the paper the bread had been wrapped in and began to fold it. 'Dear old Gaga. I miss her, but I also feel relieved! Now she's gone, I've got my freedom back, I can travel. We wouldn't be sitting here now, in this beautiful place, if she was still with us…' Mum stretched out her darkly tanned left arm and gestured at the site. The gold wedding band which she'd never removed flashed in the sunlight and I wondered, for the umpteenth time, why she didn't go to a jewellers and get it cut off. Could it be that, eight years post divorce, she was still burning a candle for Dad?

'How about you, darling,' Mum asked, 'd'you miss Gaga?'

'I think I do.' I brushed the crumbs off my shorts and shifted into a squatting position as we lapsed into silence. I found it strange that Mum could speak almost casually now about her mother, although I knew she'd felt burdened by having to live every minute of her life with Gaga in mind. She'd needed the money, too, which Gaga had left her. It had allowed her to move back to London, after thirteen years in Sussex.

A large bee hummed over a purple thistle at the foot of our block. When I saw Gaga in dreams she was a frail, pale-skinned figure staggering towards me with an anxious expression in her eyes. I felt she was trying to tell me something, but I couldn't understand what it was. I would wake up with a sense of guilt as if, by not grasping her meaning, I was letting her down.

Our patch of shade was shrinking. I shifted further back beneath the fig tree, propped myself against the trunk and stared at Mum. She was seated at an angle to me, surveying the ruins with a thoughtful look. A tabby cat with a long tail padded its way towards her in the heat, negotiating the cratered surface of the rock. Mum picked up the last few morsels of feta and held them out on her fingertips, making coaxing noises with her lips. Wherever she went, I reflected, there was always a cat who saw her coming and wanted her to stroke it. Soon she was rubbing the back of the tabby's head with one hand, while it ate the feta from the other.

What was it, I wondered, about Mum and cats? When we lived in Sussex during my teens, she'd often complained that our cats were a 'tie', and a 'nuisance,' while treating them like royalty. No tinned food for Pussy and Tinky – my short-haired tabby and her long-haired black daughter, who belonged to my sister. Instead, every two or three days, Mum downed her paintbrushes and walked to the butcher's to buy them fresh offal.

On Sunday afternoons, Mum used to sit on the sofa in our small living room, with a cup of tea, stroking Pussy's head as she tried to read *The Guardian*. Pussy would be curled up beside her in the shape of a horse chestnut, purring softly with a beatific smile on her black lips and pink nose. If I sat down beside them, Mum would caution me to be careful not to squash Pussy. I didn't exactly feel jealous; but sometimes a little indignant. Would *I* squash Pussy? *Really?*

I mused on this as I sat watching Mum feed feta to the tabby. It was a thin, mangy creature and gobbled it up as if that were its first meal of the day. Could Mum's consideration for cats – and especially our cats, both of whom had now passed on, have had something to do with the fact that nobody, bar Gaga, had been particularly considerate to her? I was thinking of the years when we lived in Chichester in West Sussex. My sister and I were going through the self-centred phase of adolescence and Dad, far away in London, took Mum's role as primary carer of his children for granted. Pussy was a motherly creature, and it struck me now that by being kind to Pussy, Mum had been modelling how she herself would have liked to be treated.

Like most cats, ours had remarkable powers of telepathy. When we came back from a weekend in London, they would be waiting as we drove into the street. Pussy sat perched on the gatepost with her white paws neatly pressed together and her green eyes trained on Mum, while Tinky, slightly more aloof, lounged in a flowerbed, flattening Mum's helibores against the soil. As we got out of the car, Pussy would stand up, arch her back, wave her long tail in the air and stretch her nose towards Mum, to greet her with a kiss.

In the little 1930s house which was our home in those days, my favourite room was Mum's studio. She said a studio had to have northern light, which meant she got the front room, and the smaller room at the back of the house became our sitting room. We didn't question this: it had an open fire and was cosy in winter.

Even when Mum wasn't painting, an atmosphere of deep concentration lingered in the air of the studio, enhanced by the ever-present smell of turpentine. When I arrived home from school in the afternoons, if the house was quiet I pushed open the studio door and inhaled deeply. This was my coming home smell, the one that told me I was back in the place where I belonged, in the painterly world which all but ceased to exist when I was at school. Sometimes Mum would be seated at an easel on the far side of the room with a paint-stained rag lying on her lap, squinting at a canvas with half closed eyes; but mostly by the time I got home she'd finished for the day and was standing by the electric kettle in the kitchen, waiting for it to boil. If the studio was empty, I'd tiptoe over to the plan chest to look at her big wooden palette, on which shiny slicks of colour lay waiting to be used. I liked the flat shapes Mum's palette knife left in the paint.

At the end of each day, Mum turned her big wooden easel to face the wall. This was partly so that passing neighbours couldn't see her work, but also to reduce the risk of dust sticking to the wet paint. I glanced at the back of the canvas, tiptoed out and joined her in the kitchen. No matter how skint we were, she always managed to provide something sweet to eat when we got in from school, and I was always hungry.

Having lived in London, my sister and I found Chichester a claustrophobic place in which to spend our teens. The thing that made it bearable was the proximity of the South Downs, ten minutes' drive up the road. Mum took us up there a couple of times a week. She'd park our rusting car at the bottom of Chalkpit Lane, just beyond Lavant village, and we'd walk up the long white chalk track leading to the Trundle. Anna and I didn't always feel like a walk after a long day at school, but once we smelled the damp, chalky air in autumn or the dry, warm air in summer, we resigned ourselves to the effort and begrudgingly enjoyed it.

I was fascinated by the chalk. It reflected whatever light was in the sky, dazzlingly white on a clear day, with pale grey shadows; a creamy magnolia when the sky was overcast. I loved the fact that you could pick up a piece and draw with it. As a surface it was pleasant to walk on, not too hard, with plenty of loose fragments to kick in front of you; and when I fell behind Mum and Anna, I liked to watch the clouds of white dust billowing around their ankles. In summer, cow parsley and Alexanders grew on the banks to either side of the track, interspersed with nettles, purple thistles and clumps of lavender-tinted scabious. And to either side the sheep-cropped land rolled away in a broad, grassy meadow.

When Anna turned eighteen she went to live with Dad in London. From then on it was just Mum and me taking walks on the Downs. By now I was in full rebellion mode, mildly anorexic and frostily silent much of the time; but from time to time, I'd let down my guard and there'd be moments of meaningful conversation. On a Sunday afternoon in the October of my 'A' level year, we walked through a remote valley near Singleton, under a glowering grey sky. We were crossing a field of winter wheat on a footpath when I turned to Mum and asked her, straight out, if she wouldn't like a new man in her life.

I'd long been wondering why Mum hadn't found herself a boyfriend. It was eleven years since she and Dad had first separated, when I was six, and a year since their much-delayed divorce had finally come through.

Mum gave me a funny look and quickened her pace. 'All the men I meet are married.'

'So?' My teenage style was blunt and uncompromising.

'I'm not going to have an affair with a married man.' She twirled the key ring with the car keys on it round her middle finger.

'But why not? Everybody else does.' At seventeen I'd seen enough to be cynical about how married adults treated each other.

'No. I'm not prepared to put another woman through what I went through.' Mum's usually melodic contralto voice deepened noticeably, until it was almost gruff. 'Definitely not.'

I stared at her. 'So… have you had a married man after you?'

Now she stopped in her tracks and looked me in the eye.

'Yes, if you must know.' Behind her, a cool wind rippled through the small, green shoots. 'It's happened twice in the last year.'

'Really?' I was suddenly impressed, not least by the fact that she'd kept the matter secret up to now. But not surprised: at 54, Mum looked much younger than she was.

'One of my students made a pass at me last summer. And then there was' – she met my gaze, then stopped herself and looked away. 'Well, never you mind who. In London.'

'*Really*?' Now I grinned at her. 'Well done, Mum, bravo!' I felt a surge of pride. So there *were* men out there who saw the beauty and wit of my remarkable mother.

Mum giggled. 'That's very sweet of you, darling, but the only 'bravo' is for the fact I turned them down.'

'But did you really have to?' I persisted. 'Maybe their marriages were falling apart?'

'No.' Mum pulled her shoulders back and gazed at the horizon. 'I'm not going to be the one to finish off some poor woman's marriage, whether or not it's on the rocks. Men will always tell you their marriage is in trouble, even if they've no intention of leaving their wives. "Oh poor me, my wife doesn't understand me…"' She mimicked a tone of masculine self pity. 'I've heard it so many times! No way. I'm not going to be a fool.'

That conversation came back to me as I sat on our boulder in Sparta, watching Mum stroke the tabby cat. Then an unsettling thought popped into my head. Maybe now, after all these years of solitude, Mum *would* find herself a man. She was free as a bird these days, with neither mother, nor daughters, nor even cats to weigh her down. What if a man who was genuinely available should cross her path: a widower, or a man long divorced? Mum was in her element here in Greece; and her palpable enjoyment made her all the more attractive.

Oh God, I found myself thinking, what would it be like to go home for the weekend and find an unfamiliar man in our kitchen? What if I didn't like him? Or, even if I did, what if he didn't get it that when I came home I wanted to have Mum to myself?

Chapter 2
Gaga in a Grey-Blue Dress

EARLY IN OCTOBER 2018 I moved *Self Portrait in Browns* into the house and borrowed Sheila's portrait of Gaga from my sister. I brought it home in the car, lovingly draped in acid-free paper, and hung it on the wall of my writing shed. This was the first time I'd looked at it in several years; and as my eyes came to focus on the contours of the face, I had the spine-tingling feeling that the real, living Gaga was with me.

It was a work of subtle colours. The grey-blue of Gaga's plain tweed dress was close in tone to the pale sage green of the wall behind her and the equally pale greys of her short, permed hair. The sage green paint had been laid down deftly with a palette knife, leaving square and rhomboid marks that lifted slightly at the edges, creating their own irregular shadows. A string of small pearls hung limply from Gaga's neck and rested against her chest. Light struck the face from the left side of the picture only, giving colour to the right cheek and rendering the curls of hair at the right temple almost white. The left side of the face was in shadow – achieved with a hint of the same green used for the wall – and a grey line extended up the side of the neck and into the hair around the ear.

My sense that Gaga was with me in the room was strong enough to make me look away, in unexpected shyness. But a few moments later I turned back towards the painting and tried to figure out why I found it so powerful.

It was something to do with the illusion of shadowy depth which Sheila had created around the eye sockets. There was a remarkable tension between, on the one hand, the watery eyes surrounded by near-translucent grey skin and, on the other, the firm, confident mouth.

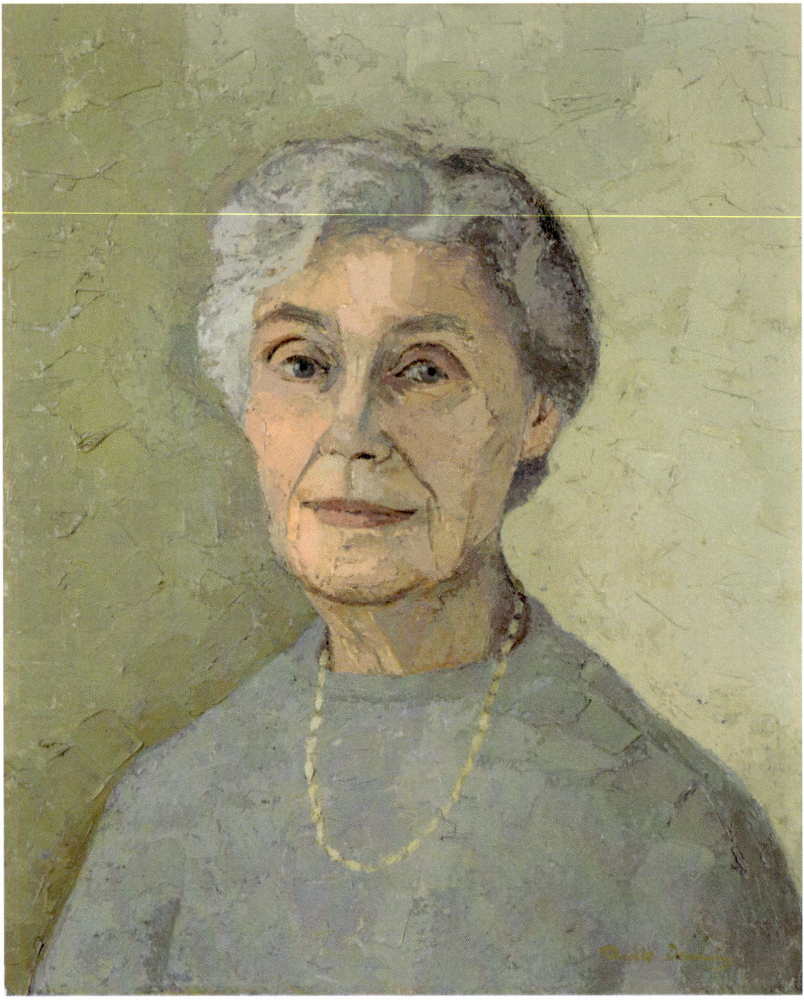

Gaga in a Grey-Blue Dress, 1969

As a young child I'd often heard Dad – and sometimes Mum too – criticise Gaga behind her back: she was prone to fretting about her fragile digestion, while he ate anything and everything; she owned stocks and shares, while we lived on a shoe-string; she read *The Telegraph* whereas Dad and Mum read *The Guardian.* And although the watercolours Gaga sometimes painted were 'rather good', she only did it as a hobby – my parents had no time for 'Sunday painters'. From time to time Mum would bridle and defend Gaga against these slights; but I was left with the impression that both my parents saw her as a cossetted figure who hailed from a bygone age which they'd left far behind. Sometimes Anna and I would join in the mockery, amusing our parents by imitating our grandmother's posh accent and the nervous way in which she drove her pale blue Dauphin. Later, in my teens, I discovered Gaga to be a capable, intelligent woman, whose stable lifestyle and consistent kindness was providing much-needed support to Mum. It was true she had some health worries, and her political views were dubious, but she didn't force them on us. Recently, going through family papers, I'd learned that Gaga had been unremittingly generous with her money, supporting Mum with an allowance from the outset of her marriage, at a time when Dad was earning almost nothing.

As to her attitude to painting, like many women of her generation, Gaga had been raised to repress her needs and hide her talents for the sake of others. I doubt whether she protested when my grandfather told her she was wasting her time with her watercolours. He wanted her to focus on managing his medical practice and running the family home.

A striking feature of the portrait was the sharp slope of Gaga's narrow shoulders – if you rolled a grape down the side of her neck it would soon hurtle to the floor. It was the same angle that I'd found so striking in a photo of her taken around 1911 after she finished her education at Cheltenham Ladies' College. Mum kept the photo in a silver frame on her dressing table. Gaga stands in a calf-length white dress with her arms hanging down and her hands clasped loosely in front of her. Her shoulders plunge from her neck like ski slopes and the serenity of her smile suggests nothing in the world has ever upset her.

Now I gazed at Mum's portrait thinking how lovely my granny looked, how calm, how real.

In 1969, the year when the portrait was painted, I used to walk to Gaga's house after school every Tuesday. It was a long way, and my leather satchel weighed heavily on my shoulder. When I arrived Gaga would have the table laid for tea, a round of home made scones cooling on a wire rack, and the kettle on the hob. I'd kiss her powdered cheek and dump the satchel on one of the damask-covered arm chairs with their hard, arching armrests and squishy cushions. Gaga was so different from Mum – more formal and reserved, even a little shy – and her polished mahogany furniture spoke of a world I'd never experienced. Mum was the link between that world and mine, but Mum wasn't here. At 12, she said, I was old enough to form my own, independent friendship with my granny.

Gaga's scones had a floury crust and soft, fragrant centres. I would cut my first scone open with one of her bone-handled knives and reach for the butter while I answered her questions. She loved to hear that I was doing well at school and I was happy to boast of my achievements. After the scones it was either Angel cake or Rich Tea biscuits. The latter were often stale, but I was too polite to say so. Then we'd go out in the garden to admire the climbing roses Gaga grew, until Mum came to collect me in the car at half past five.

At last I turned away from the painting, booted up the laptop and started work. But an hour later, when I looked at it again, I came to the same conclusion: the power of the portrait derived from the way Sheila had captured both the vulnerability of her mother's incipient old age *and* her remaining vigour. The chin was strong and firm; the cheeks were full; a neat cleft, painted in a darker version of the sage green of the wall, dropped from the centre of the nose to the wide, firm mouth. The upper lip was pressed lightly to the lower one and there was a kindness in the expression, a warm, brave frankness, with the hint of a smile.

*

Gaga's early life wasn't easy. She was born Daisy Emdin in 1893, the only child of Archibald Emdin, an engineer in the Royal Navy, and the feisty Katie Johnson, a woman who dressed in full length, rustling black silk and kept her husband on a short leash. Archibald was of Jewish descent, but this fact was kept well buried. Despite rising to the rank of Rear Admiral, he never dared to cross his wife and was too weak to protect Daisy from her mother's domineering behaviour. Archie and Katie belonged to a non-conformist church in which they worshipped 'Jehovah'.

Towards the end of the Great War (1914–1918) Gaga accompanied her parents to Malta, where Archie was to be stationed. In the capital, Valletta, she met and married a young Irish surgeon, Frederick Denning, who was working in one of Malta's naval hospitals. Gaga's new husband went by the nickname 'Bum' and she now abbreviated 'Daisy' to 'Dee'. Born in Sligo in the west of Ireland, Bum was the eldest of twelve children of an Anglo-Irish doctor and his cold, harsh wife. The couple were devout members of the Plymouth Brethren, a conservative, non-conformist Protestant sect. Bum and his siblings had endured an isolated, ascetic childhood, barred from mixing with their Catholic neighbours, in which horse-riding and fox-hunting were the only pleasures. Bum was probably more deeply scarred, however, by his experiences as a young naval surgeon tending dying servicemen on the HMS Princess Royal in the Battle of Jutland in 1915 and later in Malta.

*

Sheila was Bum and Dee's first child. She was born in a nursing home in East Grinstead, Sussex, on 24 February 1920.

By now Bum had abandoned surgery for general practice. In those days prior to the creation of the NHS, GPs worked privately from surgeries in their homes. Although he was no socialist, Bum worried about the ability of his poorer patients to manage his fees and asked them to pay him one penny a week in exchange for a year-round GP and midwifery service.

Over the next eight years, the family moved around the country, from Kent to Cambridgeshire to Suffolk to Gloucester, with Bum buying and selling a surgery-cum-home roughly once a year. It was an unsettling existence and Dee hated the moves, but Bum paid little attention to her wishes. He justified each upheaval by saying he wanted to hunt with a new pack of hounds in the village or town they were moving to.

Bum was a popular doctor. He encouraged his patients to tell him their troubles, whatever the presenting ailment. He would listen attentively, and then prescribe a bottle of 'pink medicine' (water mixed with cochineal) which Dee prepared in the outhouse. Many patients returned to the surgery a week later, saying the medicine had done them 'the world of good' and could they please have a second bottle.

In 1928, Bum bought a house and practice in Frampton on Severn, a village set in one of the most peaceful stretches of rural Gloucestershire, on the flood plain of the river Severn. The village is famous for its half-mile long village green, bordered on one side by the wall and trees of Frampton Court, an eighteenth-century Palladian mansion. The Sharpness and Gloucester canal lies a quarter mile to the west of the village and, behind it, the wide and treacherous river.

Bum and Dee were happy in Frampton and made a lot of friends. Bum hunted with the Berkeley Hunt while Sheila and her younger brothers, John and Bay, enjoyed the freedom of the countryside.

The new family home was a large, white house with a generous garden and an annex for the surgery. The children were fond of climbing onto the garden wall and running along it until Bum

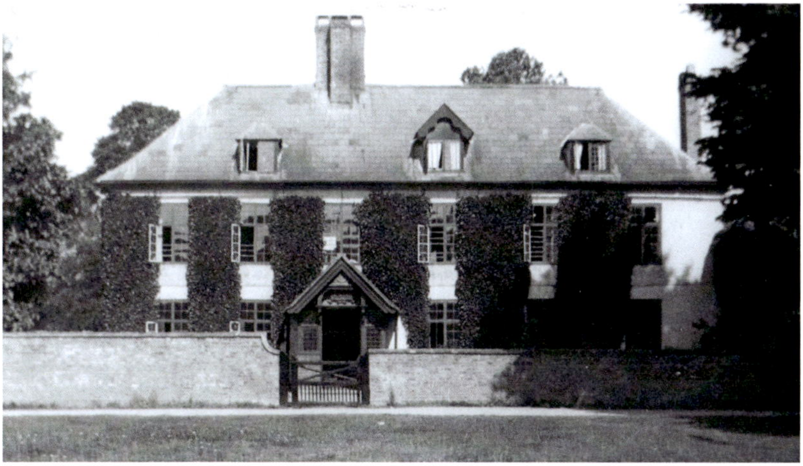

Russell House, Frampton on Severn, c. 1930

dashed out of the surgery to squirt them with water from his ear syringe.

Dee ran the house with the help of a couple of maids and a cook. As Sheila later wrote in her autobiography:

> *We had no electricity, but a multitude of paraffin lamps, large and small. These had to be filled and cleaned every morning, and my mother would do this herself as she said she could not trust the maids to do it properly, and the lamps would smoke. I think there were between 20 and 30 in all. There were tiny lamps called fairy lights which we had in our bedrooms, with small frosted glass shades. We had paraffin stoves for heating.... The bathroom was Arctic, but we knew nothing else and thought that this was in the nature of things. No-one had heard of a shower*[1].

---

1 Sheila's unpublished autobiography spans the years from 1920 to 1950; she wrote it in her eighties, motivated by the pleasure of looking back at her childhood and her desire to share her memories with my sister, my son and me. Passages from the autobiography appear in italics, as do Sheila's poems.

As a child I was fascinated by the knowledge that when my mum was as small as me, *her* mother had had the assistance of a maid and a cook. The thought produced in me a sense of awe, because it seemed to mean that Mum had been born in a social milieu of a different order from the Bohemian one in which I was growing up, where money worries were never-ending and everything we had was second-hand or borrowed.

When I reached my teens, I noticed that Mum struggled with relatively simple domestic tasks – ones which my school friends' mothers would take in their stride – such as defrosting the fridge or making sure we didn't run out of toilet paper. Eventually it dawned on me that, as a child, Mum had never seen Gaga do these things.

In rural Gloucestershire in the late 1920s, having a cook and a maid was a mark of being middle class, but it didn't place you among what Sheila called 'the gentry'. At eight, she became aware of this when she was sent to study with eleven year old Henriette Clifford at Frampton Court. Henriette's father had been killed in the Great War, and her widowed mother employed a woman called Molly Saleby as a governess. Two other girls studied with Henriette and Sheila: the daughter of a local squire and the vicar's daughter from neighbouring Saul.

Sheila was the youngest of the group by three years, but discovered that she was more academically gifted than the other girls.

> *I soon made friends with the vicar's daughter, Primrose. As I was the only doctor's daughter, we were kindred spirits; we did not feel ourselves to be gentry, which the other two did, or so we thought. Molly, our tutor, was also a clergyman's daughter. I was very happy in my lessons.*

Sheila may have been happy in her lessons, but when Anna and I were quite young, she impressed upon us how much she'd suffered at the hands of Henriette.

'Henriette was *beastly* to me!' she exclaimed one evening as she lifted a chocolate pudding out of the oven and placed it on a wire rack to cool. Anna and I were watching expectantly from the kitchen table. In those primary school days, we both had long straight hair that flopped across our eyes, but it didn't escape our notice that the edges of the pudding were burnt onto the sides of the baking dish. A faint smell of cinders wafted towards us.

'She never let me forget, for a single moment,' Mummy went on, wiping her hands on her blue and white butcher's apron, 'that I was merely the doctor's daughter.'

To me the name Henriette sounded peculiar, as if it belonged to a boy, not a girl. I bridled with indignation: how dare this person pull rank on Mummy? But as she told us the details, wincing, while pouring chocolate custard over the steaming pudding, I understood that it was worse than merely pulling rank: the person had upset Mummy so much that she'd wanted to flee to the nearest toilet, bury her face in her hands and sob. That was how I felt when I got teased at school – usually because I was annoyingly good at spelling. I would have preferred not to know about Mummy and Henriette; but it was too late, the cat was out of the bag.

Many decades later, I've forgotten the details of how Henriette tormented Sheila; but I know that rhododendrons had something to do with it.

'Even now, after more than thirty years,' Mummy declared as she handed each of us an island of cake floating in custard, I can't stand the sight of those hideous bloody flowers!'

*

Horse riding was a big part of life at Frampton. Bum kept horses for himself and the children and encouraged Sheila to compete in local shows and gymkhanas. At weekends he took her hunting with him and pushed her to ride the friskiest mount available. Sheila loved to ride, but the frisky pony was too strong and she couldn't control it. She never forgot the terror she felt as it leapt a hedge, shoulder to shoulder with six other horses, nearly throwing her from the saddle before crashing into the chaos of an unknown farmyard.

For Bum, the danger was part of the appeal. When he wasn't hunting, he liked to hack around the Vale of Berkeley[2].

One winter's day when the local countryside was flooded from heavy rain, Dad decided to take John and me out for a ride. John's pony was on a leading rein but I was a free agent. We went along the banks of the canal until we came to a place where the field on our right was so flooded that it left only a narrow tow path between the canal and the other sea of water. Nothing daunted at first, Dad set off along this path where there was just room for his horse and John's pony. I followed behind them.

Dad soon had second thoughts, however, about the wisdom of this. He decided to turn round and retreat, and so told me to turn first, as I would now be in front. But my pony had other ideas. In turning it fell into the canal and struck out immediately for the opposite bank. I fell off but luckily was able to clasp my arms round my pony's neck, and so together we arrived at the far side and somehow managed to struggle out onto dry land.

*

In 2010 I moved with my son to a town only twenty minutes' drive from Frampton, on the edge of the Cotswolds. When I'd had my fill of walking in the hilly beech woods near our new home, I began to explore the lost world of meadows, hamlets and canal to the west of the M5. I found an intriguing landscape of

2 The area around Frampton on Severn.

water birds, cattle and enormous skies, with almost no traffic and precious few walkers.

From time to time I would drive through Frampton, park beyond the village and walk the ten mile periphery of the river's giant meander. Twenty feet above the water level, the path followed the river bank through small copses and green fields. I loved to stretch my eye muscles on the sea-like expanse of grey water, frightening though I found it's swirling currents. I loved the silence, the birds of prey, the sense of space.

One day in 2017, a couple of years after Sheila's passing, when I was still missing her a great deal, I drove to Frampton and walked around the village in search of her old home. It took me some time, because I was looking for the modest type of building which I thought would have housed a doctor and his family in the 1920s. Eventually, I realized that my idea was wrong. In the precise place described by Sheila in her autobiography, close to The Bell pub and directly opposite Frampton Court, I found Russell House. It was very large with a generous front garden, an imposing porch, and a row of six grand sash windows across its width, on both the first and second floors. Freshly painted white, the place was on a different scale from anything I'd ever known Mum to live in.

It was a warm October afternoon and I could feel the sun on my cheeks. At last I turned my back to the house and gazed at the creamy, Cotswold stone wall of Frampton Court, towered over by huge oaks, beeches and chestnuts, their leaves turning yellow. This is what Sheila would have seen every morning, as she crossed the green on the way to her lessons.

My curiosity satisfied, I decided to follow a footpath leading away from the village green in the direction of the canal. It took me onto a narrow path between back gardens, then into a field with a stream running down one side. Five expensive-looking ponies with close-cropped coats and neatly-trimmed tails stood grazing in a group.

I crossed a style and clambered up a bank. There below me lay the canal, glinting in the sun. Houseboats were moored one behind the other and reflections of trees shifted on the surface of the water.

An hour later, after re-tracing my steps, I sat alone on the forecourt of The Bell, gazing across the green at the gold and yellow leaves of the Court's trees and the intense blue of the sky, which was only just beginning to fade.

A stream of four wheel drives was rolling into the village. Whatever it had been in Sheila's time, Frampton today was a mecca for the rural wealthy. I finished my drink and strolled back towards Russell House. Planting myself in the middle of the green, I spent a long time counting and re-counting the two rows of tall sash windows. Above them, three dormer windows set into the roof suggested substantial attic rooms. How was it possible, I asked myself, that my mother, who at the end of her days had owned only a former council house on the outskirts of a town, and who for years had kept her kitchen cupboards virtually empty, had started life in such grand surroundings? Or rather, *why*, when born into relative affluence, had she allowed herself to become comparatively poor?

In broad terms, of course, I knew the answer. Mum had chosen painting in preference to a profession that might have given her a regular income; and divorce had more than halved her resources. I'd been brought up to believe that creativity was more important than making money, and although the insecurity of my childhood had propelled me into becoming a lawyer, I broadly shared my parents' values. But the grandeur of Russell House brought home to me just how much comfort and security Mum had given up.

Chapter 3
Three Girls and their Ponies

ONE DRAB NOVEMBER MORNING in 2013, when Mum was 93, we were sitting side by side on her old white sofa at her home in Bradford on Avon. An atmosphere of peace and calm pervaded the house, the only minor disturbance coming from the rattling and whirring noises emitted by the very ancient fridge.

I asked Mum at what age she'd first started to draw.

'Very early. I was interested in drawing portraits of people who were sat in front of me from a very young age – probably five or six. My parents understood that all children like drawing and we were given paper and pencils. I drew lots of horses, too.'

I knew about the horse drawings: the margins of Mum's old school atlas, which we'd consulted in times of international crisis throughout my childhood, had been crammed with pencil sketches of horses' heads.

Mum's expression was thoughtful. 'In general my parents were tolerant of whatever we wanted to do. They were very liberal with us: they let us run wild in the countryside.'

But Sheila and her brothers' happiness was short-lived. In 1932, Bum moved the family to the Cotswold town of Cirencester and Sheila, aged 12, was sent to boarding school. John (now 'Joe' to the family) had gone away to school the year before (at the 'brutally young age of eight', as Sheila later put it) and Bay would soon follow.

For reasons which are hard to fathom, Bum and Dee chose a school for Sheila on the far side of the country, in Felixstowe on the Suffolk coast.

Fleet House School was a small establishment run by two unmarried sisters, the Misses Aubrey Jones. Here, to my surprise, I was happy; it was, in fact, a lot of fun. The other girls were from similar backgrounds, not so gentrified as at the Court, and I made some close friends. There was also a culture of naughtiness, which I found very enjoyable. There was a system of Order Marks, dished out for various offences, and once a week these were read out, in order of numerical attainment, to the whole school at morning assembly. Our aim, as naughty pupils, was to come top with the most black marks; we were made to stand up and say what the offences had been. I was proud to achieve this whenever I could: I was considered heroic as a result, and so became fairly popular. I suppose I escaped being expelled because I was good at my school work.

Sheila's ability to draw was appreciated at Fleet House.

'I started to look at people and draw them. I discovered I could get a likeness, so I was in demand. My nickname was 'Skinny' – which I quite enjoyed – and my friends would say 'look what Skinny's done, it's quite like so and so…'

As a young teenager, Sheila grew slim and leggy. She felt it was unfeminine to be nearly six foot tall and used to stoop deliberately when school photographs were taken.

I asked what she drew with.

'Pencil on paper. And sometimes watercolour. It was a delightful little school,' she mused, her eyes lighting up, 'we were deliciously naughty.'

'What sort of thing?'

'One of my friends came up with a dare. We had to go up to the bathroom and fill our mouths with water, then walk up and down the stairs. If you spoke, the water would come out. The idea was to continue walking up and down until a teacher came, and if she spoke, you had to answer. There was one poor woman, Miss

Upsher-Smith, who was very shy, rather ugly, not very confident and terrified of us girls. We were vile to her.' Sheila raised her eyebrows slightly to indicate a modicum of sympathy for the teacher. But the curve of her lips betrayed amusement.

'What did you do?'

She raised her eyebrows another notch and hesitated for a second. 'We spat water all over her.'

'Really?'

Mum raised her index finger and pressed it against the bridge of her nose, a trace of embarrassment in her eyes. 'Yes, really,' she said calmly. 'And there was another teacher called Kitty Baker. We used to shout through a half closed door "Kitty, kitty, kitty!" as if we were calling to a cat. She would blush and look frightened.'

'Poor woman!' I stared at Mum. 'But it sounds like a rubbish school. Were you sent there because you were a girl?'

'I don't think so. My parents saw I was clever, especially when my younger brothers were born.'

'Weren't the boys clever, too?'

She pursed her lips. 'John was clever, certainly. Bay was more of a practical man. He was a good musician, but he wasn't clever in a bookish way.'

The boys wrote to their sister frequently, with disarming affection. John, aged 11, wrote in May 1934 from his prep school on the south coast:

> 'My Dear Skin
> I hope you are very well.
> It was a lovely day on Saturday and we played cricket...
> Thank you so much for your letter… and the stamps. I have over 700 stamps in my album…
> I am sleeping in the same dormitory as last term with the same boys…
> I am writing with your pen that is why the writing is so bad…
> With lots of love from Joe.'

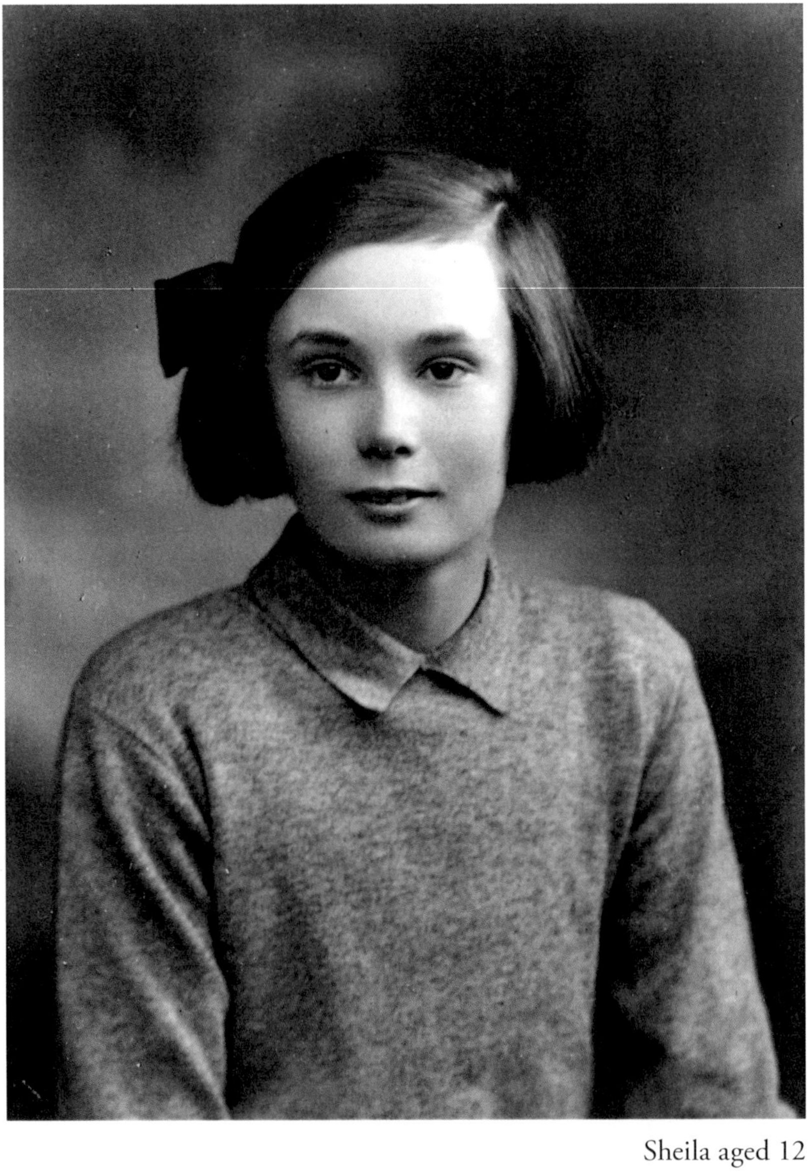

Sheila aged 12

*

With all three children away at boarding school, Bum now embarked on further house moves, initially to Highworth in Wiltshire. In the summer holidays, trips to the river Thames at Lechlade became the favourite family outing.

> *We would go there on summer afternoons during the school holidays, often several times a week. We would all pack into a small car; we would take our swimming costumes, sometimes our wind-up gramophone with a few '78s, and invariably our tea. This was usually the same: a large white loaf and the bread knife, a pound of butter and a pound jar of strawberry or raspberry jam, probably home-made. Also of course thermoses of tea and bottles of milk.*
>
> *After a bumpy ride over bridges at Inglesham we would arrive at the Trout Inn at Lechlade and hire a punt for the afternoon. Everything would be piled into it, including a rug for the picnic, and we would set off, Dad punting, for our favourite parking place, soon named by us Cow Beach, where we would moor. This was so-named because of the cows that frequented it from the field on the river bank. They came often to drink, to look at us, and to relieve themselves, either in the water or on the opposite bank.*
>
> *Hygiene never troubled anyone's mind in those halcyon days. We were soon all in the river with the exception of our mum; she felt it was too cold, usually, and busied herself with laying out the tea. When we had all had enough of the water, we came out dripping to towel ourselves, and sat down on the rug ravenously hungry. The entire loaf and the whole pot of jam would vanish very quickly, and then it would be back in the punt to the Trout, and home in time for evening surgery. No-one ever became ill from the cow-infested river...*

Less enjoyable for Sheila were the frequent occasions during school holidays when she was sent to pay social visits to the local families befriended by her parents.

'All I wanted to do in the afternoons was curl up and read a book,' she told me, 'but my mum had always accepted some invitation or other for me and the boys, and off we would have to go.'

'To do what?' I gazed at her.

'Play tennis. Croquet sometimes.'

'Which you were crap at, I imagine?' I smiled. Both Mum and I were too long-limbed and ill-coordinated to do well on a tennis court or a croquet lawn.

'I wouldn't say "crap"', she replied with a look of mock offence. 'I hit the ball every once in a while.' She raised her eyebrows, causing the hairline of her thick silver bob to shift noticeably backwards. 'Let's say I was better at reading books...'

'Would you get a sumptuous tea?'

'Yes, the teas were good; but usually I was bored stiff by the conversation. I would use any excuse I could think of to leave early.'

*

Bum and Dee changed their minds about schools almost as frequently as they moved house. After two happy years at Fleet House, Sheila was moved to a small school in East Sussex, of which she said:

> *I did not like it, I missed my wicked friends; and after only two terms I was taken away again. This time it was to be Westonbirt...*

Near Tetbury in Gloucestershire, Westonbirt was one of the most expensive girls' boarding schools in the country. Had Sheila not won a scholarship, it's unlikely Bum could have afforded to send her there. But she wasn't happy. Most of the girls were from seriously wealthy backgrounds and they were

> *fanatical about games, which I detested, so subjects of conversation were severely limited. They were also very uninterested in any lessons, so I learned to disguise my pleasure in learning...*

Sheila enjoyed her classes in English, history, French and Latin, all of which were well taught. Best of all were the art lessons, taught by a young woman called Sylvia Marshall.

'I was so miserable at Westonbirt,' she told me, wrinkling up her nose. 'Until I was taught by Sylvia Marshall. She really saved my life.'

'What was she like?'

'She was lovely. Quite young and very *sympatica* to all of us, as she wasn't much older than we were. We loved her. '

'A good teacher?'

'*Very* good. Inspiring, I would say. She really took an interest in a little group of us who liked painting, and encouraged us. She had us painting in water colours and oils, and gave us talks on the history of art. And a couple of times she took about six of us to London. We went to the National Gallery to look at old masters in the morning, then we had lunch, and in the afternoon we went to Cork Street, to contemporary galleries. I learned a lot.'

Sylvia Marshall submitted a large watercolour by Sheila to an exhibition of children's art in London, where it was accepted and hung. It was a study of three girls picking blackberries, with their ponies.

I'd never seen a watercolour by Sheila until she took me into her studio and showed me this painting; and the purples, blues and greens which dominate it were not colours I associated with her work. I stared at it for a long time, fascinated both by the way it spoke of her rural, horsey childhood and the way it revealed her emerging talent for drawing and composition. The three girls,

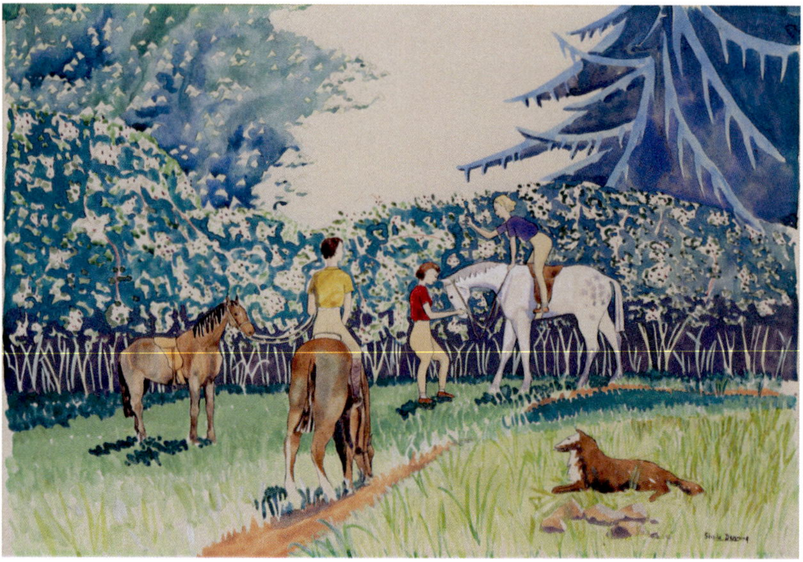

Three Girls and their Ponies, 1935

slim and svelte in their beige jodhpurs, privilege oozing from their perfect white skin and neat haircuts, had brought their ponies to a halt in front of some bushes which were dark with blackberries. One girl was standing up in her stirrups reaching for fruit, while her friend held the pony's bridle; the friend's mount waited quietly to one side, waiting for his rider to return. The haunches of a third pony, complete with rider, occupied the centre ground.

Sylvia Marshall was largely responsible for Sheila's decision to train as a painter.

'Did you ever discuss the idea with your parents?'

'My parents wouldn't have wanted to even talk about it. They never thought painting was an intelligent occupation.'

'But Gaga painted!'

Sheila pursed her lips. 'Yes, but only as a hobby.'

*

In 1936, Bum moved the family to the small town of Cricklade in north Wiltshire, buying a spacious house on the High Street known as Stonecroft. A door in the garden wall lead directly into the churchyard of St Sampson's church, which had a large, square tower. Sheila was given one of the four bedrooms in the attic, with one window looking out into the country and another looking across the garden.

> *For my new bedroom, I was bought a suite of new bedroom furniture, a dressing-table with a large mirror, a wardrobe and a small chest of drawers, all to match in 'limed' oak. I was delighted with these; I spent many hours studying myself in the mirror, trying to reassure my lack of self-confidence – I was sixteen – that I was personable.*

When I first read this passage in the autobiography, I was taken aback. How was it possible that in 1936 Sheila had considered her family poor in comparison to the families of Westonbirt girls, when her parents could afford to buy her three pieces of new oak furniture for her bedroom? When I was a teenager in the early 1970s, the idea of acquiring a new piece of furniture was unthinkable. Anna and I listened to tales of Mum's childhood with awe and a trace of irritation: by our standards, having a housemaid and a cook made her wealthy, whatever she said. We, by contrast, were the children of feckless artists who'd never worked out how to earn money: it was *we*, not she, who were 'poor'.

But although there was money for bedroom furniture, Bum now began to complain of the difficulty he was having in paying the children's school fees. Apparently unaware of how this made them feel, he complained, to their faces, that they were 'killing the goose that laid the golden eggs.' It was partly the resulting sense of guilt that stopped Sheila from telling Bum and Dee how unhappy she felt at Westonbirt. She was greatly relieved, after taking her 'senior Oxford with Matric exemption', a form of qualification for university entrance, to leave school for good in the summer of 1937.

PART TWO

OCTOBER 2018

Dr Roberts stood by the kitchen door at Ivy Cottage, smiling up at me. She was petite and young with curly brown hair and I felt excessively tall. 'Let's try Sudocrem,' she said in a quiet voice, 'and the gluten-free diet. I'll pop back to see Alan again next month.'

'Thanks,' I replied, 'we really appreciate your help.' My rudimentary knowledge of elderly care included the fact that any sign of developing bed sores had to be watched very closely. I watched from the doorway as she picked her way along the flagstone path and crossed the muddy lawn. Then I turned to Christian, Dad's main carer. He was already seated at the laptop, searching the Tesco website for gluten-free items which he thought Dad might eat. 'Is the diet going to be a pain?' I asked.

'Not at all!' Christian glanced up. 'Just a matter of checking the ingredients on each item, and avoiding the ones that contain wheat. I don't think Alan will even notice…' A look of amusement spread across his face. 'Beer might be a problem… but hopefully I can find one that's suitable.'

Christian was the most 'can-do' man I'd ever encountered. Warm, German, brimming with energy and kindness, it was he who held together the arrangements for Dad's care. Nominally, I managed Christian and the other two carers, while Anna looked after Dad's money; but on a day-to-day basis, Christian shouldered the responsibility. And when Dad flew into one of his periodic rages, Christian could handle it. Sometimes he even saw the funny side.

I put the kettle on and stood by the old Belfast sink. On the far side of the window, a millstream rushed a metre from the cottage wall, disappearing through a mossy stone culvert to pass under the lawn.

Christian looked up. 'Are you going to sit with Alan?'

'Yes, for half an hour. Then back to work.'

'He may be sleepy. He was wide awake with Dr Roberts, so that's probably done it for this morning.'

'Sure.' I quite liked sitting with Dad while he slept. It took away the pressure to make conversation, and gave me space to process my thoughts. I made my tea, crossed the living room and peered through the stained glass panel in Dad's studio door. His favourite Schubert lieder were playing on the CD player, while he lay on his back in a deep sleep. I leant my shoulder against the door to pop the catch, flicked off the music and tiptoed round the bed.

The office chair creaked as I sat down, but Dad barely stirred. His cheeks were grey and hollow, his breathing quiet.

My eyes traced the pale brown stripes on the freshly-laundered pillow cases; I could tell that Christian had plumped the pillows before arranging them behind Dad's head. Behind the bed, a collection of ointments, vitamin jars and pill boxes were lined up on the deep window sill according to size. It was Germanic, and masculine, but gave a pleasing sense of order. On the bookshelf beside the bed, heads of Michaelmas daisies arched this way and that from a tall vase – brought, I assumed, by some devoted friend. For a bedridden man of 96, Dad still received a fair few visitors.

When I put down my tea and stood up, my gaze landed on a framed, black and white photo of Bianca, Dad's mother. He'd spoken about her recently, in the present tense, as if she was one of the people who dropped in from time to time.

I'd barely known Bianca. I remembered her as a formidable woman of 80 with an elegant white perm, happily divorced and living in a West London bedsit in the home of a friend. Some years later she stayed with us after an operation, and my parents nursed her in the room next to mine. Early in the mornings I used to hear her rhythmic voice through the wall, reciting The Lord's Prayer with vigour and conviction.

The woman in the photo looked about 40. Pale curls framed her large face; her cheekbones were as prominent and impressive as Dad's, but well-covered with taut flesh and perfect skin. The carers had positioned the photo so that Bianca's calm, gracious smile looked down on him. I studied her face, bemused: she was now the young, strong one, watching over her fading son.

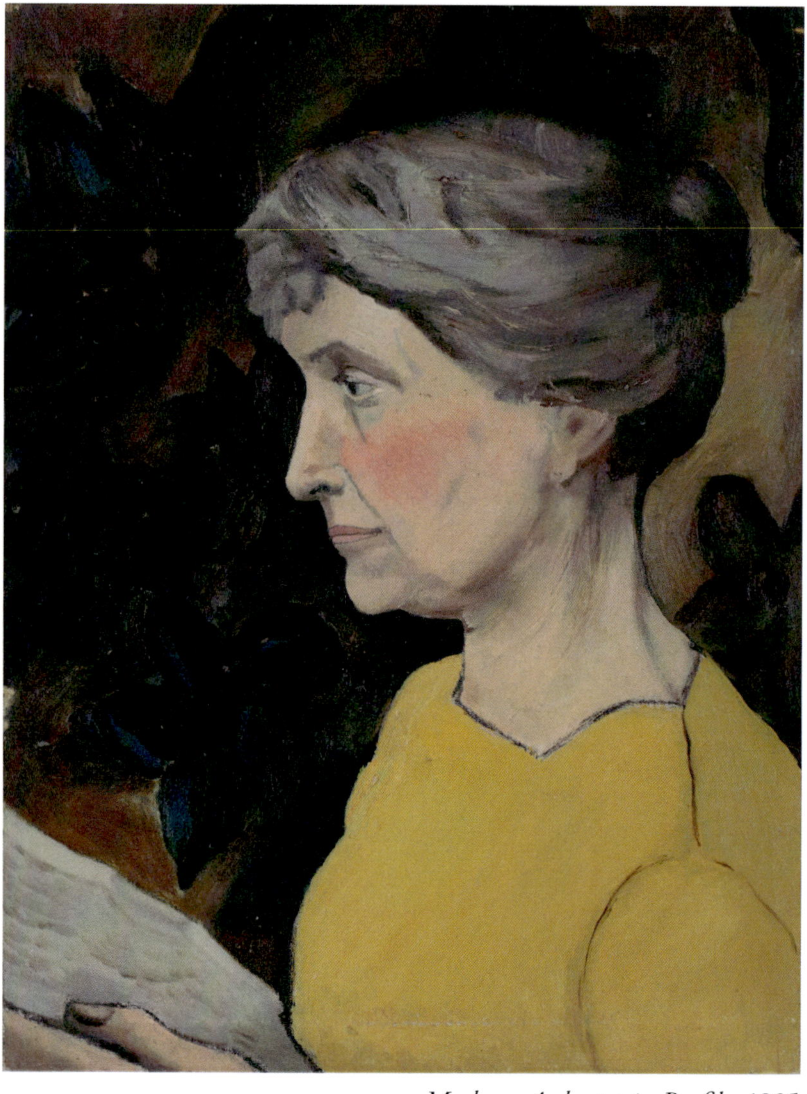

Madame Aubertot in Profile, 1935

Chapter 4
Madame Aubertot in Profile

IN 1937, Bum hit on the idea of sending Dee and Sheila on a long summer road trip through northern France, at the end of which Sheila would go to live with a French family in Paris for the winter. The fact that Hitler and his National Socialist party were on the ascendancy in neighbouring Germany doesn't seem to have perturbed him.

Mother and daughter set off at the end of June in a small Morris Eight with Dee at the wheel. It was the pair's first visit to the continent, and initially Dee was very nervous about driving on the right. How would she find her way south out of Calais? But with Sheila beside her reading the road signs, Dee relaxed and the pair spent a happy time visiting the great cathedrals of northern France at Abbeville, Amiens and Beauvais. Sheila's French came on fast, helped by the fact that Dee relied on her daughter to do the talking. After a few days in Rouen, the pair drove south to visit the chateaux of the Loire at Amboise, Chambord and Azay-le-Rideau.

> *We liked the French and we liked the food. Our money went a long way. With something like regret we turned north-west in August to meet Dad and the boys in St Malo in Britanny.*

After a holiday at St Lunaire, the whole family accompanied Sheila to Neuilly, just outside Paris, with Bum now acting as chauffeur. In contrast to Dee's slow and cautious style of driving, Bum's was 'perilous' and even 'exceeded that of the Parisians in speed and brio[1]'. In Neuilly, Sheila was delivered to her new French hosts,

1 Quoted from Sheila's autobiography.

the widowed Mme Aubertot and her daughter Yvonne, who lived in an apartment at 15, Rue du Marche.

> *One entered number 15 through an archway, past the concierge's office, and then climbed the stairs to the Aubertots' first floor flat. It had a typical French pre-war interior, with dark heavy wooden furniture, uncomfortable chairs and no sofa.*
>
> *I felt at home with the Aubertots from the first day. Madame was a tall and lovely Norman woman who supplemented her income by offering a generous hospitality to young women sent by their families to improve their French. Yvonne did not have her mother's beauty and charm; she was short, stunted even, possibly a bit backward and plain to look at. But both she and her mother were kindness itself. I was soon addressed as "ma petite Sheila" and, as I was the tallest of the household, I liked this flattery.*
>
> *Mariette the maid was a charmer: young, pretty, sprightly and a very good cook. She introduced me to many dishes that I had never heard of; though the ménage was frugal, the food was delicious. If she thought I particularly liked a pudding she would make it again as often as she dared; I remember having Diplomate*[2] *about once a week. Chocolate I had as my breakfast drink; this was made in the proper way, by placing solid chocolate block in the cup and pouring boiling water over it.*

One morning in 2014 when I dropped in for a cup of tea, I asked Mum what she remembered about her stay in Paris, all those years ago. She'd had her hair cut the day before and her silver bob fell in a sharp line across the back of her neck.

---

2 Diplomate is regarded as a *'dessert gourmand'* and consists of leftover bread and *viennoiseries* (pastries) drenched in a sauce made with egg, cream, cocoa and chocolate.

'I had a great time with Mme Aubertot. She used to give me an hour's French tuition a day, as well as conversing with me constantly. She used to make me read out loud and I wrote pieces in French which she corrected. And she gave me dictation: "*Dictee, Shaylagh*?"' – she opened her mouth extra wide to mimic the way Mme Aubertot used to pronounce her name. 'I was soon thinking and dreaming in French.'

'What did you do the rest of the time?'

'I did exactly what I wanted.' Mum's eyes shone. 'I went off alone after breakfast and came back for supper. I went to museums and cafes and sometimes I sat and painted outdoors.'

I loved Mum's paintings of the Seine. There was one of a series of very tall, angular, turn-of-the-century office buildings beside a bridge, painted in greys and dull blues against a heavy, white sky; it had the depressing quality of a city enduring the depths of winter. In another, a low bridge spanned the river, beneath a pale blue sky painted – almost sculpted – in thick swirls of paint that created a sense of movement and warm air. In the foreground a series of

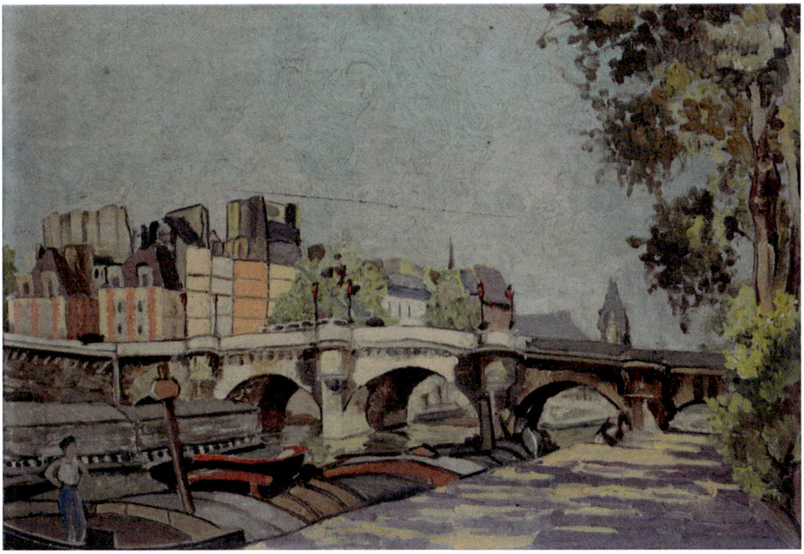

Bridge over the Seine, 1938

wooden boats jostled against a wide quay, on which long purple shadows were cast by overhanging trees. A loosely drawn male figure stood in one of the boats. In the background, apartment blocks with tall pointed roofs and skylights were rammed together at slightly wonky angles. These two paintings had hung on our wall when I was a teenager, providing me with a visual backdrop for the books by Simone de Beauvoir and Jean Paul Sartre which I was reading. These, I told myself, were the quays where the pair used to stroll in the evenings, deep in conversation about politics and philosophy.

'Did you just sit by the river and paint?'

'More or less.' Mum wiggled her eyebrows with an air of excitement. 'I bought some old paintings on canvas from a street stall and primed over them; then I sat out on the quays with my paints. I had comments and criticism galore, but never any hassle. I was very struck by the difference between painting outdoors in England and in France. The English, if they saw you painting in the street, looked embarrassed. They'd avert their eyes and walk by; whereas in France you got a crowd behind you, making informed remarks. Men in overalls – workmen – would say things like: "*Ici ca marche; mais la-bas, pas tellement, Mam'selle*," ("This bit works, but that bit doesn't really work, Mam'selle") – and they were usually right. I'd ask if the person was a painter and he'd say "*non, je suis ouvrier, mais je connais la peinture mam'selle*" ("No, I'm a workman, but I know about painting, miss.") The crowd didn't bother me, they were very friendly; and my French was pretty good by then.

'On one occasion two men were watching me paint. One said to the other, "*Ce n'est pas mal, n'est ce pas?*" ("It's not bad, is it?") The other replied "*Pas mal, comme l'auteur d'ailleurs*" (It's not bad, and the artist's not bad, either!) He thought I couldn't understand. I turned round and said "*Merci*!"'

When she wasn't at her easel, Sheila went to the Louvre, the Musee de l'Art Moderne and other galleries and museums. She also went to lectures on literature at the Alliance Francaise. Once a week she bought a ticket for the Loterie Nationale and one day she won a prize. She spent the money on theatre tickets, taking Madame Aubertot and Yvonne to see *Le Corsaire*.

Sheila painted a portrait of Madame Aubertot. Madame sits in profile, holding a letter, against a background of dark brown wallpaper. Her features are lean and angular, her expression tranquil; the sharp yellow of her dress brightens what might otherwise have been a sombre painting. Studying it one morning in my writing shed, I noticed what I thought were pencil lines outlining the thin, rather sad lips. This surprised me: in her later portraits, Sheila wouldn't have dreamed of using a pencil on canvas, even in the first hour of roughing out a portrait.

It's possible that Madame Aubertot was the first portrait in oils Sheila ever painted, having only made portraits in pencil when she was at school. The shadows beneath the jaw and on the back of the neck are entirely convincing, as is the sculpting of the cheek and chin. The wallpaper is problematic because the dark blue and brown flowers have a three-dimensional quality and swim out into the room from the lighter brown ground; but the effect is a nice contrast with Madame's serious demeanour, giving the painting a touch of playfulness.

*

When we cleared Sheila's house after her death, we found a large quantity of personal letters in the bottom drawer of her oak bureau, carefully tied in bundles with scraps of white tape. Thinking they might be useful for my project, I took them home in a giant cardboard box and stowed it under my bed. In late October 2018, somewhat nervous as to what I might find, I carried the box down the garden to my writing shed and opened it up. Here, scrawled in dark blue ink on sheets of thick, off-white cartridge paper folded into uneven squares, lay so many clues to the story of my mother's early life. I spent the short, darkening days of November going through the bundles one by one, peering at postmarks, sorting, reading and making notes, with my black cat Rameses and the roaring of the woodburner for company. The most faded of the envelopes, with postmarks from the 1930s and early 1940s, contained letters to Sheila from Bum, Dee, Joe and Bay. These helped me to fill out the account in the autobiography of Sheila's life before and during WWII.

In June 1938, she left the Aubertots and went home, promising to stay in touch with her new friends by means of letters. But her adventures in Europe were not over. Through an agency, Dee now arranged for Sheila to go to Munich to live with the Heuck family for six months, to learn German from scratch.

With the benefit of hindsight, this plan seems extraordinary. In March 1938, while Sheila was enjoying herself in Paris, Hitler had annexed Austria; and by the late summer he would be making serious threats to occupy the Sudetenland in Czechoslovakia, on the pretext of protecting its German-speaking population. The persecution of German Jews was already driving many to flee and the major pogrom of Kristallnacht would take place before the end of the year. Of her family's awareness of these developments, Sheila wrote:

> *Jewish refugees were arriving in London and America, among them many distinguished artists and musicians; and no doubt the government and the Foreign Office were better informed [than we were]. As for us, we heard Hitler's speeches on the radio and we saw him on the newsreels in the cinema... We saw the notorious Berlin Olympic Games of 1936*[3]*. We did not like what we saw or heard, but of the concentration camps we heard nothing.*

---

3 The Olympic Games of 1936 were hosted by Germany in Berlin and used by the Nazis to promote an image of a new, strong Germany, while hiding their policies towards Jews and Roma. Calls for a boycott of the games due to Nazi policies were unsuccessful.

By the time Sheila set off for Munich in August, it was apparent to many that war was likely. But not, it seems, to Bum and Dee.

> *I was to arrive in Munich during the summer holidays and Dad, scenting another adventure, decided to drive me there across Europe, but to have some fun on the way. So we set off in a small open car, another Morris 8, with brother Bay, who was thirteen and due to start at Wellington College in September, sitting on the back seat.*

After driving through France, Switzerland and Austria without once buying a newspaper – a curious omission, in the circumstances – they arrived in Munich and found their way to the Heuck family's apartment. Frau Heuck and her daughter Gerti greeted them warmly, but immediately presented Bum with a telegram from Dee.

> *I do not remember the exact wording, but the message was plain enough. 'Do not leave Sheila – come home at once – war is imminent.'*

Bum was shocked into silence, while Frau Heuck stood in the hallway saying "*Der Krieg ist schrecklich,*" ("war is terrible"). Although her visitors spoke no German, she managed to get across to them that Sheila could not stay.

The Dennings thanked Frau Heuck, got back into the Morris 8 and drove as fast as they could to the German border at Strasbourg. They felt some relief at crossing into France and stopped to snatch a meal in a restaurant, where Sheila overheard their fellow diners talking of war. Pressing on via Reims, eventually they reached Calais and boarded the car ferry for Dover.

Late one afternoon, I was sitting in my writing shed, drinking tea and going through letters from the cardboard box. The light was fading at the windows but the stove was going and a delicious heat had built up around me. In between two faded envelopes I found a folded sheet of very fine, translucent paper, yellowed with age. It didn't look like a letter and when I opened it out I saw that it was the telegram, sent by Gaga from Cricklade in August 1938.

RETURN HOME IMMEDIATELY
RETURN MUNICH LATER = MOTHER

The sight of these words gave me a funny feeling in my stomach. Sheila had told me the story of her abrupt departure from Munich many times; but this piece of paper served to convert it from a piece of family folklore into something real. I read the words again. Why had Gaga suggested that a return to Munich later might be possible?

I got up, opened the iron door of the stove and tossed in a log, enjoying the crunching sound as I dropped the heavy catch. In August 1938 Gaga wouldn't have known that the war, when it came, was going to last six years.

But she didn't mention Sheila by name in the telegram. My clever grandmother appreciated that, if something went wrong and the telegram was intercepted, it would be better if the German authorities didn't have her daughter's name.

*

In late September 1938 the crisis over the Sudetenland was averted without war by the diplomacy of British PM Neville Chamberlain (who would later be much criticized for his policy of appeasement). But for the time being, Sheila's travels were over.

> *A strange year now followed. A strange year, doubtless, for all the people of Europe. We in England went about our usual business. Chamberlain announced that he had brought back "Peace in our Time" from Munich. We tried to believe him. Meanwhile, rumours of evil omen were*

> *coming out of Germany, and Jewish refugees from Nazi persecution were arriving in our country, almost daily*[4]*. We heard Hitler's speeches on the wireless and picked up his fanatical anger. We asked ourselves about the wisdom of the peace settlement that had been made at the end of the Great War, the "war to end wars". There was a growing sense of foreboding.*

Sheila spent much of the next year in London, returning to her parents for weekends and holidays. In London she lodged with her cousin Joy Westendarp, who was newly married to an actor and beginning her career as a literary agent.

Joe wrote to Sheila on 2 October from Haileybury, his public school. He began by teasing her about her close shave in Munich; then asked what she was planning to do next.

> 'It is quite obvious to me that you will never make a secretary… I can't see you as one. It would be much better if you got a degree or took painting up really seriously…'

Taking up painting really seriously was exactly what Sheila intended to do. Having secured Bum's agreement to support her, she now enrolled at the Westminster School of Art, in Victoria.

To put this in context, a handful of women from well-to-do families had attended London art schools from the turn of the twentieth century. Among them were women whose names are still well known today, such as

---

4 One of these was Emil Rueb, a distant cousin of my father. Emil fled Nazi Germany on 14 September 1938 and stopped in London before travelling on to the USA. He travelled at the urging of his parents, who hoped he would be able to bring them to join him. Emil's story is the subject of *All for You: A World War II Family Memoir of Love, Separation and Loss*, by my cousin Dena Rueb Romero, published by She Writes Press in 2024.

the painters Vanessa Bell[5], Gwen John[6] and Sylvia Pankhurst[7]; but many others have been long forgotten.

At the turn of the century, the training women students received was circumscribed by social attitudes. The focus was on figurative painting, but working from a nude model was considered unsuitable for women, with the result that classes had to be segregated. Women were forced to draw from plaster casts in overcrowded studios, while their male counterparts worked directly from life and received more individual attention. Scholarships and exhibitions were more likely to be given to men than to women. And, after completing their art school training, women struggled to be taken seriously as professional painters, since 'professional' status was only accorded to those who lived by selling their work. A few women did this, but many succumbed to the pressure to get married.[8]

---

5 Vanessa Bell, 1879–1961, founder member of the Bloomsbury group, studied at the Royal College of Art from 1901-1904. She worked in London, East Sussex and the south of France, producing still lifes, landscapes and figure paintings over a sixty year career. She also produced decorative work for the Omega Workshops. Bell's sister was the writer Virginia Woolf.

6 Gwen John, 1876–1939, a Welsh painter, studied at The Slade School of Art from 1895 – 1898, which at that time was the only art school which took women. Gwen John spent most of her life in France, where she produced a number of portraits of mainly female sitters. During her lifetime her reputation was eclipsed by that of her brother, Augustus John, but in recent years there has been renewed interest in and appreciation of her work.

7 Sylvia Pankhurst, 1882–1960, studied painting at Manchester School of Art and the Royal College of Art. Among other subjects she painted women at work in factories before becoming drawn into full time work as an activist for women's suffrage.

8 Carolyn Trant, *Voyaging Out – British Women Artists from Suffrage to the Sixties*, pp8–9.

Sheila's memory of The Westminster remained very clear when I asked her about it one morning in 2013.

'The Westminster was an excellent school with a scintillating cast of teachers. There were many well known painters on the staff, both men and women. In fact, in 1938 there were more women teachers there than at Camberwell, where I trained after the war.

'In those days, art school teachers weren't expected to have teaching qualifications: the important thing was that they were active, working artists. Gertrude Hermes, the illustrator, was on the staff[9]. So was Mervyn Peake, the author and illustrator[10]. I knew him slightly. He taught illustration and did funny drawings of grotesque people and animals. And there was a painter called Blair Hugh-Stanton[11].

'As a student you were left fairly much to yourself. They didn't lay down the law about how to paint, although I was told by one tutor that line drawing was not acceptable, which I found very discouraging. They started everybody off with still life: you weren't allowed to go straight into the portrait class.'

It was probably while she was at The Westminster that Sheila painted *Cabbages, Apples, Potatoes*[12], which we found among her work after her death. It had a special intensity, as if it had been painted in a mood of rapt concentration. The outer leaves of the cabbage were dark purple and crinkly, with a frill along the edge. Both the colour and the texture were utterly convincing, yet the work was painterly rather than photographic in quality.

---

9 Gertrude Hermes (1901–1983)was a wood engraver, print maker and sculptor.

10 Mervyn Peake (1911–1968) was a writer, illustrator and artist, best known for the Gormenghast trilogy.

11 Blair Hughes-Stanton (1902–1981) was a wood engraver and illustrator. He illustrated some of the work of D.H. Lawrence.

12 *Cabbages, Apples, Potatoes* can be seen on Sheila's website www.sheiladenning.com

On the weekends when Sheila visited her parents in Cricklade, she found that life was continuing much as before. There were the usual dances at Cricklade's Memorial Hall, built in 1933 with a superbly-sprung dance floor, in memory of the fallen in the Great War.

The most popular of the winter's dances was the local Hunt Ball, to which the Denning family always went.

> *… I was "sitting out" beside the dance floor watching the dancers and listening to the band which was playing on the stage. The singer was performing a song from a favourite Fred Astaire and Ginger Rogers film. I was suddenly struck by the words, and began to listen more intently. My heart seemed to stop, and a cold chill ran through my body.*
>
> *She was singing:*
>
> *There may be trouble ahead,*
> *But while there's moonlight and music,*
> *And love and romance,*
> *Let's face the music and dance.*
>
> *Before the fiddlers have fled,*
> *Before they ask us to pay the bill, and*
> *While we still have the chance,*
> *Let's face the music and dance.*
>
> *Soon, we'll be without the moon,*
> *Playing a different tune,*
> *And then there may be tear drops to shed*
> *But while there's moonlight and music*
> *And love and romance*
> *Let's face the music and dance.*
>
> *"What is going to happen?" I thought as I sat there. "To all of these beautiful young men, and women too, dancing here*

> *tonight. And I have two brothers..." I have remembered that moment, that song, through all the years that have followed.*

*

Back in London, Sheila was unable to study painting full time for long. Early in 1939, Bum told her he didn't want to go on paying her fees. He'd never wanted her to go to art school, he claimed; he'd wanted her to go to Oxford, take a degree in English literature and become a teacher. If she wanted to continue, she would have to find a way to fund herself.

'I was annoyed, because we'd made the plan together and now he'd left me in the lurch. I refused to be leaned on. I said "No, dear Dad, I'll support myself and carry on".'

Help was at hand. By now Bum's youngest sister, Sheila's Aunt Vere, was married to the successful fashion photographer John French, whose work regularly appeared in Vogue, Harpers and other leading magazines[13]. Vere was only ten years older than Sheila and the couple were sympathetic to their niece's desire to study art. Given her height and fabulous looks, John offered to get Sheila work as a fashion model.

When a garbled version of this idea reached Joe, he wrote to Sheila from school, in protest:

> 'My darling Shee,
> I hope you are very well.
> Have you got this photographer's model job yet? I hope not.
>
> I may be rather conservative, but I would rather I did not see your face looming up in *Picture Post* advertising Colgates!

---

13 John French (1907–1966) was known for his fashion and portrait photography and for pioneering a new form of fashion photography suited to reproduction in newsprint.

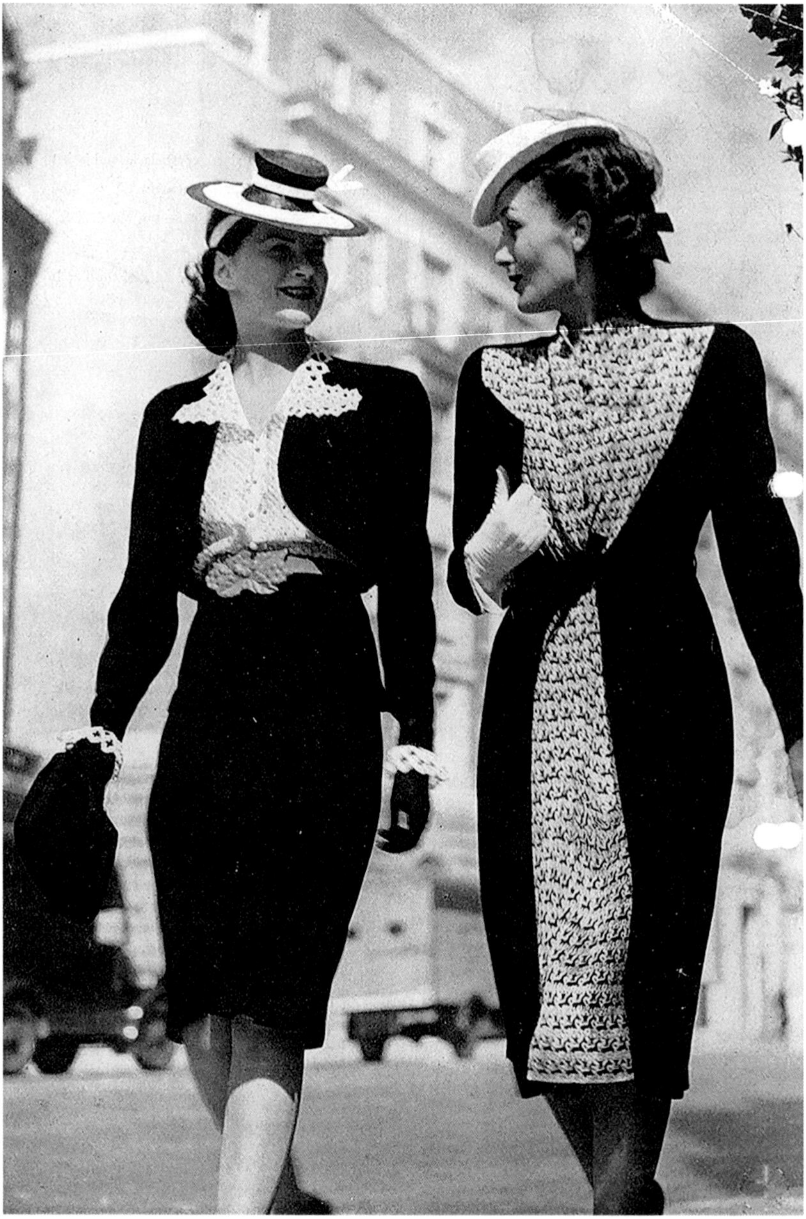

Sheila (on the right) working as a model, 1939

> Money is hard to EARN, but it is very hard to earn if this is the price to be paid. However I may be an ignorant schoolboy, wholly unqualified to write on this topic...'

There was never any question of Sheila's face being used for advertising: John French's contacts were in the world of fashion. He sent his photographs of Sheila to several agencies and bookings began to come in. But Sheila found her new job uninspiring:

> *Far from being the glamorous profession of adolescent dreams, the "work" when it came was precarious and tedious. I had to supply my own hats, shoes, handbags, gloves. This was hard enough. They often wanted to take outdoor shots, which entailed travelling to Kenwood or such; when there we waited sometimes hours for the weather to do the right thing. I remember a particularly tedious day waiting for a breeze to blow my hair in a certain direction.*

In between modelling jobs, Sheila continued at the Westminster. When things went well, it was Dee she wrote to:

> 'Drawing was grand today and he (Millard) said I had "the right spirit". Ok and I *must* tell you what Mr Jamieson[14] said last Thursday. Don't think me horribly conceited, but I'm still as pleased as punch about it, and must let off steam to someone! About my painting, this was. He came and looked at it with Miss Bruce, and he said – "That's *very* nice" (in his little Scotch accent)- "that part there is really lovely." Then he looked at me and said "She's going to be a painter." I went about in a trance for the rest of

14 Robert Kirkland Jamieson (1881–1950), a Scottish landscape painter, was head of the Westminster School of Art for most of the 1930s and became head of St Martin's School of Art in 1945.

the day! Personally *I* didn't like what I'd done at all, and didn't think it was nearly as good as other bits which have brought forth no remarks!'

*

On 1 September 1939, Hitler's army marched into Poland. On the morning of Sunday September 3rd, the entire Denning family were at home in Cricklade.

My mother and I, John and Bay, had crossed our garden to the door in the wall that led directly into the churchyard. We were sitting in our usual pew, the boys in their grey flannel suits. The vicar climbed into the pulpit and looked at us all for a moment.

"I have to tell you," he said, "that at eleven o'clock this morning, Britain and France declared war on Germany."

So, it had happened at last. The promise of peace in our time had proved hollow; the hope had been a false one, as we mostly knew in our hearts that it would be. The years and months of foreboding were over. Much would now be broken. For our family, as for countless others, our lives as we had known them would be shattered for ever.

Chapter 5
Death to the College of Art

FOLLOWING THE OUTBREAK OF WAR, Sheila's brothers packed their trunks and went back to school as normal. Joe was sixteen and a half and had just one year left at Haileybury. Bay was barely fifteen and had three years to go at Wellington.

Initially, Sheila remained with Bum and Dee in Cricklade, where local families were busy receiving child evacuees from London. Sheila later described the children as

> *a source of amusement, annoyance, worry, interest. Some of them we heard did not know that milk came from cows…*

The evacuees were sent to the local school, where

> *their street wisdom must have been a contrast to the slowness of the local children, and a challenge to their teachers.*

No evacuees were sent to live with the Dennings. Bum was soon working very hard as the only doctor for the expanded population of the town, and Dee took on the task of running the child welfare clinic. Sheila, for her part, volunteered with the local Air Raid Precautions Service, or ARPS, in Swindon. This was

> *a standing-by affair with a list of instructions as to what to do if bombs should start falling on Swindon. There were two or three men and myself and we sat, at night, in a kind of caravan, brewing endless mugs of tea and playing cards… It was tedious but cheerful and convivial and I quite enjoyed it, especially as I was the only woman.*

By now a strict blackout had been ordered, due to the risk of air raids.

> *Bales of black cloth appeared in the shops and we all draped our windows carefully. Special masks were available for car headlights, allowing only a small central beam; we had to drive with great caution, and no street lights were allowed, anywhere.*

It was six miles from the ARPS caravan near Swindon railway station to Cricklade. On one occasion Sheila was obliged to walk home in the blackout, as the bus wasn't running; she was overcome with terror as she walked down Blunsdon Hill in pitch darkness. On another occasion, when a bout of 'flu kept her from her duties for a few days, she received a note from her colleagues:

> *"The sun has lost its light, the moon its lustre – Please soon return to the dejected cluster of ARPS."*

When I first read this passage in the autobiography a few weeks after Sheila's death, it delighted me. I imagined my beautiful mother, aged nineteen, with her smooth skin and dark wavy hair, surrounded by adoring young men clutching mugs of stewed tea. It was the adoration which meant the most to me. I'd always felt stung by my father's failure to treasure my mother as the special woman she was; I found the idea that other men had seen her beauty and valued her friendship profoundly comforting.

After several months in the ARPS, during which there were no air raids on Swindon, Sheila wanted to play a more challenging role in the war effort. In 1940 she joined the women's branch of the army, known as the Auxiliary Territorial Service (ATS). Since she had a driving licence, she was quickly appointed to the Field Ambulance Nursing Yeomanry (FANYs) and found a post as a driver of staff cars.

> *The FANYs... had a history of which they were proud; in fact they considered themselves a cut above the ordinary*

ATS. They had been drivers of ambulances and cars in France during the first World War. We were given an embroidered band with the letters FANY to wear on our uniform tunics.

Sheila was posted to Edinburgh, where she lived in a 'lovely Georgian house' in the centre of the city. Initially the work was routine, but in November 1940 she wrote to Dee saying that she and some of her colleagues had been promoted.

> 'Darling, I've been put on Command driving, isn't it exciting! Several of us had a driving test on Friday… and we all got through except one. We shall still do some pool car driving, but quite a lot of Command driving as well. A few people who have been here some time are rather annoyed. This week I'm to drive the Ferry car from one part of Battle Head Quarters (BHQ) to another, it's a kind of taxi that goes back and forth every half hour, about 7 miles between. I've been initiated into the secret of the whereabouts of the BHQ which is highly secret information which one does not tell a soul. Most important people are always dashing from BHQ to the other place. I shall probably become a spy and sell my information to the highest bidder. As well as ferrying we might also go on tour all over Scotland which will be good, but death to the college of art.'

Not only the college of art, but all creative activity by Sheila was put on hold for the duration of the war; I found nothing she painted between 1939 and 1946. She was soon driving officers of the Scottish Command to visit military units in far-flung places, on trips which sometimes lasted several days.

The officers were mostly charming and entertaining passengers. They did not hassle us unduly, except for one

> *short, stout major who insisted that I stayed in the same hotel with him and made a pass at me.*

'Fraternisation' as it was called, between male officers and female drivers, was strictly forbidden. In order to reduce the risks, the drivers were given a list of bed and breakfast accommodation in farmhouses where they were expected to lodge separately from the officers. Sixty years later, Sheila still remembered the plentiful food.

> *... the high tea in the farmhouses was a revelation to me: bread, home-baked, farm butter, scones, cakes, biscuits, perhaps some scrambled eggs and ham. Food rationing had only just come in...*

Sheila understood how much food mattered to her adolescent brothers, and did her best to send them little treats. Bay wrote from school:

> 'My darling Shee
> Thank you so much for the chocolate, it is too good of you to save it up. Is it plentiful still in Edinburgh? I love shortbread, it was lovely, the stuff you sent me last term.'

Sheila led a busy social life in Edinburgh, as she wrote to Dee:

> 'On Thursday night six of us went out to the most unspeakably awful troop concert at Craigmillar. The AMPs invited us, and fetched us in an ambulance. It was in a large hall packed with troops, their wives and sweethearts, and the atmosphere was unbelievable. I don't know what they were all smoking, something very strong and smelly, and about half way through the concert our eyes began to close up and smart so we all sat with our eyes shut and of course they thought we were asleep with boredom. There was a facetious

> compere, a terrible female with a pale voice who sang ballads, and a slinky fifth-rate glamour girl who danced an Eastern dance in a very Folies Bergere costume to the intense delight of the troops who whistled and cat-called and shrieked. Whistling (fingers in mouth) is always a sign of approval in the Army. It went on for or at least six hours, then at last they took us home in the ambulance which was what we were fit for.
>
> 'From Friday till Sat I had 24 hours leave so could wear clothes again. I wore my black frock to the Grosvenor where I went to a dinner-dance with James. James is a tall and handsome Scots laddie whom I met at Milly's cocktail party, he wears a green glengarry and trews (tartan trousers) and looks very beautiful. He is most amusing but will call the Grosvenor the Gruvvenor. He comes and has coffee with me at Crawfords in the middle of the morning instead of doing any work. I tell him this war will be won by the women! We met Norah (one of our officers), Margaret Allan and 2 friends of Jimmy's at the Grosvenor and had a very fun party. Then we went on to the St Giles grill and caroused until 3 in the morning.'

Dee was missing Sheila a great deal and was thrilled to get her letters. She, too, wrote frequently, describing the trials and tribulations of daily life in Cricklade, where she was frequently called upon to help evacuees and was having trouble retaining a maid and a cook. At night she lay awake listening to planes flying overhead and worrying about her sons, who sometimes insisted on driving to local dances in the blackout.

Occasionally, the grim reality of the war in Europe impinged on Sheila's life in Edinburgh, foreshadowing things to come. In early June 1941, she heard news of a family friend whose son had been stationed on HMS Hereward when it was bombed by the

Nazis off the coast of Crete. She wrote to Dee:

> '... poor Olivia came to stay with the Hillards when she heard about Tom, I think he is the elder one. She was terribly upset, Mave had to ring her up and tell her about it – Olivia came over to Edinburgh at once and found she'd arrived in her bedroom slippers. He may be a prisoner of course. I think they took some off the Hereward.'

By now, Sheila had applied for a transfer to Oxford. Before leaving Edinburgh in late June, she spent a weekend's leave with an army friend, Maggie Davidson, on a farm near Glasgow belonging to the latter's aunt:

> 'I hitch-hiked over from Edinburgh to Glasgow yesterday morning. Great fun. I went in uniform to make things easier. Got a lift for 3 or 4 miles along the road from one man, then started to wander along slowly, no traffic at all. (Sunday morning). Suddenly there was a noise like a Heinkel[1] and a Ford brake full of men went tearing past at 80 m.p.h. To my astonishment it pulled up, taking about a mile to do it in, turned round and came back. It was full of the most comic-looking tough guys I've ever seen, driven by a very fat man with what one can only call a jolly face – rather like Nurse Gray only vastly good-humoured. So in I got, suitcase and all. There were 5 of them – I thought at first several of them were other hitch-hikers like me, but no, they all seemed to be related, and were on their way to Stranraer. It was a perfect hitch-hike – the Glasgow road is long and straight and we tore along at between 70 and

1 A German warplane.

> 80. They were charming and so funny and couldn't have been more kind… They took me all the way to Glasgow Central Station, and from there I got a bus to Johnstone.'

*

As a young child, I was aware that my parents had lived through something important and intriguing known as 'the war'. I noticed that they liked to talk about it and got into the habit of pestering them for tales of their adventures, usually at bedtime. It proved an effective ruse to extend the day; and I found the stories gripping.

'Tell me about that soldier, in the street!' I'd had my supper and knew that any minute now I'd be told it was time for bed.

Mummy winked at me. It was 1964 and she was standing at the wooden clothes rack, which she'd placed in front of the coal-burning stove in our living room in London, in an attempt to get the washing dry. 'Ha. That little squirt.' She picked up a pillow case, pulled out the corners and put it back on the rail. 'Well, one day I was walking down the street in my uniform. In Edinburgh.' She pulled back her shoulders, thrust her nose into the air and took a stride towards the sofa, where I was lolling on cushions, sucking my thumb. 'Like this. I'm minding my own business. And then suddenly I hear a man's voice, from the road.' She raised her eyebrows and opened her eyes extra wide. 'I'm on the pavement, and he's on the road. He's in uniform too; but he's so short, he has to trot to keep up with me.'

I began to giggle, propping myself up on an elbow to be ready for the punch line, which I knew by heart.

'"Hey miss!" the man shouts at the top of his voice, as if I'm miles away. "*Isn't it cold up there*?"' Mummy glanced down at me on the sofa. 'So I swing round to face him, and I swat him with the back of my hand.' Now she wacked a damp tea towel so hard that it fluttered from the clothes rack to the floor. 'And the little soldier lands flat on his back, in the gutter.'

I convulsed with laughter. I felt not a shred of sympathy for the man; he'd got precisely what he deserved for trying to insult my giantess of a mother.

One evening, I was sitting in the bath in our damp basement bathroom, which had mould growing on the walls. The door was open and Mummy was wandering in and out, tossing items of dirty clothing into the triangular-shaped wicker laundry basket that stood in the corner; and gently chivvying me to wash myself. My sister was already tucked up on the top bunk of the bedroom we shared, reading a Noel Streatfield novel.

'Mummy,' I began, picking up my wet flannel and arranging it over my raised knees. 'Did you actually fight anybody, in the war?'

'No, darling,' she replied. 'Women didn't fight; that was for the men.'

'But you were in the army. So you must've been a soldier, mustn't you?'

Mummy stood facing me, her back to the basin. It was summer, and she was dressed in a green cotton shift with a leaf pattern on the fabric. Her arms and shoulders were bare and I could smell that sweet, slightly sweaty smell of hers that I found reassuring. 'I was a Junior Commander, by the end of the war,' she replied, raising her eyebrows with an air of mock pride. She'd been to the hairdresser that afternoon and her dark brown hair stood out around her face in a *buffon*. 'But I wasn't a soldier in the sense of having to fight.'

I had no idea what a Junior Commander was; and I was hoping to get her to sit down, on the old wooden chair that lived beside the bath. 'So what did you actually *do*?' I fixed her with serious eyes and refused to look away. After a moment's hesitation, she stepped towards the chair.

'If you hurry up and wash, I'll tell you.'

Still gazing at her, I took the soap from the edge of the bath and worked up a lather between my hands. The bath water was none too warm by now, but if I asked her to turn on the hot tap, she might forget my question.

She picked up the pumice stone and turned it over with her long, slim fingers. "The most exciting thing I did was stand on the roof of a tall building, watching out for fire bombs. Did I tell you about that?'

The cake of soap slipped through my fingers into the water.

'It was utterly terrifying, but it was a job that had to be done and I was ordered to take my turn.' Mummy kneeled down on the bathmat, plunged her long arm into the water, retrieved the soap and gave it to me. 'Hurry up, love, or there won't be time for a story.'

My sister and I both loved being read to, but the real life story Mummy was telling was much too gripping to forego. And I could tell that her legs were aching. She suffered from varicose veins and hated to stand on one spot for long, especially on the cold concrete of the bathroom floor. Now, to my delight, she sank onto the chair and leaned towards me.

'Did some fire bombs land while you were standing on the roof?' I spread the soapy lather over my chest and arms, my eyes still fixed on hers.

Mummy shook her head, and the new buffon wobbled, releasing a whiff of hairspray. She must have spent the afternoon with her head inside one of those space-age spherical hairdryers, while I was at school. That was very unusual: normally she washed and dried her hair at home, to save money.

'No darling, nothing landed while I was on duty.'

I felt rather disappointed. 'But… was the building really, really tall?' When Mummy took us into central London to see art exhibitions, the buildings we passed were huge.

'A good few storeys. I had to climb up a ladder onto the roof.' She leaned towards me and swooshed water over my shoulders, washing away the soap.

I pictured her standing precariously on a steeply sloping slate roof. 'Wasn't it very hard to keep your balance?'

'No darling, the roof was flat, with a railing all the way round. It was quite safe – so long as the building wasn't hit.'

'Did you stand there all night?'

'About two or three hours at a time, after the air raid siren went.'

'But if a bomb had landed, what were you supposed to do?' I wasn't going to let this go. It sounded at once appallingly dangerous, and terribly exciting. And it made Mummy into a major hero of the war.

'I was supposed to rush down into the building, to raise the alarm.'

'But Mummy, if a bomb had landed, wouldn't they have heard it?' I pictured a lot of people in different rooms, going about their business, then a loud crash and a woosh of flame.

Mummy grimaced. 'Probably. Come on darling, time to get out.' She stood up, produced a towel and held it out invitingly. In my mind's eye I saw her shimmying down the ladder in her army uniform, yelling for all she was worth, and the people rushing down the stairs and out into the road. Slowly I stood up in the bath and tugged at the chain to let the dirty water out. Then I climbed onto the rim of the tub and into her arms.

Chapter 6
Self Portrait in a Red Scarf

ONE OF THE MOST STRIKING paintings we found in Sheila's studio was a small self portrait painted on a canvas board measuring just twelve inches by ten. The head in the painting was only life size, yet the image pushed at the edges of the board with unnerving power. Sheila wore her hair wrapped in a red cotton scarf chequered with a fine gold thread. She'd knotted the scarf on the crown of her head; in front of the knot, a permed quiff of dark brown hair framed her forehead. Sheila's brow was smooth, the eyebrows plucked in perfect arcs, the amber eyes perfectly balanced, the nose small. The pursed, unsmiling lips were soft and full, coloured with a dark pink lipstick only a shade lighter than the scarf.

Sheila must have painted this portrait shortly after the war, although the date wasn't written on the back. It was the earliest painting of hers in which it was clear she'd used a palette knife: the gold thread had been cross-hatched onto the scarf with a small, delicate blade; and areas of the forehead and temple revealed the marks of a knife. In the bottom right hand corner, the initials 'SD' appeared on a stylish slant, painted with a fine brush in the same pinkish-gold employed on the cheeks and neck.

It was a delicate, exquisite bit of painting in which my mother captured both the quality of her own beauty and the sorrow that gripped her in her mid-twenties. Her steady gaze was somewhere between aloof and wary, the regard of a highly intelligent woman trying to come to terms with a profound shock.

The days I spent in my shed reading through the family letters eventually convinced me of what lay behind the sadness in Sheila's

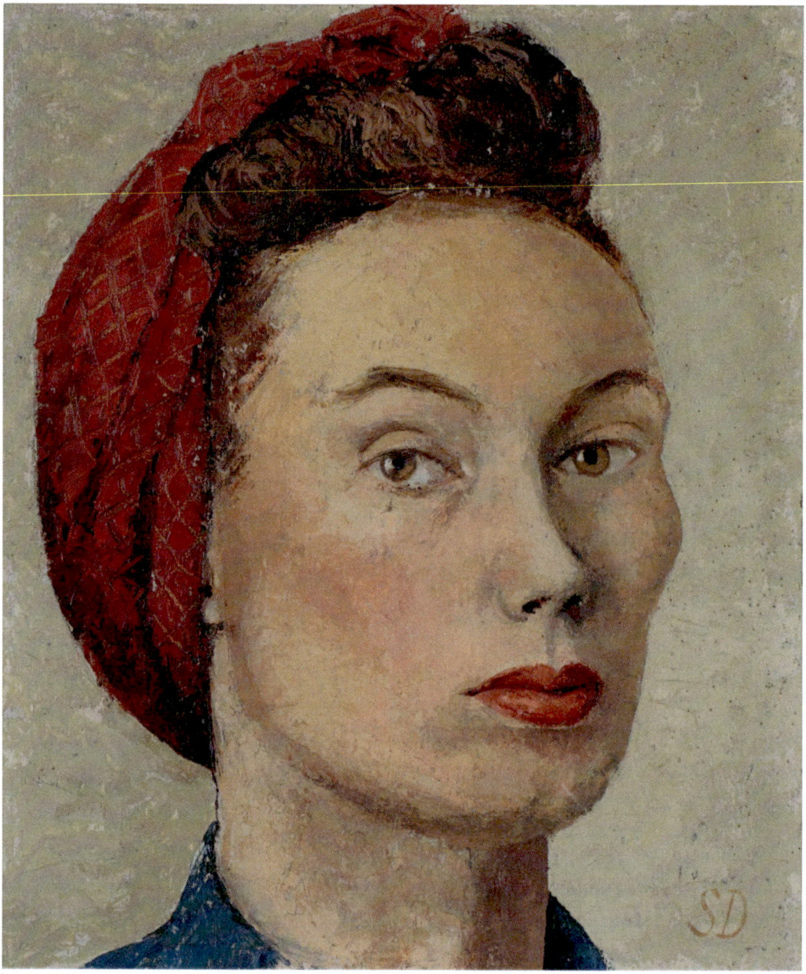

Self Portrait in a Red Scarf, c. 1946

face, in both *Self Portrait in Browns* and this painting, which I call *Self portrait in a Red Scarf.* It was a tragedy I'd known about since childhood; but I'd failed fully to appreciate its impact on Sheila.

Most of the wartime letters were encased in diminutive, off-white envelopes bearing the head of George V on the brown, penny halfpenny postage stamp. As I took out each letter and waved away the cloud of fine dust that rose into the air, the daily life of the Denning family became more concrete in my mind's eye. I could see my grandmother in her mackintosh hurrying in from the child welfare clinic, speaking to cook in the kitchen, then hurrying to the dining room to check the table had been properly laid for lunch. Bum would appear any minute, tired and hungry after morning surgery. And here was my uncle Joe, aged seventeen, in his grey flannel trousers and waistcoat, handing his mother the latest letter from Sheila.

In the autumn of 1940, having just left school, Joe observed his parents' lives with the critical eye of one who was ready to set off into the wide world. He wrote regularly to his sister:

> 'Darling Shee
> I hope you are well and having a good time. I gather you are from your letters which Mama awaits eagerly... Bum does nothing but fish in wet or fine weather. He has caught about a dozen pike between 2–3½ lbs. He has bought a new reel which is a great success.
> 'Ma does nothing but work...'

Joe was trying to make plans for his future and told Sheila he was considering becoming a solicitor. To study law he needed a credit in Latin, which he'd not taken at school, so he signed up for a 'crammer' in Kent. He was also mulling over which branch of the armed forces to opt for when he was called up. While studying for his Latin exam, he received advice that he'd make more money as a barrister than a solicitor. He mentioned this to Sheila and she arranged for him to meet the barrister father of a school friend, who was a King's Counsel (KC).

Joe went to London the night before his meeting with the KC. After seeing an early showing of the Charlie Chaplin movie *The Great Dictator*, he took the tube to Gloucester Rd, hoping to find a cheap hotel. He lost his way in the blackout and then the air raid siren sounded. Later he wrote to Sheila:

> 'It was about 8pm and I didn't know where I was or where the hotel was, and so... I ran to Earls Court and went down the tube for the night! It was a grand experience. I slept on a bunk of hard wood with a soldier above me. Tubes went on until midnight, lights stayed on all night, but hot drinks and refreshments were served and I enjoyed it. I slept in my clothes with my overcoat under me. I would not have missed it for the world, so cheap...'

Despite his rough night, Joe was excited by watching the KC in court the following day and made up his mind to opt for the bar. He was concerned, however, about whether Bum could afford to support him during his studies. With hindsight, it seems unlikely that a man who had managed to pay for both his sons to board at expensive public schools would have baulked at putting one of them through university; but Joe took nothing for granted.

Around this time, he learned of a Royal Air Force scheme whereby young men were sent to university for six months, at government expense, prior to training as pilots. Joe decided to apply for the scheme and, with a certain diffidence, put Oxford as his first choice of university. He was just eighteen.

Dee was unhappy about her teenage son applying for the scheme, which was tantamount to joining the RAF. All British men aged 18 to 40 were liable to conscription, with exemptions for certain 'reserved' occupations and for certain medical and veterinary science students. It's not clear to me how Joe could have delayed joining up; but Dee and Sheila believed he could have done. Dee passionately wanted Joe to wait, whereas Bum encouraged Joe to apply for the scheme.

When Joe heard that his application had been successful, he wrote to Sheila:

> 'I feel such as must a tadpole feel on the eve of turning into a frog, for I am going to Oxford on April 15th 1941! At the stupid old government's expense! I am feeling awful about enjoying the luxuries of the idle rich undergrad in the middle of a war, but I suppose the Air Ministry don't mind otherwise they would not send me up...'

In October 1941, having completed the university part of the scheme, Joe was sent briefly to Canada and then on to the USA, where he underwent six months' training in the Arizona desert. This was the ideal place to train as a pilot, due to the consistently clear skies. Joe was accompanied by at least one childhood friend from Cricklade, Peter Arkell; but his departure must have felt quite momentous to the Denning family, none of whom had ever travelled outside western Europe. Joe wrote to Sheila from his base at Falcon Field near Phoenix, complaining that he was unsure how to deal with his parents' anxiety:

> 'I get constant request for news about flying. What do Mum and Bum expect me to tell them? ... tell them I spend my time looping the loop or anything else that appeals to you. Actually the schedule is fairly wide and includes night flying which is quite fun although I prefer to be firmly asleep in bed, formation flying which is the greatest fun, navigation. Cross country. Etc. You see, they would hate to know I fly at night (at least I suppose they would!) so just cool them off! I have just soloed on the new plane I am flying which is a Basic trainer it is a

> low wing monoplane with a 450 HP engine. It is a joy to fly and I am feeling rather lucked up. I am certain in fact to be washed out if I am too optimistic! Well, I hope that is enough flying news, so tell the family as little as possible…'

By the summer of 1942, having completed his sojourn in Arizona, Joe returned to England as a fully trained 'Pilot Officer'. He was nineteen and a half and, travelling home to Cricklade, found things had changed. Dee had taken a job in the Censorship Office in London, where she spent her time checking the contents of letters and parcels destined for servicemen in POW camps behind enemy lines; Sheila had trained as an army driving instructor and was working in the home counties. Bum alone remained in Cricklade, still the town's only GP.

On at least one occasion in the summer of 1942, Sheila and Joe met up in London.

Joe wrote to her shortly afterwards, from his RAF base at Peterborough:

> 'I did so enjoy our weekend in town. Wasn't it heavenly. We really must repeat it again soon.
>
> 'At the moment I am trying hard to be a good little boy. Very little smoking, no drinking and no women. Just flying…'

But such moments of shared leisure were few and far between. For the most part, Bum, Dee, Sheila, Joe and Bay were living separate lives, as their various contributions to the war effort demanded. Bay had turned eighteen in August and was making enquiries about joining the Royal Navy, while Joe was frequently moved around England by the RAF.

By the autumn of 1942, he was stationed at RAF Old Sarum, outside Salisbury, close enough to Cricklade that he could travel home for short visits. It was now dawning on Bum, it seems, that his son would soon be flying sorties over enemy territory, facing much greater risks than in Arizona. When Joe was moved from Old Sarum to Gatwick airport, Bum wrote to him on 7 November in terms which, with hindsight, suggest a premonition of what was to come.

> 'My darling Joe.
> I hope you had a good lunch and a pleasant run down to Gatwick. We miss you very much…
> Bay… says you are now on active service. He says the CO is a very good fellow. Gatwick is in Cox's beat and either he or a friend will look you up and give you some advice. He says you must not let them get on top of you and you must keep your eyes skinned – must not be a fool – or words to that effect. Cox is friendly – very interested in you – means to help you all he can. I know you will be a good chap as you have always been. We are tremendously proud of you, but of course a bit anxious. Now my dear old boy – I wish you the very best of luck. I have always loved you very much. No one could have a better son, or a better friend.
> Drop me a line sometimes, and God Bless you.
> Bum'

Just one month later, in the late afternoon of Monday December 7th, Bum received a phone call from an official at the War Office. Joe had been sent out that day from Gatwick on an armed recce[1] over northern France and had not returned. This was his first operational flight, in a single seater Mustang. The Germans had

1 An 'armed recce' had dual goals. The pilot officers were tasked with flying relatively low in order to observe the situation on the ground and report back on it. If they found suitable targets, they were to fire at them. If their planes came under attack, the instruction was to refrain from returning fire and if possible to remove themselves.

not claimed Joe's plane as among those shot down that day and Pilot Officer McGhee, who had flown alongside him in another Mustang, had seen nothing to explain Joe's disappearance. Joe was now officially 'missing'.

Bum made frantic phone calls to Dee and Sheila in London. Sheila promised to meet her mother and bring her home from Paddington to Swindon. She later wrote:

> *I shall never forget that day… we went to Paddington to ask about train times. As usual during the war, there were no time-tables; one never knew when a train would come. They thought there would be a train going to Swindon that evening – we should come back at, say, nine o'clock.*
>
> *We had hours to fill in. We walked endlessly round the streets near the station, slowly, looking again and again in the window of a chemist, which was closed. I remember still the large glass containers filled with coloured water, blue, red, gold. We walked sometimes arm in arm, each trying not to cry for the sake of the other. We were too agitated to sit down, even had there been anywhere to sit. To keep moving seemed the only way to fill the endless hours.*

Nothing in the family letters told me how Bum, Dee, Sheila and Bay got through the days that followed. Even in her autobiography, Sheila says very little.

> *… messages of hope arrived from officialdom as well as messages of sympathy. 'Missing', they said, was not necessarily the end, there might still be good news, we should not give up hope.*

But as time went by, there was no more news.

> *No-one ever claimed to know what had happened... Had he been shot down over Normandy? Had he gone down into the sea, without trace? Had we but known, we could*

> *have given him burial in our hearts. After a time… my mother and father appeared to have accepted that Joe was dead… I think that my father's heart was truly broken…*

Sheila outlines how, in the early months of 1943, despite the uncertainty about their son's fate, her parents picked themselves up and carried on. Bum continued to care for his patients, while Dee returned to her job at the Censorship Office.

> *They went on hoping for some news of Joe, but none came. My father as yet showed no physical signs of the distress he was feeling, but we knew what he suffered, and he would often weep. I think he probably also had a sense of guilt, for not supporting our mother in her desire to prevail on Joe to wait a year before joining up.*

*

Needing a break from the solitary work of reading family letters, and overwhelmed by sadness about Joe, in December 2018 I visited my friends Claudia and Ian in Cornwall. As we sat and talked in the long, dark evenings, while the wind ripped across the garden and battered the outside walls of the house, Ian told me of his interest in military aviation. He suggested that we access Joe's war record from the National Archive, via the internet. This is what it said:

> Two Mustangs, PO C.B. McGhee and PO J.A. Denning both No. 26 Squadron left Gatwick 14.10 hours 7 December on RHUBARB operation. PO C.B. McGhee area railway Abbeville, Amiens, Beauvais, Grandvilliers. One locomotive destroyed, seen to explode and pieces fly into the air. Two locomotives possibly damaged hits observed on engines also about 20 covered trucks hit. Encountered accurate RED GREEN and YELLOW FLAK

> from AIHT. Guns fired after aircraft had passed over their positions. P/O J.A. Denning area railway targets in Fecamp, Mirville, Doudeville St Valery. P/O J.A. DENNING did not return from operation. NO RT [radio transmission] message was received from him. PO CB McGhee landed Gatwick 15.30.

'It's possible,' Ian told me gently as he rolled a cigarette between his fingers, 'that your uncle's plane sustained damage from the anti-aircraft fire reported by PO McGhee, and crashed later as a result.'

'But wouldn't McGhee have seen it go down?'

'Not necessarily; it would have depended on the weather.'

'Early December.'

'Exactly. They took off from Gatwick at ten past two in the afternoon. By 3.30, when McGhee landed, it would have been dusk.'

'And possibly foggy, at that time of year.'

'Easily.' He paused. 'But it's strange that the Germans didn't claim your uncle's plane.'

To me, the failure to claim the aircraft could only mean one thing, but I found it too distressing to speak of. Joe's plane must have plummeted into the Channel. I could imagine no worse fate than to be trapped, alone, in the tiny space of an aircraft cockpit with a huge weight of water pressing on the doors and windscreen.

*

Very little correspondence has survived from the years 1943 and 1944. A handful of letters give the impression that life went on as usual. Dee wrote to Sheila with accounts of a busy domestic life in Cricklade, compounded by her job at the Censorship Office; Bay wrote of his new existence in the navy, his duties, his travels and his girlfriends. Even Bum, whose enduring grief Sheila describes later in the autobiography, wrote letters packed with trivia.

On 5 December 1944, after giving a detailed account of wintry walks in unsettled weather, Bum wrote baldly to Sheila:

> 'It is just two years today (Thursday) that DOJ [Dear Old Joe] left us – I have put a notice in *Times* and *Morning Post* for best date 7/12. I put his school motto rather than anything else and hope you approve. It seems so futile somehow. I enclose some rather lovely lines and hope you will like them.'

Missing, presumed killed

There is no cross to mark
The place he lies.
And no man shared his dark Gethsemane
Or, witnessing that simple sacrifice
Brought word to me.

There is no grave for him;
The mourning heart
Knows not the distribution of its prayer.
Save that he is anonymous, apart
Sleeping out there.

But though strict earth may keep
Her secret well
She cannot claim his immortality;
Safe from the darkness
Whence he sometime fell
He comes to me.

Pamela Hall

*

It would be difficult to overstate the impact on Sheila of Joe's disappearance. My sister and I were born in 1955 and 1957 respectively, some 13–15 years after the event. In response to my childhood questions about the war, Sheila told me endless stories; but she spoke very little of Joe. All I knew was that her favourite brother had set off on a flight across the English Channel and not returned. It was perhaps because she spoke so little of him that, when I noticed the grief-stricken look in her eyes in the painting *Self Portrait in Browns*, I failed to make the obvious connection.

Throughout my childhood, two large black and white portrait photos in silver frames faced each other on Gaga's walnut side table. To my eyes, the faces of the two young men were quite similar, but I knew which one was Joe and which was Bay. Occasionally, if I was left alone in the room, I would steal up to the photo of Joe and study his face closely. I hoped in this way to discover the secret of how he'd met his end. But the photo showed me only a glimpse of who he was, not how he died.

I have a copy of Joe's photo propped on my desk now, as I write. It shows a smooth-skinned young man in a grey flannel jacket, his shoulders twisted at an angle, gazing into the middle distance. He is neither looking at the photographer nor avoiding the latter's gaze and his expression is passionately serious. He has a head of luxuriant dark hair, neatly combed above a high forehead, bushy eyebrows and clear, candid eyes. His cheeks are sharply chiseled, tapering to a firm but narrow chin; his nose is straight, his mouth full.

Despite the permanent and insistent presence of the photograph, I don't recall either Sheila or Gaga speaking of Joe in any detail. When Sheila reached her eighties, this changed. She went into a process of looking back over her life, going through old letters and papers and thinking a lot about her childhood.

During one of my visits when we were sitting together, in reflective mood, she told me that she had been thinking 'a great deal' of Joe. She had still not abandoned the hope that one day, answering a knock at the door, she would find an old man who, having previously lost his memory, had now recovered it and come to find her. Hearing these words, I felt the full force of her sadness. Sheila felt life had cheated her of the love, support and companionship she might have given to and received from Joe; and the sense of loss was becoming sharper as she moved into old age.

PART THREE

DECEMBER 2018

I was in an upbeat mood. It had been a sharp, frosty winter's day and I'd been for a run on Rodborough common on my way to Dad's, enjoying the sensation of the cold air cutting into my throat. A delicious warmth hit me when I entered his room, pumped out by two electric heaters and a couple of logs burning slowly in the grate. Dad was sitting up in bed in his grey fleece hat with the duvet pulled up across his chest. His face lit up when he saw me.

'Well, I never! What a surprise!' The tone was faintly mocking, but friendly.

I stepped towards the bed and squeezed a bony hand which lay, as if forgotten, on the paisley blanket which covered the duvet.

'How's things, Dad? Keeping warm?'

Dad's olive green fleece was zipped up to the chin, and a pair of fingerless gloves lay at the ready on his tummy. He felt the cold acutely now, even though he never left his bed.

'Just about,' he replied, shifting his shoulders against the pillows. They remained broad and powerful-looking, even while the rest of his body was shrinking. 'And you? Are you cold? Come and warm up by the fire.'

'I'm fine, it's very warm in here and I've just been for a run.' I glanced towards the windows, where the light was fading fast. 'It's lovely out there.' It was almost Christmas and the days were short. 'Shall I close your shutters?'

'Yes, please.' Dad's eyes followed me as I stepped towards the windows on the far side of the room. I liked handling the shutters. They spent their days folded against the thick stone walls to either side of the windows, like the wings of waiting angels. It pleased me to open them out across the shadowy glass and drop the metal latches into place.

'You're looking very trim,' Dad smiled approvingly as I pulled up the chair on castors and sat down.

'Thanks, Dad.' I studied his face. The gaunt look of the last few weeks had all but vanished. 'You don't look so bad, yourself!' I half wished I'd brought my drawing book. How was it that at 97 a man could seemingly drift close to death and then revive? But then, Dad's carers gave him Rolls Royce care, within the limits of what was possible in a draughty stone cottage.

The door opened and in walked Charlie, today's carer. 'How about a drink, Alan? It's gone six o'clock. Fancy a beer?' He glanced at me. 'You can have one too, Teresa, we've got lots.'

Dad was gazing up at Charlie with a look of amusement. 'A beer?' he repeated slowly, as if he'd never been offered one before and wondered what it was. 'Yes, alright then, yes, I will.'

'It'll do you good, Alan,' Charlie added, tossing me a wink as he went out the door. A moment later he was back with two glasses of beer and a plate of oatcakes. He swung Dad's special table across the bed and placed his glass and the plate in front of him.

I watched as Dad took a couple of swigs.

'Mm,' he said, 'delicious.' Then he turned to me. 'Won't you have some?'

'I've got some, Dad, look.' I lifted my glass and lent forwards to clink it against his. With some difficulty, he broke an oatcake in two and put it in his mouth. He'd lost a lot of dexterity in his fingers over the years. "Determination", I reflected, should have been his second name.

'Have one of these,' he told me, gesturing at the plate. 'Very good with beer.' I didn't really want one, but I took one anyway. A collection of crumbs was forming on Dad's fleece, and I leant forwards to dust them off. As I did so, he turned his big brown eyes on me and offered me his glass.

'No thanks,' I replied, 'I've got my own.' He gazed at me with a soft, beneficient smile. Then he pushed the plate of oatcakes in my direction.

'Have another one, they're very good.'

'No, really, I'm not hungry right now.' I steered the plate back into the centre of his table. 'These are for you, while you're waiting for your supper.'

'They're very, very good.' Dad went back to shoveling fragments into his mouth.

When he'd finished, he rested back against his pillows and gazed around the room with an expression of satisfaction. I wasn't in a hurry and was wondering what might be a good subject of conversation. I decided to explore how aware Dad was of his age, a subject that had long intrigued me.

Resting my forearms on the bar at the side of the bed, I leaned forwards. 'D'you know how old you are?' I began.

Dad gave me a sharp look. 'Why, how old am I?'

I took a deep breath. 'You're 97! What an achievement that is!' We'd celebrated his birthday the week before, and I'd made him a chocolate cake which he'd eaten with great relish.

'No, no, no!' Again the big brown eyes were turned on me, this time with a look of disbelief and a measure of indignation.

'You are, Dad! You were born in 1921 and now it's 2018. You'll be 98 on your next birthday!' And if you live another three years, I thought to myself, you'll get your telegram from the Queen. I didn't dare say it out loud, because that would be tempting providence. Generally I wasn't convinced he'd survive that long, but this evening anything seemed possible. 'Why,' I added, 'how old d'you think you are?'

As I spoke, Charlie returned, bearing another tray with Dad's special plate and cutlery. The smell of home-made fish pie wafted towards me.

'We're discussing Alan's age,' I told Charlie. 'He doesn't believe me that he's 97.' I turned back to Dad. 'So, go on, how old d'you think you are?'

Dad glanced up at Charlie with a faintly anxious look, then cast his eyes around the room while he considered the question. 'Eighties, I suppose,' he said slowly, as if it was a matter to which he hadn't given much thought. 'Early eighties…'

'No, Dad, you really are 97. And it's something to be proud of!'

What Dad did next astonished me. Staring at me with a look which blended amusement and outrage in equal measure, he lifted his right arm from under the covers, turned his bony white hand on its side like the blade of a knife, and, very slowly, swung it towards my neck. He stopped when he got there, but the meaning of the gesture was utterly clear: it was a karate chop, intended to silence me.

My reference to his age had hurtled him back to those long years when he saw me as his troublesome younger daughter, the one who sometimes challenged his domineering behaviour.

Chapter 7
A Life of Threadbare Richness

IN THE EARLY PART OF 1943, Sheila completed her Officer-Cadet training. By now, in addition to grief about Joe, she was struggling with the dearth of cultural and creative activity which characterized war-time life. She began to take an interest in the work of the Army Education Corps (AEC), a body tasked with improving troop morale with concerts, films and art exhibitions. This led to her applying for a commission with the AEC, who posted her to Bulford Camp on Salisbury plain. Here she was given a free hand to organize whatever cultural events she chose.

> *At last I had found my niche in this hard and uncongenial world of Army life. I soon had a circle of friends of all ranks, kindred spirits, writers, musicians, painters, intellectuals, Jesuits, all of us struggling to make life bearable in this strange place. There was a small unit of Royal Army Medical Corps (RAMC) paramedics and ambulance people who were also training as parachute jumpers, in the event of our possible invasion of France, and this small group seemed to consist largely of semi-pacifist intelligentsia, among whom we found many friends… I made a lifelong friend in Private Mary Harper*[1]*; and of the men, John Cope, who took up with Mary, and Mac, who took up with me, and Charles Slaughter, a Jesuit training for the priesthood…*
>
> *We organized what we wanted, naturally, and I don't think we had huge audiences among the rank and file. But we started a film club, and affiliated ourselves to the*

1 Mary Harper became a print maker and textile designer after the war.

British Film Institute; they proved most efficient and sent us 'Battleship Potemkin', 'Dr Caligari' and many other films... We started evenings we called 'Words and Music' which combined readings of poetry and prose (read by us) with music played... on gramophones – each evening based on a vague theme. These events took place in a small hut furnished with hard uncomfortable chairs, but to us they were the breath of life.

While much was going on in the outside world, Sheila and her friends at Bulford felt they were playing a waiting game. Rumours were rife as to what the military were planning, but security was good and no information was leaked. It wasn't until Bulford's RAMC paratroopers were ordered to an unknown destination, in May 1944, that it became apparent that something major was about to happen. Sheila's boyfriend Mac would never return from the D Day landings on June 6th.

While she was at Bulford, Sheila was exposed to pacifist thinking for the first time, since many of her new friends were Quakers. She had long been unhappy about the British policy of bombing German cities, and in February 1945, she and her friends felt outraged by the fire bombing of Dresden.

We were winning the war in Europe, so why was it necessary? Some of us felt that Dresden amounted to a war crime.... These cities were not military targets; old men and women, young women, young children and babies, were being killed in their thousands, and to what end? I did not want any more part in it; and early in 1945 I requested to be allowed to 'resign my commission' – in short, to leave the army. After some help from the Central Board for Conscientious Objectors, and appearing before a military tribunal to state my case, I was allowed to leave in April 1945.

When the war ended a couple of weeks later, Sheila decided to volunteer for relief work on the continent. She applied to join the Quaker organization the Friends' Relief Service (FRS).

> *At this time… the condition of very many people in most European countries, was dire indeed. Malnutrition was rife almost everywhere and its consequences were disease, weakness and death. The Allies began to send in supplies by ship and by air as soon as humanly possible – certainly before the end of May. In Holland the supplies arriving by boat had to be broken into to feed the dockers before they had the strength to unload the cargo.*

Sheila was hoping to work in Germany 'to try to repair some of the damage I felt we'd inflicted on the German people'. But before completing the FRS training course, she received an urgent message from Dee. Bum had had a heart attack while delivering a baby by forceps in a rural cottage and had been rushed to hospital. She must please come home at once.

Bum survived, but needed a prolonged rest. Since Bay was stationed in Sierra Leone with the navy, it fell exclusively to Sheila to provide support to her parents. With some reluctance, she cancelled her trip to Germany and took a post with the Quakers near Godalming in Surrey, from where she could travel to Cricklade at weekends. The work involved sorting, packing and dispatching to Europe donations of second hand clothes, for use by refugees and displaced people. Sheila and her new colleagues, who were all male, lived and worked in a large wooden hut on a country lane. One of her co-workers was a man called Peter Garnett.

> *Peter was the cook and made the most delicious chocolate puddings, fairly often, at my request. He was from a middle class Yorkshire family, a serious-minded young man, not a Quaker but a somewhat High Church Anglican who was*

> *intending to become a priest. We became friends, fell in love and decided to marry.*

In November 1945, Peter took Sheila to Yorkshire to meet his parents and over the next few weeks wrote her a stream of passionate letters. But in early January 1946, he told her he was gay and could not go through with the marriage.

When I was growing up, Mum told me all sorts of things about her personal life, most of which I didn't need to know, but she didn't say much about Peter. With Mac, the RAMC paramedic she'd had an affair with at Bulford, it was different. I can still remember the look of pain on her face one Saturday afternoon when I was quizzing her about the war. It was 1965 and we were out for a walk on Wimbledon Common.

'Poor Mac,' she said very softly, 'he was a real sweetie.'

'What happened to him?' I was eight years old and sometimes too curious for my own good. We were following a well-trodden path towards a group of chestnut trees bedecked in pink and creamy candle blossom.

She sized me up with an uneasy expression. 'He went to France, darling; and he didn't come back.'

I heard the sadness in her voice and didn't seek any more detail. But my thoughts went in the inevitable direction: what if Mac *had* come back? And Mummy had married him? Mac would have been my father. I didn't like my real father very much when I was eight. He could be nice at times, but his temper terrified me: he would erupt in bouts of violent anger at the smallest provocation. And he frequently upset Mummy so much that I had to invest huge amounts of energy trying to comfort her. The idea that I could have had a different daddy was quite appealing. What was he like, this Mac? I had the impression he'd adored Mummy. Would he have loved me, too? Would he have been kind? My school friends' fathers never seemed to shout like Daddy did. Would Mac have brought me presents? Taken us out to lunch? Daddy was permanently skint and could never buy us anything, not even the shoes we needed for school.

This train of thought gave me funny, fluttery feelings in my tummy as I trotted beside Mummy, trying to keep up with her long-legged strides. It was quite pleasurable to imagine a life that might have been, but all the while the knowledge that it wasn't the way things were threatened to drag me back to cruel reality. Then in a blinding flash I saw the flaw in my thinking. If Mummy had married Mac, she would have had different children and I wouldn't have been born at all! That was a deeply disconcerting thought.

*

At some point in 1946, Sheila left the FRS and returned to London, living with her cousin Joy and signing on as a part time student at Heatherley's School of Art. She was hoping to apply for a War Service Grant to study painting full time.

London was now a bleak city of exhausted, bereaved people, heaps of rubble and badly-damaged buildings. The winter of 1946–1947 was bitterly cold:

> *Rain fell on the streets and immediately froze. The pavements became sheets of glass on which one could hardly walk. Life was difficult and austere.*

It was in this environment that Sheila wrote her poem *To the World's End.*

I had to go
To the World's End[2] *in the unexpected snow.*

I saw how the flakes fall dark
And hard as pieces of steel from the winter sky,
And I more used to deathfall than sudden snow.

More slowly than steel they fall
But feel for the grey prisoners no pain,
Having lain their indifferent clothing of alien snow.
Snow has no pain nor pity.

Than charity more cold, its fierce ground-light
Shines harsh to search the eyes that come and go.

Light beating from the ground
Has found our falsehood and revealed our fear
That here we walk on death we daily sow.

I shall not go
Again to the World's End in the unwelcome snow.

She was starting to paint again. Among her work from this period we found an image of the dark interior of an abandoned church, painted on a canvas board. I turned it over, hoping to learn the year it was produced. There was no date, but the words 'Bombed Church' appeared in Sheila's elegant, sloping capitals, followed by an address in Queensway, W2. In a very thin layer of paint, applied with brushes, she conveyed the gloom inside a building which had been hit in an air raid. Two majestic, dark red pillars framed a diminutive altar table, behind which an altarpiece and crucifix in dull browns stood below a broken window. The broken glass was partially covered with planks of wood. Above, the sky was visible and the silhouette of a pigeon perching on the window frame suggested that life went on, in the city beyond the building.[3]

---

2 A district at the Fulham end of the Kings Road in London.

3 *Bombed Church* can be seen at www.sheiladenning.com.

I began to wonder about Sheila's state of mind in the months and years immediately after the war. I knew, because she told me, that she'd felt very low, depressed even, during her studies at Camberwell from 1947 to1951. Now I was becoming curious about when this low mood started. As to the cause – I assumed it was the combination of the loss of Joe, on which she now had more time to dwell; the loss of Mac; her rejection by Peter and the realisation that her once very solid and loving family would never return to what it had been before the war.

In a letter written by Bum to Sheila in November 1950, he refers to her seeing a psychologist, a development about which he is clearly not too comfortable:

> 'I do hope your psychologist has been able to help you. Don't dally with him too long but get cracking. God helps him who helps himself – I think that effort overcomes weakness and leads to strength – hesitation and compromise only make one neurotic so get cracking my honey and don't keep picking and spying on yourself...'

By 1946, my grandfather had made a partial recovery from his illness, but when he exerted himself he continued to suffer minor heart attacks. Being unable to work, he had sold the Cricklade house and moved to Ireland with Dee, claiming that his motive was to avoid paying UK income tax, but no doubt he was also seeking an escape from painful memories. Rather than buying a new home, my grandparents chose to stay in a series of guest houses, initially near Dublin and later in Counties Clare, Galway and Sligo. Bum wrote to Sheila frequently:

> 'I am sitting in the window 70 yards from the sea – overlooking the Bay. Sea is a sort of indigo blue – the pier is a blaze of sunshine and granite. Houth in the distance

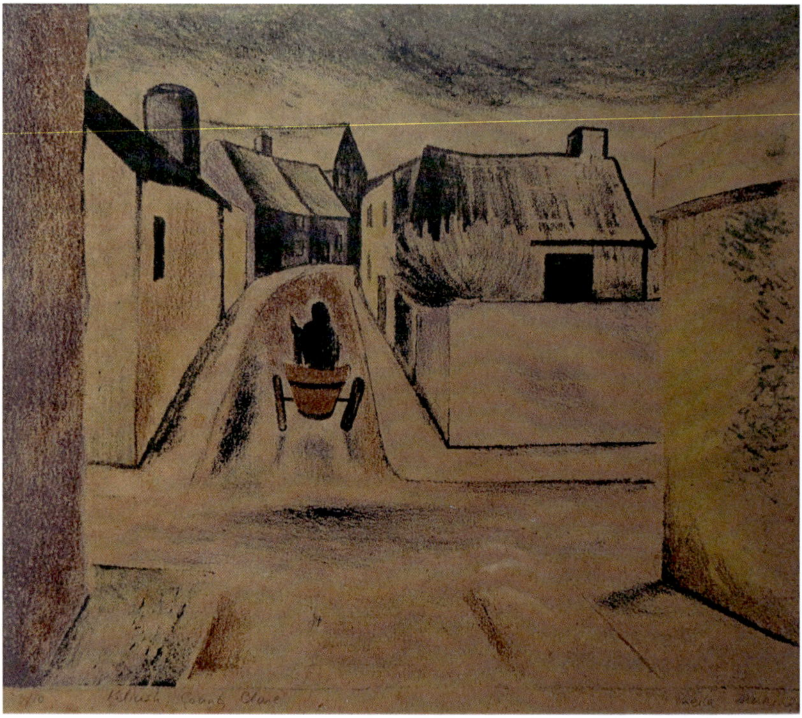

Irish Pony Cart, c. 1947

> is dappled with white houses, green fields brown heather and grey cliffs. Altogether very pleasing and peaceful…
>
> 'It is marvellous too to be getting better… Of course I have to go easy and not walk more than ten miles or so at a time…'

Sheila visited her parents several times in their new surroundings and discovered that she felt very much at home in Ireland. After spending a week prowling around Dublin in September 1946, she picked up a sympathy with Irish Republicanism which would last to the end of her days. It comes through in her poem *Dublin Landscape.*

The Liffey slaps the stone piers,
Laps gently the steep wall
Under the Parapet, under the Four Courts.
A soft blue sky between the curling clouds
Shines in the water; houses of pink and grey
Nudge, poke and jostle for room along the quay.
Small slap of uncovered feet
Of children who chase, or drag with a limping lag,
Or pull their wheeled boxes rolling across the stones.

Here among the driftwood of foreign trinkets
Behind the winking window of the blackened shop
Shout still the strident yellow broadsheets,
And on the shelves the books smoulder with
an ancient trouble.

Here is a country all contained
Within a little space.
Where, in what other city,
Can one come from the many-coloured river
Into the richly-peopled streets,
And hear at once the cold cry of the seabird,
And see beyond the squares the sudden mountains?

It was possibly in one of the Irish guesthouses that Sheila painted Bum, sitting in a deep armchair drawn up close to a small grate in which a fire burns. It's a sketch more than a finished painting, and was made on the back of a landscape painted on hardboard. Compared to the grandfather whom I dimly remember, Bum looks relatively young, albeit with a receding hairline and soft grey hair. He's leaning back comfortably in the armchair, his legs stretched out towards the blaze, and his eyes focused on a newspaper which he grips firmly in his right hand. The tawny beige walls of the sitting room blend softly into the lavender beige of the carpet; a small table, just big enough to hold a cup and saucer, sits beside the armchair. Behind Bum's chair, a large and comfortable-looking couch with a couple of fat cushions nestles against the wall; both couch and cushions are covered in a sage green fabric, the same colour in which Sheila outlined the shape of the armchair and the shape of her father's head.

Sheila loved walking as much as Bum. From time to time, during visits to her parents, she would go off by herself for long walks in the mountains, delighting in the country people whose paths she crossed. One of her stories was about a very tall, red-headed man who reared up from behind a dry stone wall to greet her. He was utterly well-intentioned, just pleased to meet an unfamiliar woman who was almost as tall as he was.

'They're a fine people, the Irish,' Mummy told me one evening when she was standing at the sink in her butcher's apron. She wiped her hands on the kitchen towel, stepped towards the window and stooped down to the crate of half pint bottles of Guinness she kept on the floor. She said she drank Guinness to help with her thyroid disorder: Bum had told her it was full of iron and would do her good. I found the bottles intriguingly dark and they made a nice clinking sound if you jumped or skipped on the floorboards next to them. I watched in fascination as Mummy took the bottle opener out of the drawer, prized off the frill-edged metal lid and poured the black, velvety liquid into a tumbler. Her eyebrows moved up towards her hair line as the pale brown froth rose swiftly up the sides of the glass, propelled by the force of the fizzing drink. Any second now the froth would zip over the top and cascade down the sides of the glass. But it didn't, for once, and Mummy glanced at me with an air of triumph as she raised the glass to her lips. 'And they have the gift of the gab. Lots of poets, writers, playwrites among the Irish.'

I was a bit young to appreciate this. What I wanted to know was, when were we going to *go* there? At seven, I'd never been further than West Wales and I was impatient to visit this magical land that she talked about. Daddy had recently bought a second hand gypsy caravan and parked it in our back garden for Anna and me to play in. It was a tiny cart with a curved roof, giant, rusty metal wheels and shafts between which a pony could be harnessed. The outer walls were painted a faded, mottled, raspberry pink, a colour which at that age utterly delighted me, as did the idea that the wagon (as Daddy called it) had once been home to a Romany Irish family. Mummy often told me how, in the west of Ireland, tinkers still roamed the country lanes in wagons like ours.

The first swig of Guinness left Mummy with a beige moustache. As she licked her upper lip, she said, 'One day, darling, when we've got a bit more money, we'll go to Ireland for a holiday. We'll rent a gypsy wagon and a horse and we'll spend a couple of weeks ambling round County Mayo or County Clare on the back roads.'

'Will we sleep in the wagon?' I liked the idea that all four of us would sleep together, in a heap; but it was hard to imagine. Mummy and Daddy often joked about wanting to place a board down the middle of their double bed to divide it into two; and anyhow, Daddy was away lots of nights.

Mummy took another swig and smacked her lips together. 'I expect so, yes.'

'Can we go this summer?'

She frowned. 'No darling, not yet. We need to save some money first.'

On the strength of this I found an empty jam jar under the sink and started a collection to pay for the holiday. Everytime I saw either of my parents with what I thought might be a spare penny or two, I urged them to put it in the jar. But spare pennies were a rarity in our house and the collection never got beyond one and sixpence.

*

Early in 1947, Bay married his wartime sweetheart, Anne Prunier. He was just twenty two and painfully aware that Bum did not approve. He wrote to Sheila before the wedding, pleading with her to support his bride, who had picked up on her future father-in-law's negative feelings towards her:

> 'Will you be able to get down to Brighton on the Thursday afternoon and give Anne moral support for Thursday night as well as Friday. You see although Mother feels O.K. about us getting married now, Bummy is sure to be Bummyish and that will upset Anne as it certainly did for the last two weeks of my sick leave. I'm afraid Anne was unhappy and felt her presence resented, if you see what I mean.'

Sheila had little in common with Anne, but did her best to be kind. Bay and Anne's plan to emigrate to Africa meant that she would soon be left alone to carry the burden of supporting Bum and Dee.

After the wedding Bum and Dee returned to Ireland and, in April, Sheila visited them in County Clare. The harsh winter was at an end and she took long walks along the coast. An intense and beautiful poem came out of this trip, *Slow rolls the green Atlantic.*

Slow rolls the green Atlantic to the land's beginning,
And harsh the wash of wave on the iron shore
Beneath this tower, below these cliffs of Moher.

Such power in bark and beat of ocean's tread
Makes ground-bass to the slow single melody
Of a life of threadbare richness. So constant a moving pattern

Has entered the earth and hides in the heave of the plain;
Look there like foam lie lurking the Aran islands –
In these black cliffs discern the swirl of the petrified sea.

Sheila also made drawings on her trips to Ireland. One of her loveliest works is a lithograph based on one of these. It shows a man in a tiny cart, pulled by a pony along a narrow village street. The poverty of the village is apparent from the diminutive scale of the houses, beautifully conveyed with firm lines, shading and patches of colour. The wheels of the cart spin at perilous angles, and its bottom is only a few inches above the road. Somehow, Sheila manages to give the impression that the cart is bouncing in and out of ruts. The driver sits hunched in his bucket seat, black hair blending into a black jacket, one ear of the pony visible over his left shoulder. Above the houses, a wild sky threatens rain.

Chapter 8
Spirit Levels and Plumb Lines

IN SEPTEMBER 1947, Sheila's War Service Grant came through and she was able to enroll as a full time student at Camberwell School of Arts and Crafts in south London. Bum was in no position to help her and she would inevitably be short of money, but she was determined to manage. She shared a flat in Willesden Lane, north London, with a friend she'd met in the FRS.

> *My grant was £3 a week, which had to cover rent, food, travel and everything else. We were to live largely on spaghetti and to walk instead of taking buses, though Camberwell, being in Peckham, was too far for this.*

Camberwell was regarded as one of the best art schools in London; but in 1947, like most other British art schools and universities, it was in a strange situation. Some of the staff and many of the students were newly demobilized, having lost 6 or 7 years to the war, and the age gap between demobilized staff and demobilized students was relatively small. A second group of students were fresh out of school, aged 16–17. The gulf in life experience between the war veterans and the school leavers was so vast that the two groups rarely mixed[1].

---

1 Vera Brittain describes a comparable phenomenon in *Testament of Youth*, when describing her experience on resuming her studies at Oxford after the Great War. She was one of very few students at Somerville who had served in the war (as a nurse) and, as such, says she was shunned by the younger women students who were just out of school.

Camberwell had continued to function throughout much of the war and had many well known artists on its staff. In 1947 the head of painting was William Coldstream[2], who, with Victor Pasmore[3] and Claude Rogers[4], had set up and run the Euston Road School of drawing and painting from 1937–1939. There, the emphasis had been on representational painting based on close observation. Some of the artists in the group had been members of the Communist Party and others, though not Communists, were staunchly left wing. They'd reacted against the avant garde art movements of the 1910s and 1920s such as vorticism, cubism and surrealism and sought to create an art of social relevance which was easily understood by ordinary people. In 1947, this group of painters dominated Camberwell. Pasmore, Rogers and Lawrence Gowing[5] taught painting and John Minton[6] headed the Illustration department.

It's not clear that there were any women on the staff at Camberwell in 1947. John Alford's painting *The Teaching Staff at Camberwell*,

---

2 William Coldstream (1908–1987) studied at The Slade under Henry Tonks and was a member of the London Group and, later, an official War Artist.

3 Victor Passmore (1908–1998) was educated at Harrow, studied painting at evening classes, became friendly with Coldstream and Rogers and was elected a member of the London Group. In later life he gave up teaching in order to paint full time.

4 Claude Rogers, (1907–1979), studied at The Slade and exhibited with the London Group and the London Artists' Association.

5 Lawrence Gowing (1918–1991) studied at the Euston Road School in 1938 and was teaching at Camberwell by 1943. He went on to an illustrious academic career at Durham, Newcastle, Chelsea and The Slade.

6 John Minton (1917–1957) was a conscientious objector during WWII and began to teach illustration at Camberwell in 1943. Minton travelled widely through Europe, the Caribbean and North Africa and became well-known as a book illustrator.

painted in 1952, depicts a group of seven be-suited men standing about in a studio bristling with easels. The bespectacled figure of Gilbert Spencer, who became Head of Painting in 1950, holds centre stage. He stands with his left hand in his suit pocket and his right hand raised in a gesture of such overbearing authority that one can hear him loudly pontificating on the faults in the student painting on the easel in front of him[7]. It does not take a great leap of imagination to grasp that a female student with even a modicum of self doubt would have struggled in this environment.

Sheila describes how, in 1947, new students were subjected to a strict regime of working from observation, according to a quasi-scientific method.

> *I was set to draw in the cast room, in which were life-sized casts mainly of Greek sculptures. We had to do some months' probation here before being allowed into the Life Room. I soon discovered that the Coldstream way of drawing was the most favoured by the tutors. This seemed to be based on sight-sized drawing arrived at by rigorous measurement. Spirit-levels and plumb lines (a weight attached to a piece of string which, when still, gives a vertical line) were approved; also "negative spaces" – ie the shapes between limbs, for example, in a figure. I remember Coldstream sitting down to look at my drawing, once, and saying – "You see the space between the arm and the body? Doesn't it look like a puppy-dog's head?" I could see that it possibly did, but reflected silently that it was the human being that interested me and not the puppy-dog.*

Coldstream's strict observational approach was to have a major influence on British art education for decades to come. At its best it led to the production of strikingly accurate representations of

7 The painting is reproduced in *Camberwell, It's Students and Teachers, 1943–1960*, Geoff Hassell, p. 32.

subjects from life. Some were beautiful, while many exuded a profound coldness.

Sheila didn't enjoy Coldstream's method, but felt it had some value.

> *I learned to draw carefully and to observe exactly, under this discipline, and I think that up to a point this was useful…*

She wasn't the first student to struggle with the rigidity of the Euston Road group's approach to painting. Erica MacDonald, who started at Camberwell in 1943, under a different group of teachers, later described her experiences thus:

> We were an odd assortment of students, being either very young… wounded ex-servicemen and refugees… In two terms in a badly bombed, badly lit, cold school, they taught me to draw – really draw. The thrill and excitement of that! Later the Euston Road Group came onto the staff… The newcomers to the staff viewed my fluency and ease in drawing with grave suspicion, especially as I was only aged fifteen. I thought they totally disapproved of my work. Pasmore decided to teach me to paint and one day set up a still-life in a room of my own for five hours. When he returned I had finished my first ever painting, bottle labels, highlights and all and enjoyed every minute. Pasmore's reaction was one of absolute fury –"you've made painting easy and it should be difficult", was the burden of his objection. After a night of tears, the only conclusion I came to was that my crime was enjoying painting and working too fast…[8]

Bernard Dunstan[9], who taught at Camberwell from 1950, said of the 'Camberwell way of drawing',

---

8 Geoff Hassell, *Camberwell School of Arts and Crafts, Its Students and Teachers, 1943–1960*, p. 215.

9 Bernard Dunstan (1920–2017) was an artist, teacher and author.

> I was impressed by its intensity and uncompromising attitude – no mere approximation or guessing – but appalled by its rigidity and desperate slowness.[10]

When Dunstan started to teach a life class, he said

> I was baffled by students who drew in such a doctrinaire way; always sight-size; sometimes seeming to get no further than the collar-bones after a morning's work, going laboriously round the outline of, for instance, a foot, with no thought of the form coming towards you or receding…[11]

One grey winter's morning in 2013, I asked Sheila to tell me what she remembered of her time at Camberwell. She was at the stage of life where long conversations were tiring; but on this subject she became animated.

'You weren't allowed to do life painting till you had a thorough grounding in life drawing,' she told me, picking up her mug of Barleycup and cradling it between her hands. She was sitting at the head of her long, narrow dining table, in a bentwood chair which had once belonged to Gaga and had now become almost an extension of her body. The joints of the chair creaked softly when she moved. 'And you had to study anatomy,' she went on, 'which I found very useful.'

The plan chest in Sheila's studio housed two detailed drawings of the human skull, on which every bone was labeled with its medical name. She'd made these as an art student and kept them for more than sixty years.

'Was any of it fun?' I asked. 'I mean, did you enjoy yourself at Camberwell?'

'Not really, no.' She wrinkled up her nose. 'As a school it had

---

10 Geoff Hassell, *Camberwell School of Arts and Crafts, Its Students and Teachers, 1943–1960*, p. 189.

11 Ibid. p. 189.

a very narrow focus. If you weren't preoccupied with tone[12], as opposed to line, you weren't seen as a proper person. So they never thought I was much good.

'Most of the teachers spent their mornings in the pub. I remember Victor Pasmore sticking his head round the door of the life room at eleven am and shouting at the whole group of students, "Mind you all put in the hands and feet!" He was dying to have his first drink with his pals. He didn't even bother to go round the room and look at what we were doing.'

'Are you serious?'

Sheila's ability to express herself by moving her eyebrows had not diminished with age. Now she raised them with a look of thinly veiled annoyance. 'Absolutely.' She drew breath. 'There was another teacher called Michael Salaman[13], less well known, and one morning he and Pasmore were both teaching. The first one to come round said, to quite a few of us, "Too hot, your colours are too hot, put some blue in!" Then a bit later the other one came round and said, "Too cold, your colours are too cold, warm them up!" Many of us did as we were told, particularly those of us who were less confident...'

I knew, without asking, that Sheila would have been among the less confident students. I asked how many women were in the student group.

'There were more women than men; not all the men had come back from the war, and in some areas the demobilisation was very

12 When artists speak of 'tone', they are usually referring to the relative lightness or darkness of a colour. It was through close attention to tone that the artists who dominated Camberwell in the late 1940s described the subjects they drew or painted – whether those were figures, faces or streets of houses. By contrast, an artist like Sheila, whose main preoccupation was line, uses line as their primary means of describing their subject. The two approaches are not mutually exclusive, and both can produce interesting work.

13 Michael Salaman (1911–1987) was a painter and teacher.

slow. But in 1947 many of the women were 17 or 18, just out of school; whereas I was 27 when I started, and 31 when I finished.' She sat back in the chair, resting her slim fingertips against the mug. A look of despair flitted across her features.

'Did you make friends?'

'There were two or three women like me who'd been through the war and we became friends. There were two groups of people at Camberwell: people who'd been through the war and people who hadn't. One group was the very young students on the newly-introduced student grants and the intake of staff who were very young, and hadn't been through the war. The other group, the older students and staff, were nicer.' She tipped back her head and drained the mug.

'But the male students, in general, were a bunch of…' she sniffed as she cast around for the right term, '… arrogant so-and-sos, particularly the very young ones. Several had been at the same Quaker school together, but their behaviour wasn't very Quaker.'

I shuddered, thinking how hard it must have been to do something as personally exposing as painting, in the presence of such men.

'What was the attitude of the staff towards you as a female student?'

'Hostile, definitely hostile. They were nearly all male and they were cliquey. I didn't mix much socially, I wasn't part of the clique…'

'Were female students sexually harassed?'

'Possibly. I wasn't aware of any incidents involving members of staff. But I was perhaps half asleep much of the time: I was in a state of depression, which was only partly to do with Camberwell.'

'How did you cope?'

'Martin Bloch.' Sheila's eyes brightened as she spoke. 'He was the teacher who saved my life. I'd been at the school a couple of years when he appeared. He saved me from total depression and boredom, along with half a dozen other students, who were all floundering. Bloch was a Jewish refugee from Germany, but he'd been in England throughout the war. He treated each of us as an individual, coming round to talk and listen to us. He tried to discover what your genuine gifts and interests were, and then he tried to develop them.'

'Was Bloch a good painter?' I asked.

'I never saw much of his own work, which was figurative, but yes, I think so. He was different from the rest of the staff in that he put a lot of time into teaching us – he didn't go to the pub.'

Barry Hirst[14], who studied at Camberwell from 1950–1952, said of Bloch:

> Bloch, in those days, represented the most diametrically extreme position imaginable when compared to the Euston Road. His strength as a teacher lay in his ability to "fire" his students through his unwavering sense of commitment to painting and drawing, drawing of a very different kind to that practised by other staff. This total belief in drawing was coupled to a use of "colour", which came as a merciful release to many of us. You can imagine the shock for a typical Camberwell student to be told, "Today is a pink day, paint as much of your picture pink as you dare, let the paint flow" or again "do not draw with all these measurements, preserve the naïve quality".[15]

These sentiments are reinforced by what the art dealer Geoff Hassell says of Bloch in his book about Camberwell:

---

14 Barry Hirst (1934–) artist and teacher.

15 Geoff Hassell, *Camberwell School of Arts & Crafts: Its Students and Teachers 1943–1960*, p. 199.

> Bloch had studied in his native Germany under Lovis Corinth (1858–1925) in the early years of the century and had travelled throughout Europe, meeting and working with such people as Jules Pascin (1885–1930), Marie Laurencin (1883–1956), Robert (1885–1941) and Sonia Delauney (1885-1979), Karl Schmidt-Rottluf (1884–1976) and many others. He was thus able to bring to Camberwell a far broader outlook than many of his peers. Much loved by his students, his method of teaching and painting was often derided by some members of the staff. It has been suggested that perhaps he was ahead of his time. This aside, many students were devoted to him and his methods, and his masterful understanding of how colour and light affect atmosphere. Undoubtedly his success as a teacher was in no small way due to his persuasive persona.[16]

'One day,' Sheila went on, 'Bloch said to me, "When you learn to paint freely, and fiercely, you'll be a good painter." I felt greatly encouraged. Nobody else at Camberwell had ever said I'd be a good painter. The other teachers complained that I wasn't sufficiently interested in form and tone, which were the concerns which dominated their painting. It was true that I was more interested in line.'

At the end of her four years at Camberwell, Sheila failed the examination process set by the school. This had a serious effect, not only on her confidence but on her future earning capacity, for she lacked the qualification needed to teach in art schools.

*

16 Ibid. pp. 19–20

Destructive criticism delivered by male artists in positions of authority was something experienced by many young female painters of Sheila's generation. Nora Heysen, who was born in 1911 and eventually achieved recognition as one of Australia's great portrait painters, suffered such criticism during her years studying painting in London. In her book *The Mirror and the Palette*, Jennifer Higgie describes how the Royal Academician James Bateman visited Heysen in her studio in 1935.

> 'Bateman was savage, telling Nora that her work lacked tone, her technique was mechanical, and that she was trying to evoke light and vibration "the wrong way"... she wrote to her parents about the episode, concluding that "he is biased against women painters... we nearly came to blows discussing women artists and their merits."'[17]

Heysen was well connected through her father, the Australian painter Hans Heysen. He introduced her to the painter, art historian and former director of the National Gallery Charles Holmes. When she showed Holmes some of her work, telling him she wanted to paint figures and landscapes, he laughed at her. Heysen felt crushed and devastated by his attitude, which left her 'deeply depressed'.[18]

But it would be wrong to give the impression that all women artists who studied and worked in the UK in the 1940s and 1950s were dismissed by a male-dominated art world. Joan Eardley, who was born a year after Sheila and is now recognized as having been one of Scotland's leading twentieth century landscape painters, thrived at Glasgow School of Art. She enrolled in January 1940, at a time when the school was taking very few students due to

17 Jennifer Higgie, *The Mirror and the Palette*, p. 170.
18 Ibid. p. 171.

the war and she was selected by Hugh Crawford, then Head of drawing and painting, to join a small group to whom he gave special attention. Crawford was an enlightened and empathetic teacher, who encouraged individual students to pursue the study of whichever historic artist or artists most appealed to them.

After completing her studies, Eardley was obliged to take a job as a joiner's labourer in a boat-building yard; but alongside this, and despite the war, she was already submitting drawings to mixed exhibitions in Edinburgh and Glasgow with some success. Later in her twenties, Crawford offered Eardley a post-graduate year at Glasgow School of Art, at the end of which she won two scholarships which enabled her to travel and draw in Italy and France for eight months. By the time of her tragically early death from breast cancer at the age of forty two, Eardley's skill and vision were widely recognized.

Another example of a near-contemporary of Sheila who survived art school and achieved recognition early in her painting career was the Cumbrian artist Sheila Fell (1931-1979). As a teenaged student at Carlisle School of Art in the late 1940s, Fell was told she would never make a painter and should opt for textile design instead; but later, while studying at St Martin's School of Art she began to exhibit, holding her first solo exhibition at the age of twenty four. Befriended by the artist L.S. Lowry, Fell went on to have a successful career and to be elected as a full member of the Royal Academy of Arts at age 44, before her untimely death in 1979. She is best known for her powerful evocations of the Cumbrian landscape.

*

One of the things which helped Sheila through the difficult years at Camberwell was singing. In 1948 she was invited to a concert at Friends House in the Euston Road, at which the Morley College choir were performing Benjamin Britten's *A Child of Our Time.* The conductor was Michael Tippett. Sheila was so moved by the music that she decided to join the choir.

> *I couldn't even sight-read and had never sung in a choir before. To my surprise, they took me without even an audition and I discovered that I was an alto. This casual attitude I think was typical of Tippett – so long as you could "make a cheerful noise unto God" (Gustav Holst? Thaxted?) you were welcome.*

Singing in Tippett's choir lifted Sheila's spirits; and she made new friends.

> *We rehearsed at Morley once a week, and the concerts were quite frequent – often at the Central Hall, Westminster. I soon became a close friend of Neil Tyler, who worked at the BBC; and another friend was Florence Banks. These people, who loved music, were more congenial to me than the snobbish and snooty young men at Camberwell.*

For a while, Neil Tyler and Sheila were more than close friends. They had an affair and she made a pencil drawing of him, in profile, which is so sensitive and full of character that I've always felt as if I knew him, when in reality I never met him. The man in the drawing has sharp cheek bones, slightly hollow cheeks and the beginnings of a receding hair line. Although the drawing ends at the neck, I read into it that Neil was lightly built and a couple of inches shorter than Sheila. He developed quite a passion for her and wanted to get married, but his parents objected. They felt that a woman of twenty eight was 'too old' for their son, despite the fact that he was already thirty. I'm not sure how deeply attached Sheila had become to Neil by the time he bowed to his parents' wishes; but in the wake of losing Mac

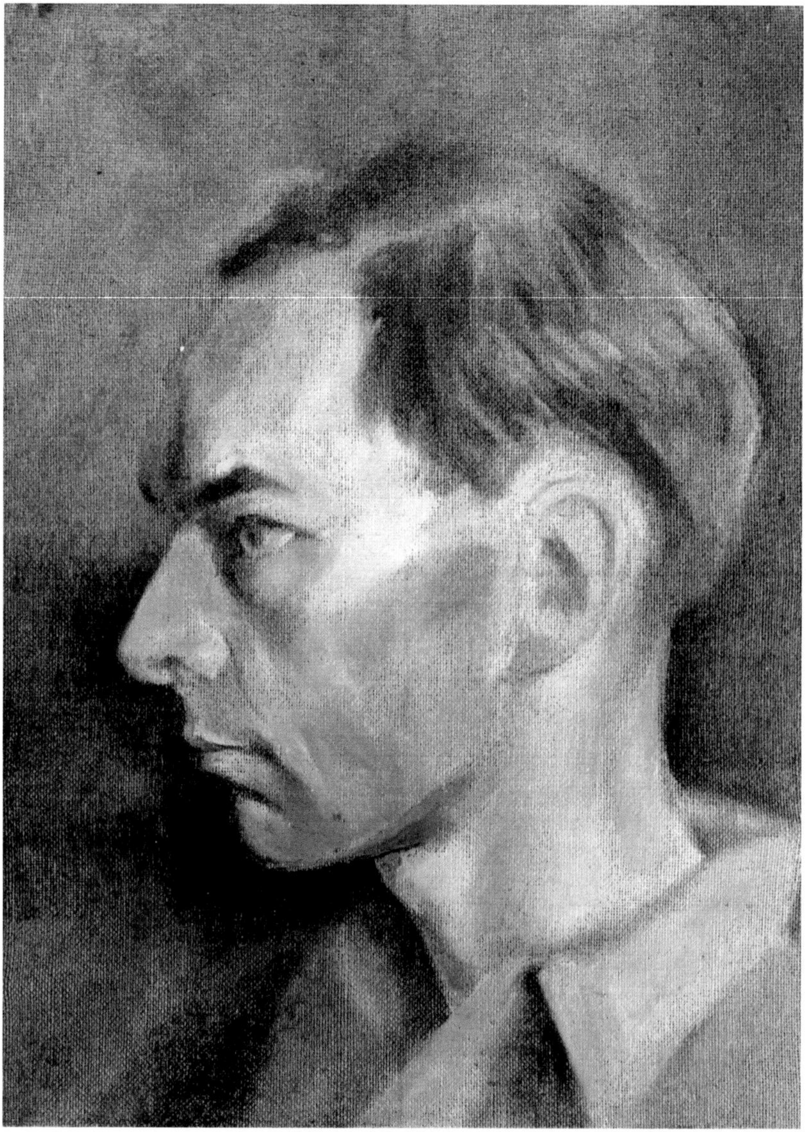

Neil Tyler, pencil drawing, *c.* 1949

and her experience with Peter, this second broken relationship must have knocked her self confidence.
I suspect that Sheila painted *Self Portrait in Browns* while she was at Camberwell. It's darkness of mood fits with the way she was feeling at that point in her life. A third self portrait, *Self Portrait in a Red Hat*, probably dates from the same era.

The latter is a hastily-painted work on board. The style is completely different from that of the other two self portraits. When she produced *Self Portrait in a Red Hat*, Sheila was painting 'freely and fiercely', if I've understood correctly what Martin Bloch said to her. It's a loosely-drawn painting of a woman dressed in blue trousers, a green coat and a red pointed hat, sitting at a table with a pot plant behind her. The colours are bright and full of energy, the paint has been slapped on at speed and the figure and background are outlined unapologetically with thick black lines. It's more reminiscent of the work of the Expressionists than of the Euston Road School.

The facial features are conveyed with brief, deft gestures. The mouth consists of two lines of black with a blur of red between them; the eyes are black-outlined almond shapes, with dabs of cobalt blue for pupils. Despite – or perhaps because of – the lack of detail, the expression comes over with great force. I see a woman wrestling with the depths of anger and despair.

It bothers me that I don't know in more detail what disturbances in Sheila's inner world produced these three self portraits, but the traumatic experiences she told me about are enough to explain the state of mind she was in, by the time she went to Camberwell. Joe was lost, yet the clarity about his fate which might have made it easier to grieve was not available. The secure and loving pre-war world in which Sheila had grown up had vanished. The last of the family homes was gone, leaving her in rented accommodation in London, while Bay was building a life for himself in Africa, and Bum and Dee pursued an itinerant existence in Ireland.

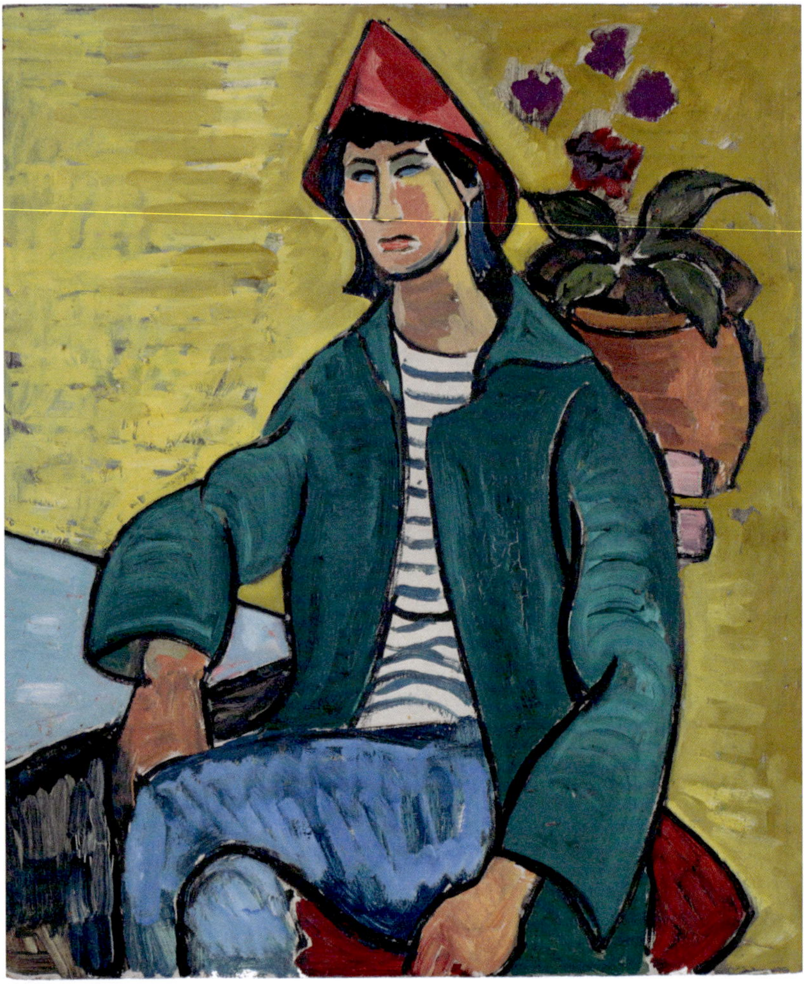

Self Portrait in a Red Hat, c. 1947

As for Sheila's love relationships, popular though she was with men, she'd lost one boyfriend to the war and two others had abruptly called off a near engagement. This series of losses and disappointments was compounded by the disillusionment she must have felt when, having waited so long to go to art school, she was given the message by most of the staff at Camberwell that she had no talent.

PART FOUR

JANUARY 2019

On a drab Friday evening, after a long and tiring day at work, I dropped in on Dad. When I walked into his room, he was lying very still in the hospital bed facing as usual towards the two large windows, on which Christian was fastening the shutters. 'Alan's very sleepy today,' he murmured. I stepped towards the side of the bed so that Dad could see me easily. There was a split second as he tried to decide who I was; then he smiled, weakly at first, and gave a small chuckle. I was relieved to hear it: a frosty reception would have been hard to take. I stooped to squeeze his hand and shot a smile at Christian, who winked at me as he left the room.

I sat down in the chair with the castors and glanced at the logs hissing in the grate.

'Shall I build up the fire?'

Slowly, Dad turned his head towards me. He looked very lean this evening, his cheeks mere shadows. 'Yes,' he murmured, 'yes, do.'

I found the bellows, removed the fireguard and started to blow air between a pair of logs. They were too close together, so I tilted one at an angle. This instantly produced a lively orange flame that played in the gap. Pleased, I sat down again, but in the few moments while my back was turned, Dad had fallen asleep. His head rested motionless in the centre of the pillow and his left eye was closed. The right one lay half open, revealing a dark pupil turned up towards the ceiling. For some years now he'd had trouble closing that right eye; sometimes he slept all night with it open.

I rested for a while, gazing at the fire and enjoying the soft roaring it made in the chimney. After a day at a computer in a harshly-lit and noisy office, nothing could be more calming than to sit in silence in this dimly-lit stone room.

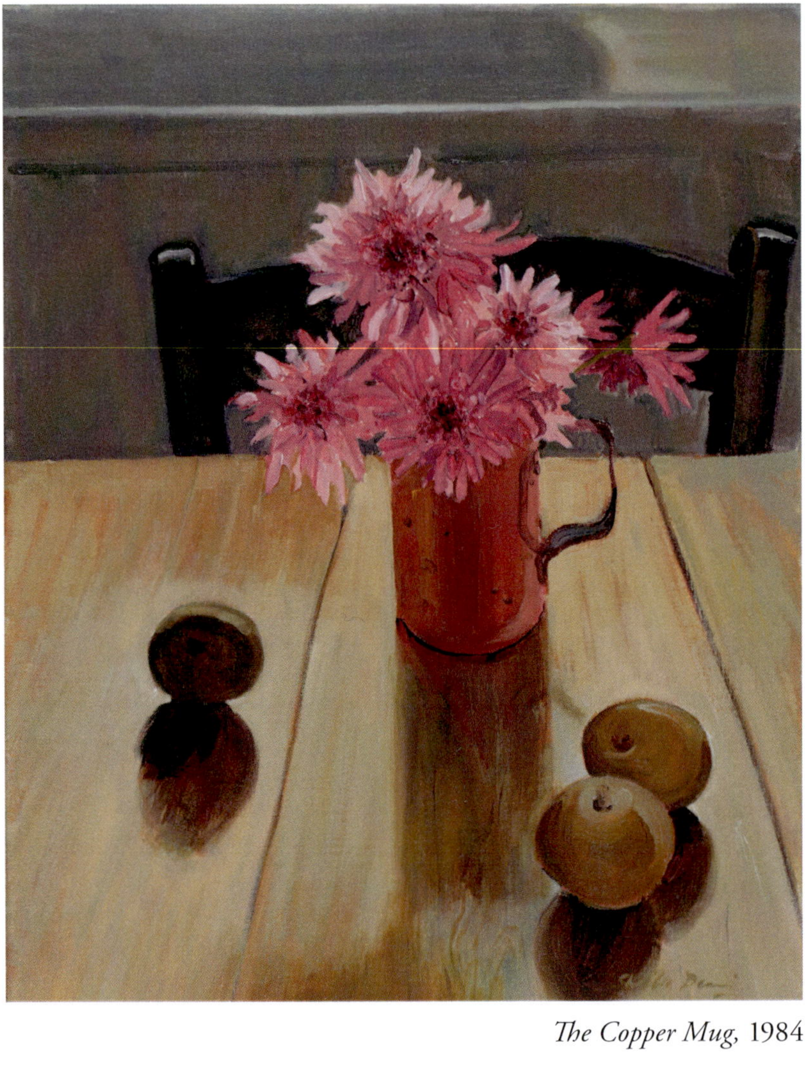

The Copper Mug, 1984

I got up, tiptoed to a rack where paintings were stored and pulled out Mum's The Copper Mug, *which had long since lost its place on the wall. With the frame propped against a bookcase, I spent a long time studying the way she'd painted the slender petals of the dahlias. I'd never shared Mum's taste for shocking pink, but I loved the way she'd conveyed tiny variations in tone. And I liked the way she'd described the thin and dented handle of the mug. That mug had been one of Mum's few treasured possessions, for as long as I could remember. In all the places she'd lived, it had always been with her, sitting on a mantelpiece or bookshelf; sometimes empty, often crammed with flowers from her garden.*

From time to time I turned back to Dad, who was drifting in and out of sleep. Every few minutes he would open his good eye and utter some words, most of which I couldn't make out. I'd rarely known him like this: his speech was indistinct, almost as though he'd had a stroke. I must ask Christian what he thought was going on.

In between the flurries of speech, Dad would sink back into the pillow and the good eye would close. He's sliding closer to death, I told myself; I'd never seen his face so haggard. The realization hurt. I looked away and checked the flame – still lively – before turning back to the painting. I was sitting with the frame resting on my knees, enjoying the curl at the tips of the petals, when Dad spoke again.

'Your mum still painting, is she?' He was trying to smile, speaking in a special tone of polite respect which he reserved for awkward questions.

My eyelids burned. We had been here before; I would have to tell him.

I put down the painting, rolled towards him on the castors and leaned forwards. 'She's gone, Dad; she's not with us any more.' Did I have to spell it out? 'She died; you've forgotten.'

A distraught look came into his eyes, making me wonder if I should have spared him the truth. 'Oh. Oh, of course.' I couldn't tell whether he was upset for himself, by the reminder that Sheila was gone and his own death was hovering close; or sorry that he'd made me repeat something painful to me.

We were sitting with our heads close together when Christian knocked and entered the room. 'Now Alan,' he began, in a warm, energetic voice, 'how about some supper?'

Chapter 9
Riverside Cottage

IN 1949, a new man arrived in Sheila's life.

> *I was sitting one day in Lyons Corner House in Rye Lane, Peckham, having my tea and my chocolate cup cake, when in limped a young man that I did not recall having seen before. How little are we prepared, often, for the significant moments in our lives.*

This was Dad, whose name was Alan Thornhill. He was the youngest child of Sigmund Dornberger, a German Jewish businessman, and Louise 'Bianca' Warren, who was Scottish. Born near Mannheim in 1872, Sigmund had migrated to England in 1897, where he'd changed his name to 'Stewart Thornhill' and become very successful as an importer of glass and china. Stewart and Louise had produced two sons and a daughter and then, after a gap of 17 years, Alan. He'd grown up in wealth and comfort, riding ponies and attending expensive public schools, but suffering intense feelings of isolation. He often described himself as having been an 'after-thought' for his parents, and an object of resentment for his brothers, who saw him as a usurper of their parents' time and money.

> *Having got his tea, he appeared at my table and asked if he could join me. He was at the Art School, he said, and had seen me there.*
>
> *He soon launched into a tirade against solicitors. He and three friends had taken out a lease on a flat in Eccleston Square, near Victoria, and were having problems with the legal arrangements. He seemed very irritated, angry in fact, with the solicitors' firm.... He had been teaching English in*

Italy at the University of Pisa, but had come to the pottery department at Camberwell because he felt the need to work with his hands. He had had a war injury which was causing his limp.

Sheila immediately saw that the young man seated at her table was troubled by a burning anger, which he had little ability to contain[1]. But he was also handsome, charismatic and brimming with energy. She would soon find that he liked to question accepted ways of thinking and prided himself on breaking with convention wherever possible. Like Sheila, Alan had been a conscientious objector by the end of the war; and he was a vegetarian.

After the subject of the Eccleston Square lease was exhausted, I don't know what my parents talked about in this, their first conversation. I imagine Alan turned his considerable charm on Sheila and showed some interest in her as a person, for when he invited her out, she accepted.

We began to see each other away from the Art School. I soon started staying with him in his flat... We seemed to have a lot in common. Sometimes I felt tense with him; he was highly critical of so many things and people that I felt disconcerted and I suppose knocked off what balance I had myself. But often he was a very delightful companion. We danced at the Pheasantry club in Chelsea, went to films, concerts, and the Festival of Britain[2].

---

1 I never got to the bottom of why Dad was plagued by such intense anger. It's possible it was a symptom of PTSD resulting from his war time experiences.

2 The Festival of Britain was a national exhibition and fair visited by millions in the summer of 1951. It was intended as a celebration to raise British morale in the wake of the years of wartime austerity and acted as a showpiece for British scientists and designers.

Sheila was quickly drawn into Alan's circle of lively friends, both his flatmates at Eccleston Square and the people who came to supper, most of whom he'd met when a student at Oxford. One of the flatmates was Shirley Hughes[3], who would later acquire international acclaim as an author and illustrator of children's books. Another was Roger 'Jimmy' James, who became a GP and author. The wider circle at that time included Tim Gibbs[4], who became a successful landscape painter and Tom Pomfret[5], a painter and illustrator.

Sheila was again living with her cousin Joy. When she caught the 'flu, Alan wrote her a note which oscillates between mockery and sympathy:

> 'Well, fancy that now! What a poor, stricken creature and me only just discovering. I tried to phone you on Sunday night but could get no reply … Are you streaming miserable and snoozing in a coma or are you having a lovely time reading and being fussed? I hope by now it has got to the stage of luxury.'

As their relationship developed, Sheila and Alan went on a series of trips to France and Italy, keen to immerse themselves in the European sculpture and painting which had been inaccessible during the war years. Alan's German Jewish roots and his memories of childhood holidays in central Europe had given him a strong sense of connection to the continent. Like Sheila, he appreciated

---

3 Shirley Hughes (1927–2022) studied at Liverpool and Ruskin School of Art in Oxford. She illustrated over 200 children's books and both wrote and illustrated another 50. In 2017 she was awarded the CBE for services to children's literature.

4 Tim Gibbs (1923–2012) studied at the Ruskin School of Art and became a landscape painter and muralist. He taught at the Ruskin, Bath and Morley College, London and was head of fine art at Oxford university from 1974–1980.

5 Tom Pomfret (1920–1997) was a painter and illustrator.

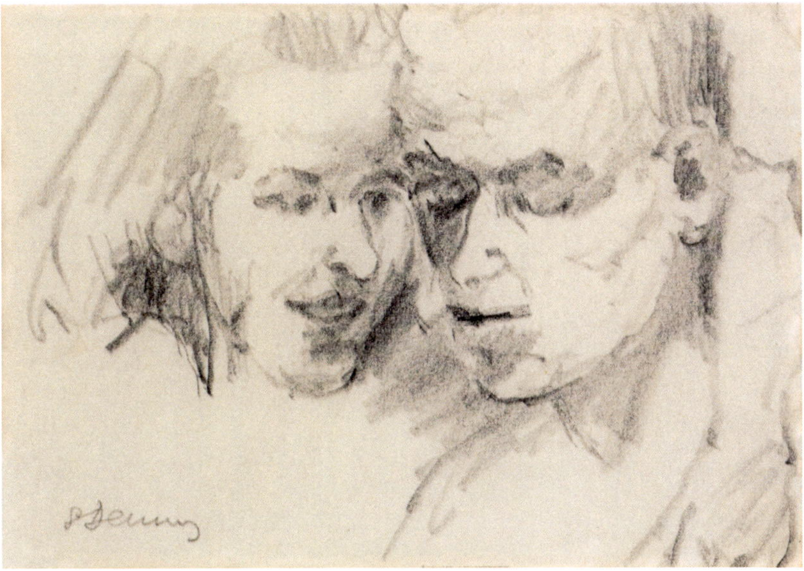

Couple on a Train, c. 1951

French and Italian food, he loved exploring unfamiliar towns, churches and abbeys and he relished conversation with strangers in his good French and fluent Italian.

Sheila's pencil drawing, *Couple on a Train*, dates from one of these trips. A simple sketch of two people in conversation with their heads close together, it conveys a strong sense of intimacy. The drawing intrigued me as a child because the woman appears to be comforting the man, who looks upset and shaken. I found that puzzling: in my childish world, men were sturdy creatures little troubled by painful emotions, whereas women frequently wept. I used to stare with admiration at the woman, and wonder what she was made of.

When Sheila was in Ireland visiting her parents, Alan wrote to her about plans for a trip to Italy:

> '… I have written to Elba saying will probably arrive on 14th, and am writing to Paris for *une chambre a deux personnes* for the night of the 12th. Have you any

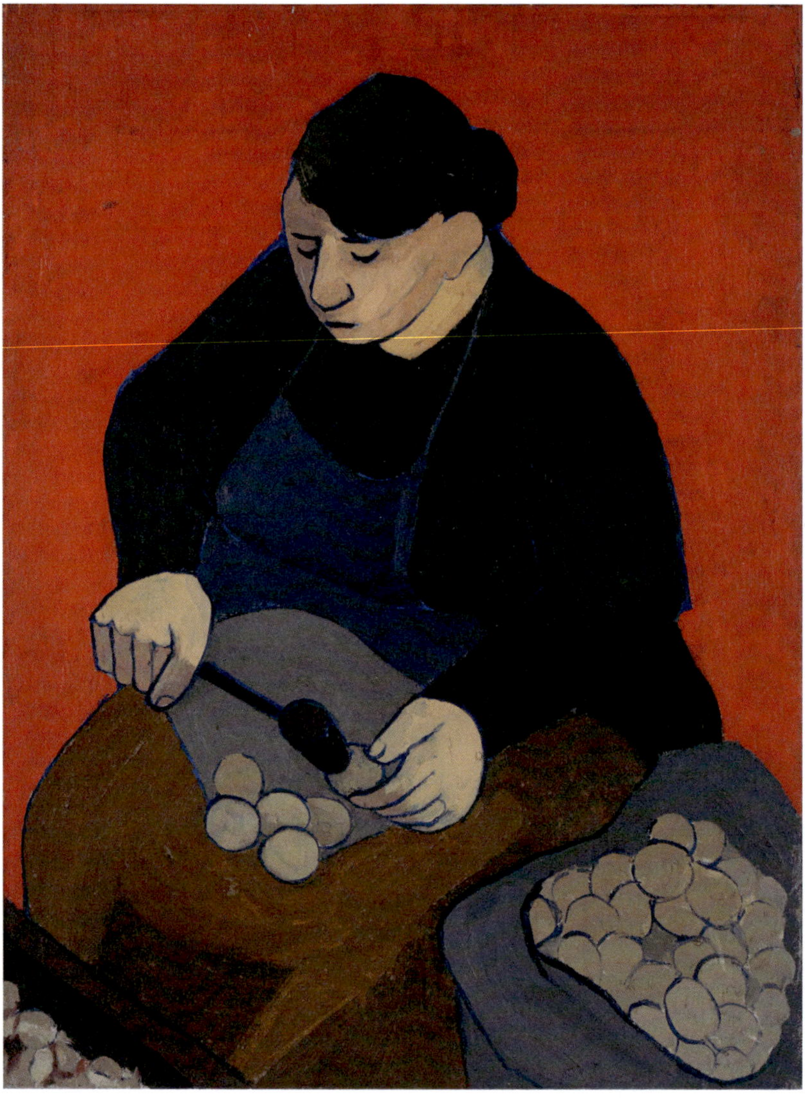

Woman Cracking Walnuts with a Hammer, c. 1949

> objections, by the way, to *Hotel des Pyrenees*? Would it be nicer to go elsewhere, I wonder? Any suggestions?'

He goes on to tell her that his friend Joy has invited Sheila to her wedding, in Sussex, and he's hoping she will accept. He wants to show her the house his father built there, in which he lived as a child.

> '…Will you come? I think it would be fun if you did… afterwards we could go over to Fittleworth and explore my old home instead of going straight back to London. Perhaps stay the night in a pub and go back Saturday.'

He ends the letter:

> 'Darling, the bottom is out of everything and I am counting the days and nights, and thinking over our story in odd moments and rather wanting the world to know that
> I love
> You. Alan/ Come back soon.'

Finding this letter was a revelation to me. I had no idea that my father had once been in love with my mother, and that her absences had filled him with impatience for her return. The impression I'd formed as a child was that his main feelings towards her were ones of irritation and guilt: irritation because she had needs and predilections which didn't coincide with his and guilt because he was in the habit of putting his needs before hers, but on some level knew he was wrong to do so. I read and re-read the letter with a sense of astonishment.

A rather lovely painting came out of the visit to Elba – either made in situ or done later from drawings made in situ – called *Woman cracking walnuts with a hammer*. Clad in dark clothing, the woman sits with a bowl of nuts perched on her lap. It's one of the least elaborate of Sheila's paintings, and oddly touching. The paint is applied thinly, with brushes, and Sheila has paid little attention to tone: the work is about large, two-dimensional shapes. The manner in which the woman, who isn't young, arches her body around the bowl speaks of a hard life of domestic labour.

*

At some point in 1950, Sheila and Alan began to discuss the idea of moving out of London. Alan wanted to study ceramics at Farnham School of Art in Surrey, under Henry Hammond[6] and Paul Barron[7]; after which he intended to start his own pottery. Sheila, for her part, had all but finished her studies at Camberwell and had no clear plan for what to do next. When Alan suggested that she too should study pottery at Farnham, part time, so that she would be in a position to help him achieve his goal, she agreed.

Working with clay would never excite Sheila in the way that painting did. But for the time being she was too caught up in Alan's agenda to tell him straight that she didn't want to be a potter; perhaps she didn't even know it. She made a few coil pots and learned to throw on the wheel; and soon she was drawn into Alan's plan for them to go into business together.

During one of Sheila's absences in Ireland, Alan found a cottage to rent within easy reach of Farnham. He wrote to Sheila:

> 'Extraordinary thatched cottage with everything abnormal and nothing normal, awaiting your mature consideration.'

Sheila would later describe the place as follows.

---

6 Henry Hammond (1914–1986) studied with the potter Bernard Leach. He then built up the ceramics department at Farnham School of Art with Paul Barron.

7 Paul Barron (1917–1983), another potter, is best remembered for his contribution to teaching at West Surrey College of Art and Design, Farnham.

> *Riverside Cottage stood in a field, at the bottom of which was a small stream which looked none too clean. Inside, a living room and kitchen, upstairs two bedrooms, in neither of which could one stand upright. I can't remember if one could even stand upright in the downstairs rooms either – probably not. There was no electricity and no piped water. There was a pump in the kitchen which pumped water from the stream. Cooking was to be done on a paraffin stove, and the paraffin had to be fetched. There was no indoor lavatory and certainly no bathroom. The bathroom, we soon learnt, was the stream.*
>
> *This earthly paradise obviously appealed to our young hearts, as we decided to rent it and to move out of London… Our landlords were the Jones family at the nearby farm. To them, we were Mr and Mrs Thornhill, it still being not quite proper to be otherwise in 1950, at any rate not in the country.*

Having built himself a basic studio to one side of Riverside Cottage, Alan divided his time between studying at Farnham, making pots at home and scything the field which surrounded the cottage. Sheila drew, kept house and went to pottery classes.

Although neither Sheila nor Alan was earning money, their decision to rent Riverside was not motivated by lack of funds. Alan had a small but adequate income from his post as a sleeping director of his father's china and glass business. Riverside appealed to him because of the months he'd spent in Italy living with a peasant family at the end of the war, where he'd acquired a positive, somewhat romantic, view of the 'simple' rural life. For him, the discomforts of life at Riverside simply added to its charm.

For Sheila, the discomforts were more of a problem; but, being in love, she put up with them. She also put up with the regular criticism she received from Alan, who found fault with both her housekeeping and her attempts at making pots.

By now, it seems, Sheila had acquiesced in a process whereby her career as a painter would be eclipsed for many years by his career as a potter and sculptor. Her negative experience at Camberwell had made her vulnerable to this and the values of the time, whereby women were expected to subordinate their ambitions to those of their men, must have played a part.

At Riverside, a lot of Sheila's time was spent simply surviving, whether gathering wood to light the fire, washing clothes in the river or finding a suitable bush behind which to dig a latrine for the day's use. For Alan, who needed no more than five hours sleep a night and had an abundance of physical energy, the more manly of these tasks were a source of delight; whereas for Sheila they soon became a burden. In 1950, even in the circles of Bohemian artists, housekeeping fell to women. Having grown up with a cook and a maid, Sheila wouldn't have been well placed to run a conventional home efficiently; and a home without running water or electricity required more of its housewife than a London flat had done.

In addition to the demands of rural life, Sheila was still struggling with grief for Joe and worry about Bum's health. She had no studio and I've found no evidence that she was painting – a state of affairs which won't have contributed to her wellbeing.

*

Sheila's autobiography ends, somewhat abruptly, early in 1952. On the penultimate page, she mentions that in 1951 friends began to ask when she and Alan were going to get married. Sixty years later, she told me that she abandoned the autobiography at this point because the prospect of writing about her marriage was too painful to contemplate. I was reminded of the day she showed me the green velvet outfit which she wore on her wedding day. I was nine or ten years old and we were having a tete-a-tete in her bedroom in London, in which, as often, her unhappiness with my father featured. She went to the wardrobe and pulled a velvet-covered hanger from the far end of the rail, from which hung something evidently weighty, beneath a veil of faded tissue paper. I felt an uneasy sensation in my tummy as I watched her, but I was curious. Before she lifted the paper Mummy turned to me, making no attempt to mask the pain which the sight of the outfit caused her and declared, 'Never get married in green, my darling. Don't be a fool, like I was.'

At that age I absorbed everything Sheila said as readily as if I'd been a sand castle assailed by the incoming tide. Right, I said to myself, no green outfits, *ever*. My heart weighed like a sharp stone in my chest as I gazed solemnly at the dark green velvet top and flowing skirt. Why had nobody warned Mummy? I demanded inwardly, burning with a mixture of rage and sorrow. Why had nobody told her to wear a different colour?

Chapter 10
Hawkley

ALAN AND SHEILA MARRIED in November 1951. Shortly afterwards they began making plans to move, as she states in the closing lines of the autobiography:

> *… we realized that we could not stay at Riverside Cottage for ever…*
>
> *We began to think about what we needed to start our own pottery. A smallish house, with good outbuildings and a garden, in the country. The precise area did not seem particularly important, and so we got onto the books of several agents over quite a wide stretch of countryside, Hampshire, Gloucestershire, even Dorset, and I suppose Surrey, near Farnham.*

One afternoon in July 1952, after looking at a couple of houses in Gloucestershire which had proved unsuitable, Sheila and Alan were about to drive back to Farnham. They stopped for petrol and Sheila bought a copy of the local paper, just in case there was something which the estate agents had failed to mention. As she scanned the property columns, Alan sat beside her, revving the car engine.

'Anything worth looking at?'

Sheila was moving her lips while she read and re-read one particular advertisement. 'How about this?' she said out loud. '"The Lippiatt Park estate", it's coming up for auction next week. "Several workers' cottages in separate lots, including one with outbuildings."' She threw Alan a smile. 'It's called "Hawkley" and was once the cottage of the estate carpenter.'

My parents found a coin box and telephoned the auctioneers. If they wanted to view the outside of the carpenter's cottage, they were told, the address could be provided. It lay in a deep valley between the villages of Eastcombe and Bisley.

Half an hour later, Alan and Sheila drove into Eastcombe, which sat just below the brow of a big hill. They parked beside the village green, on sloping ground bordering the graveyard, and strolled downhill to the old part of the village. Here the houses were linked by narrow paths, once used by donkeys. Immediately below the terraced gardens, the land plunged into the densely-wooded Toadsmoor valley, giving the place something of the charm of an Italian hill village.

It was a warm day and a couple of men in overalls were sitting outside the pub. After asking directions, Alan took the rash step of driving down the very steep and narrow lane which led to Hawkley. With each bump, my parents' spirits rose as their heads brushed against the roof of the car. To either side, the hedgerows burgeoned with ferns, nettles, rosebay willowherb, red campion and the pointed, sap green leaves and curling tendrils of Old Man's Beard, spangled with creamy flowers. Sheila caught a glimpse through a gateway of a ewe suckling a pair of lambs, soon obscured by the branch of an oak tree which hung low over the road.

At the bottom of the hill, the road petered out on the bank of a stream. The only way to continue was via a mud track, which crossed the water on a pair of planks.

'Well, I'm damned!' Alan muttered as he pulled up, shooting an excited glance at Sheila. Getting out of the car, my parents noticed a gateway leading into the front garden of a cottage, where a young woman was hanging out washing. Two small girls toddled about on the grass and a boy sat in the branches of an apple tree. The woman turned as Alan approached. 'Was it Hawkley you're looking for?' she asked, in a strong Gloucestershire accent. 'Cross the stream, sir, keep going, and you'll see it in a second, on your left. There's nobody there, sir, place has been empty for months.'

My parents thanked the woman, admired the marguerites that grew in abundance on either side of her garden gate, and made their way across the planks. On the far side of the stream, a narrow path followed the bank of the stream to right and left, disappearing among saplings of beech and hawthorn. Ahead, the mud track led sharply uphill, following the line of a dry stone wall, behind which the stone-tiled roof of a substantial cottage began to show itself. The only sounds were the shushing of the water, a faint rustling of branches and the song of a blackbird, hidden in the wood. Sheila gasped, clutching Alan's arm as she walked. Rarely had she visited a lovelier spot.

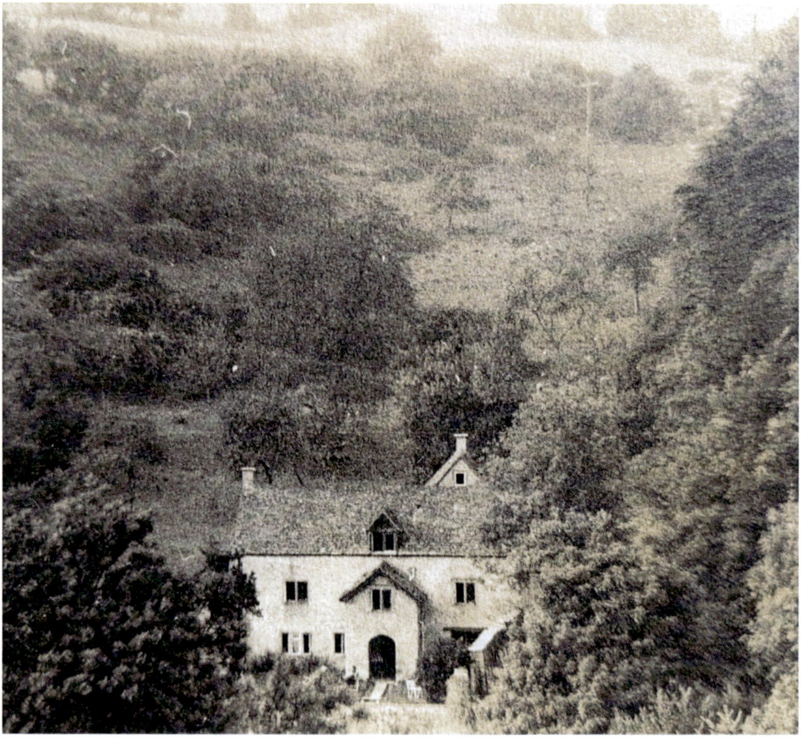

Hawkley, 1953

In fifty yards, the dry stone wall ended at an open gateway. Here, on the far side of a terraced garden, stood the cottage they had glimpsed over the wall. It was solidly built in Cotswold stone, with two windows on the ground floor, on either side of a generous porch; three on the first floor and a dormer set into the roof. Where sunlight struck the stone, it glowed light gold; in the shadow cast by the porch, the surface was a greeny-grey.

Sheila stood in the gateway, slowly taking in the stillness of the garden, the safe, sturdy feeling exuded by the cottage and the near silence of the woods. She hated noise of any kind and Hawkley's location at the end of a tiny lane seemed like a dream come true, quite apart from the unexpected beauty of the stone, the garden, the woods and the steeply rising land on both sides. Looking around for Alan a few moments later, she discovered he'd already made his way to the back of the cottage. Here he'd found three stone outbuildings and a small paddock, bordered on all sides by the woods.

*

Bum gave my parents the money to buy Hawkley. They moved there in September 1952 and Alan immediately set up Hawkley Pottery. Headed paper was printed with both names on it in equal prominence, but in reality this was Alan's project, with Sheila in the role of assistant. Alan bought a new van and engaged builders to convert the three-storey former poultry house behind the cottage into a work space. Even before they'd finished, he set up his kick-wheel and glazing table on the first floor.

There was no electricity supply at Hawkley in 1952. A neighbour was persuaded to rent out a barn connected to the grid, where Alan installed his electric kiln. Once he started making pots, every dish and plate and jug would have to be carried – perilously – across the field from Hawkley to the barn.

The war injury Alan had sustained to his lower back might have made some men think twice about the demands of the life he was taking on; but Alan was only thirty one and nothing was going to stop him. Besides, he loved physical work. In breaks from throwing pots on the wheel, he set about constructing a hard road from the place where the two planks crossed the stream, up the steep slope to the cottage. The task required more than a rudimentary grasp of engineering; but potential difficulties were pushed aside. Possibly the builders were roped in to help, as was the husband of the woman in the cottage by the stream.

While Alan was pitting his strength at the outdoor construction work, Sheila did her best to make the cottage comfortable. I doubt she had free rein to do as she pleased, for Alan held strong views about interior design and will have wanted to have his say, particularly when it came to choosing colours. Money was tight, but in the early months there was no shortage of support from friends and family. Alan's brother Paul, now over fifty and long established in Vancouver, paid for the installation of an Aga in the low-ceilinged kitchen, which had an uneven flagstone floor. Paul's wife Eve sent Sheila money to buy a set of Aga-proof pots and pans.

When she wasn't occupied in the house, Sheila did her best to help in the pottery, decorating the jugs and bowls and dishes that Alan produced. Being a good draftswoman, she could do this well enough; but orders were coming in from London department stores, which meant the pottery had to be delivered to a tight schedule. Sheila was a sensitive woman and needed a lot of peace and quiet to maintain her wellbeing; soon she was finding the pressure of commercial production difficult to manage.

*

Decades later, Sheila remembered the first couple of years at Hawkley as a time of desperately hard work. Alan had the stamina to be up with the larks, work all day in the pottery, eat and then continue working till midnight. He was excited about his new business and energy coursed through his veins day and night. When he wasn't at the wheel or carrying bowls and jugs across the field to the firing barn, he was digging a vegetable plot at the back of the house or building a coop for the geese he'd recently acquired. There was always masses to do in the pottery; when a batch of work had been successfully fired, decorated, glazed and fired again, it had to be packed in tissue paper, loaded carefully into the van, driven to London and delivered to the retailer.

Sheila struggled to keep up with Alan's pace of work, but she couldn't manage on five hours' sleep a night; and she couldn't work all day, produce a meal to the high culinary standard he expected, then continue to work all evening. Domestically, too, she was finding life difficult: for all its beauty and charm, Hawkley was not an easy place to run. Without electricity, she was obliged to do the laundry in the bath tub. To make tea or wash dishes, she had to boil a kettle on the Aga, which required constant stoking and must not be allowed to go out. For a long time, Sheila blamed herself for her 'weakness' in not being able to work at the pace of her husband; but in time she came to resent the constant criticism to which he subjected her. Years later she would write to her solicitor:

> 'I soon found that I did not come up to my husband's expectations. Indeed it was impossible to do so. If it was not my pottery work, then it was the way I ran the house and cooked which came in for criticism. Although I tried hard – too hard – to fulfil this dual role, something would always be found left undone… I think my husband could never bear the realization that he had married a fallible human being.
>
> 'This constant, daily, destructive criticism poisoned our marriage from the start.'

After some time, and with the excuse that Alan needed her in the pottery, Sheila recruited a woman from the village to help in the house; but this meant she had to work even longer hours painting designs onto dishes.

Despite the hard work and the tensions with Alan, there were elements of life at Hawkley which Sheila enjoyed. She and Alan met local artists and crafts-people through his part time teaching job at Stroud Art School, some of whom, such as the sculptor Jack Greaves[1] and his wife Millie, would become life-long friends. People heard about the new pottery in the local media or by word of mouth; some dropped in, got talking and found they had a lot in common with the new arrivals.

Sylvia Lauder, a weaver, turned up one day on foot. She lived in Stroud with her painter husband Kenneth[2] and their young son, Richard. A petite, fair-haired woman of unforgettable warmth, Sylvia was a keen walker and naturalist; my parents soon discovered that she knew the name of every wildflower in the woods. Sylvia would remain close to both Sheila and Alan for the next sixty years.

Other new friends were Margaret Holgate[3], a textile designer, and her beekeeper husband Jim, who were living two miles from Eastcombe at Oakridge Lynch when Sheila and Alan arrived in Gloucestershire. By the time the Holgates moved away to Wales,

1 Jack Greaves (1928–) studied at Leeds College of Art and the Royal College and became a figurative sculptor. In the late 1950s, he and Millie lived at Miserden in the Cotswolds but later Jack worked for many years in the USA.

2 Kenneth Lauder, (1916–2004) was born in Edinburgh. He studied at Chelsea School of Art and the Royal College. Initially his output included both painting and weaving, but later he focused on painting.

3 Margaret Holgate (1917–2014) studied at Newport College of Art and the Royal College of Art. In the 1950s her work as a textile designer included the screen-printing of silk scarves which were sold by Liberty and Mary Quant in London. Later in life Margaret became a successful jeweller as well as running a restaurant in Aberaeron, Wales.

a strong friendship had developed between Margaret, Alan and Sheila, which again would last throughout my parents' lives. Other good friends were the weavers Jerry and Joan Carter, who lived at Miserden; and Christian Ness, an architect and her scientist husband, Alan Ness.

Within a couple of years of their arrival at Hawkley, Sheila and Alan were regularly invited out to suppers and parties. Being naturally very gregarious, Alan enjoyed this greatly. Sheila, by contrast, didn't always want company; and the need to return invitations felt like a burden in her overly-busy life. She could cook, but it wasn't her favourite activity; throwing a dinner party for eight or ten people was a major undertaking which would preoccupy her for days.

There were deeper reasons to be wary of the local party scene. Some of the men believed their talent and vocation as artists gave them licence to indulge their sexual appetites to the full, marriage notwithstanding. The parties were often wild, and 'wife-swapping'[4] was considered part of the fun, despite the distress it inevitably caused and despite the small children supposedly asleep in upstairs bedrooms.

*

Bum and Dee visited Hawkley frequently in the early years, both separately and together. After returning to England they'd bought a house off the Fulham Road in London, where Dee was now settled. Bum's health remained fragile, but he'd gone back to work, taking a post with the RAF in Somerset. My grandparents loved their visits to Hawkley and wrote warm thank you letters,

4 I dislike this term intensely, because it presupposes that a 'wife' is the chattel of her husband, to be lent out at his whim; but this is the term which I frequently heard used with reference to 1950s Gloucestershire artists.

expressing delight in the character of the place. During a stay in March 1953, Bum observed how hard Sheila and Alan were working and wrote to them afterwards:

> 'I hope that you are both feeling less rushed and jaded; Hawkley will be heavenly in Spring, summer and autumn and I think "you chose well" as DOJ said to me about Mama.'

Dee wrote in July:

> 'I did so enjoy my stay with you both – you are always so very sweet and thoughtful in every way – it was lovely having those two hot days last weekend and being able to sit out all the time – I am looking forward to September now!'

For Bum, who had eaten off china plates all his life, it must have been hard to understand the peasant-style earthenware which Alan was producing; and I imagine he worried about the financial insecurity inherent in his daughter's new lifestyle. But he went out of his way to be supportive and tactful, writing in December 1953:

> 'I am so glad that orders are coming in – John Lewis and Peter Jones sound alright to me provided that they pay you a fair share. I have not dared to put your dish bordered with apples into our Sick Bay oven. I feel that it might crack or come apart. When cooked I transfer the apples to it.'

Neither Bum nor Dee seem to have noticed that Sheila was barely painting, nor the curious fact that she didn't have a studio, despite the existence of two empty outbuildings which she could have used. Perhaps they took it for granted that, with marriage, Sheila's career would have to take second place to that of her husband. They may not have understood that, if she didn't paint, she was likely to become depressed. But surely they must have seen how thin and drained she was starting to look?

Although she ate 'like a trooper', Sheila was extremely slim; and beset with an excess of nervous energy. This made it even harder than it might otherwise have been to handle the increasing tensions in her marriage, and the dawning realization that Alan was being unfaithful to her. Some of the photos of the period show her with bulging eyes and the look of a woman who is becoming unhinged. Bum won't have known about the infidelity, but it's odd he didn't insist she undergo medical tests for what, much later, turned out to be a severely hyper-active thyroid.

In February 2019 I opened the cardboard box again and started to read the hundreds of letters received by Sheila at Riverside and Hawkley, hoping to better understand that period of her life. But it was the envelopes, rather than the content of the letters, which brought home to me what happened to my mother in those two idyllic locations.

Up to 1951, Sheila's letters had invariably been addressed to 'Miss Sheila Denning'; but those she received at Riverside and Hawkley were addressed to 'Mrs Alan Thornhill'. I stared at the new name in cold dismay. I knew it had been the norm in those distant days for women to give up their names for those of their husbands; yet I felt the inherent insult as something acutely personal to Sheila. Where did my mother vanish to, in 1951, I wondered, flicking through the dusty envelopes and seeing my father's name endlessly repeated. Here was proof, if proof were needed, that she had allowed her unique and brilliant self to become eclipsed.

Chapter 11
The Potter's Wife

IN THE EARLY YEARS AT HAWKLEY, Alan's tableware sold well in several London outlets, including Heals and Henry Rothschild's Sloane Street shop, Primavera. It also created a stir in Gloucestershire. In July 1953, in its review of the annual Stroud Show, the Stroud Journal wrote:

> 'A newcomer to the Stroud show is...The Hawkley Pottery, Eastcombe. This is an interesting Cotswold industry, consisting chiefly of tableware, some of which is made from local clay. In fact, the joint owners of the business, Alan Thornhill and Sheila Thornhill, actually model clay taken from their garden. This Cotswold craft will be a welcome addition to the trade exhibits and should prove a great attraction.' [1]

A subsequent article in 1956 described how

> '...In the clear waters of the Mediterranean Mr Thornhill has seen much of the beauty of the undersea world. It impressed him so much that his designs are often reminiscent of shells or fish. What is more, he uses an oyster glaze which gives his work a distinctive appearance.'

The article goes on to report that the pottery's products were now selling 'in some of the best London and provincial shops'; and that Alan was employing two helpers:

---

1 *Stroud Journal* 17 July 1953.

> '…an Eastcombe lady and an apprentice are kept busy helping Mr Thornhill – Mrs Thornhill devotes most of her time to her small child and the home…' [2]

The 'small child' was Anna, born in June 1955.

Both my parents had wanted children, and Sheila told me that my father was very affectionate and supportive during her pregnancy; but in less than three months, the new family unit was in serious trouble.

In late August 1955, Alan set off for France, ostensibly by himself, leaving Sheila to cope alone with baby, house, garden and pottery. He wrote to her from St Malo on 30 August:

> 'Darling
> Here I am in St Malo. Dead flat crossing, had to sleep on the deck wrapped in a blanket – but it was a warm night so got quite a bit of sleep… Marvellous to get ashore…
> 'Am going to spend today here and go off to Quimper tomorrow.'

He asked Sheila to pay his bill at the local garage, hoped that the new "lady help" would prove good and told her that in an emergency she *might* be able to contact him at Poste Restante Quimper. What he carefully avoided mentioning was his travel companion, a young English woman with whom he was having an affair.

*

Despite the emotional roller coaster she was living through in her marriage, Sheila produced two paintings of Anna at Hawkley. Both are painted in a simple, brushy style, with no sign of the palette knife the use of which would characterize her later work. In

---

2 *Stroud Journal* 13 July 1956.

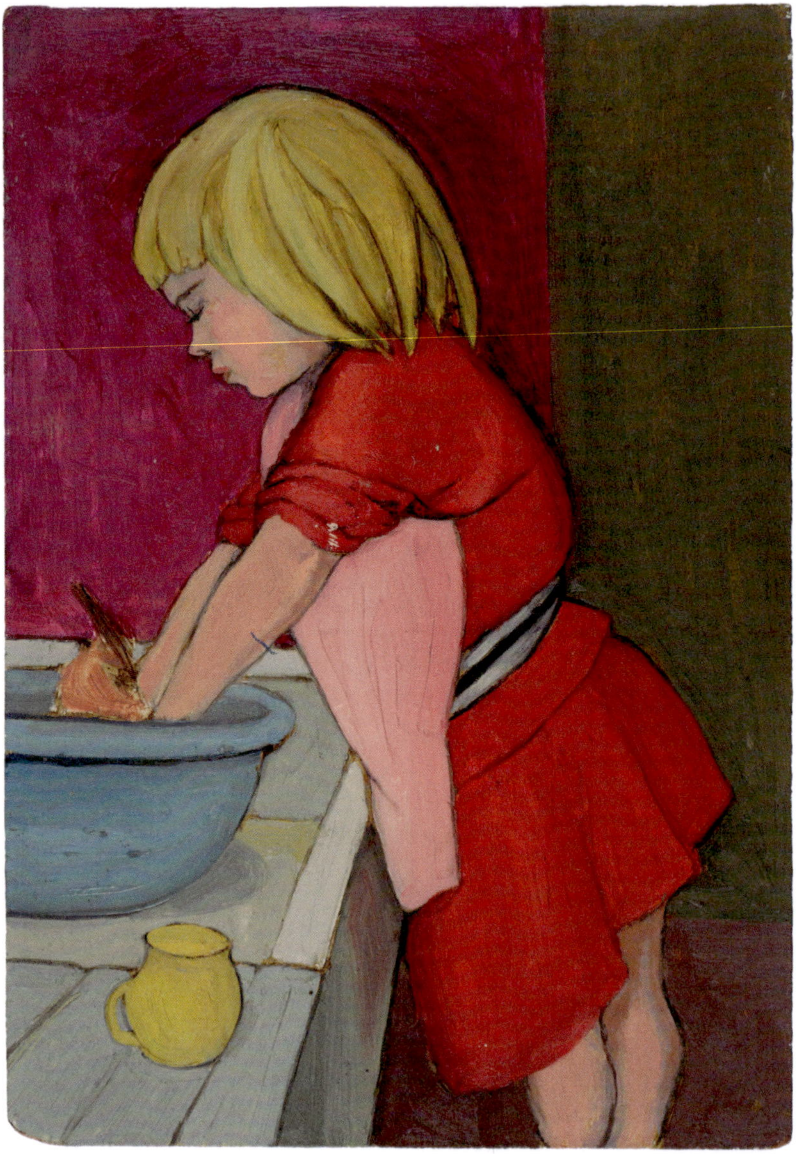

Anna washing up, c. 1958

the first, my sister is about eighteen months old. She sits in a high chair attachment fixed to the back of a red kitchen chair. Her bare legs dangle, her hair is short and such a pale shade of blond that it's almost white. One pudgy hand rests on the tray in front of her; the other clutches a large rattle, made of brightly coloured baubles. For me, the painting of the face fails to capture Anna. The gaze is fiercely serious, suggesting a worried adult rather than a toddler.[3]

The second painting is quite different and in it I see very clearly my big sister of those distant days. Wearing a crimson dress, Anna stands on a wooden kitchen chair, leaning forward at a sharp angle, her hands immersed in a blue washing up bowl. Her hair, painted in a warm yellow, falls in sharp points onto her shoulders. A pink pinafore has been tied over her dress and she appears deeply absorbed in the task at hand – washing something in the bowl. To either side we see the simple lines of a1950s wooden draining board.

*

I was born at Hawkley in March 1957, on the first day of spring, and we lived there till I was rising three. Much of my sense of that time is coloured by what I absorbed of Sheila's unhappiness and the growing conflict between her and Alan; but I do have three sharp memories which are my own. For nothing could prevent me, as an impressionable infant, from falling in love with the natural environment in which I found myself. Hawkley was a small child's paradise. In my recollection we lived out of doors, in close contact with animals and trees, earth, wind and water.

The memories date from 1959, when I was two. The first is of playing in a field where Sheila, Anna and I used to stop on our way back down the steep lane after visiting the village shop. Sheila parked the buggy just inside the gate, while I ran

3 This painting can be seen at www.sheiladenning.com

in my wellies towards an ancient pink-red tractor that stood abandoned by a clump of blackberry bushes. It had a shiny leather seat, like an old-fashioned bicycle saddle but bigger, which I could reach by climbing. I loved nothing better than to perch high up above the grass, my little hands resting on the giant steering wheel. Mummy and Anna were close by, picking wildflowers for the kitchen table, and nobody was in a hurry. The shopping was done, loaded safely into string bags and stowed under the buggy and we had all afternoon to amble homewards.

My second memory is of the flock of geese Daddy kept in the back garden. They hissed when Anna and I approached, stretching out their necks, spreading their vast white wings and noisily beating the air, until we turned and ran back to Mummy, clutching her legs for protection.

My third is of the evening when the bay horse that lived in our paddock got its head stuck in the barbed wire fence. The horse belonged to a neighbour; my parents let it graze on our land because they both loved horses and enjoyed its presence.

I don't know who was first to notice that the horse had got its head stuck. I toddled outside at bedtime, in the light of a damp summer's evening, and there was Daddy astride the horse's neck, talking to it in a coaxing voice, while he struggled to cut through the barbed wire with a pair of pliers. Mummy was quite upset by the sight of the poor horse; in my mind's eye she's holding each of us by the hand, telling us to stay very still and keep quiet, so that Daddy can concentrate on the very difficult thing he's trying to do. We see that Daddy's having trouble with the pliers and the horse is on the verge of panic; we know that if we speak, Daddy'll get cross and the horse more frightened. We stand there with our hearts in our mouths, till in the end the wire gives way and the horse winnies and pulls its head out from between Daddy's legs. It trots away across the paddock, its brown mane flying, while Daddy turns to Mummy with a look of triumph.

*

Reading the Hawkley era letters started me thinking of Lucina, the young Italian who came to live with my parents as an *au pair* in 1956, when my sister was about a year old. Lucina was just twenty, fresh out of Portsmouth art school. In February 2019 I arranged to visit her at her home in London, where she was still painting every day at the age of eighty two.

'I was a naïve, sheltered child when I went to Hawkley,' Lucina told me in a voice so soft I had to lean forward to catch her words. She sat very still in an armchair in the back room of her 1930s house, her shoulder-length white hair resting on an olive green scarf wound loosely round her neck. It was a Sunday afternoon in late winter and the dazzling, early spring light I had enjoyed on my journey across London was now fading. We sat together in the gathering dusk, preferring the darkness slowly filling the corners of the room to the harsh light of an electric lamp.

Lucina had arrived in the UK from Rome with her mother and brother, shortly after the war ended. 'When I left art school in 1956,' she told me, ' it was easier for me to go and live at Hawkley with your parents, than to do something like getting a proper job, perhaps in London.'

'Did you spend all your time with Anna?'

'Initially, yes, and later I worked in the pottery. I became very fond of Anna, and she of me; she used to call me "Bibby".' Lucina smiled. 'I took her out for walks; we'd climb the bank behind the pottery, to look at the sheep.

'Alan and Sheila were lovely to me, always kind, but I felt the strained atmosphere between them from the day I arrived.' Lucina regarded me steadily, knowing that her words would come as no surprise. 'I didn't understand the adult world at all and I found the tension between them painful. I was always trying to do my best to make things right. I'd grown up in a closed family and it was quite a shock being with them.'

'What sort of thing? Did Alan lose his temper?'

'Not exactly, his anger was very contained. He burst out with something now and then, maybe more when I wasn't there. But there was a coldness between them. Alan would make snide remarks to Sheila, about this and that. Sometimes he spoke in an icy tone. And I would think to myself, "maybe this is the way grown ups behave". I tried to turn a blind eye; I didn't want to come between these people.'

'Did Sheila retaliate?'

'Well, occasionally she would answer back; not to have a big row, but there were one or two remarks she made.' Lucina hesitated. 'He let Sheila down the most while she was pregnant with you.'

'How?'

'If an attractive female visitor came, he would flirt with her in front of Sheila.'

This came as no surprise, but it made me wince.

'It wasn't just Alan, you know,' Lucina said softly. 'Lots of people among their friends were having affairs.'

I knew that, but it didn't help. Sheila kept me very close to her in my early months and inevitably I became highly attuned to the distress she was feeling. I lived in fear of her collapse. I must have reasoned, in the simplistic way that infants do, that if I was to survive, I must protect her.

I stared at Lucina through the half light. 'Was Alan ever unkind to you?'

'No, to me he was kind… Well, perhaps once he shouted at me, and I burst into tears; but mostly he was kind.'

An uncomfortable thought was going through my head. 'Did he try it on with you?'

Lucina didn't hesitate. 'Just once. On the stairs. I slept in the attic and he tried to kiss me as I was going up to bed. I didn't kiss him back… and then afterwards he criticised my "provocative" behaviour.'

I felt a wave of disgust. My father's poor sexual boundaries had caused havoc throughout my childhood. But I was grateful to learn that Lucina had rebuffed him.

'Sheila and Alan were amazing with Anna,' she continued, 'whatever else was going on. And having a child around really helped the atmosphere. I used to think "I want to be like that, If I become a parent". Anna was lucky, because both her parents were at home.' She paused. 'Alan wasn't *all* bad, you know, he also had a kind heart.'

I knew this was true: for all his faults, at times Alan communicated enormous warmth – both then and now.

It had grown dark in the room but I could tell from her voice that Lucina was smiling. 'There was a lovely atmosphere during meals, at Hawkley. They talked to Anna all the time, encouraging her; and not just Sheila, Alan talked to her, too.' She sighed. 'I was always disposed to see all the bright things! But it was real, they definitely loved Anna.'

She fell silent for a few moments, then added: 'Hawkley was such an idyllic place. There were lovely days when your grandfather came to visit, when everybody seemed happy; and Sheila always made the best of things. She tried to cover things over; she would get on with preparing the lunch. After I started working in the pottery, it was breakfast, lunch and dinner when we mostly met up.'

Lucina leaned forward and switched on a lamp. 'Sheila and I had some jolly times together, talking about art and artists. We enjoyed each other's company; but I didn't sense in her a feeling of peace and real happiness.'

She paused. 'Some of the best times I remember were when Alan was away in London. He went quite often, to the Craft Guild, to sell pottery. He'd leave me plenty of work to get on with, painting designs on plates. In the evenings there would be just me and Sheila and little Anna, and it was very nice. We'd sit by the fire in the sitting room.'

The only room I remembered at Hawkley was the kitchen, but I could imagine the scene that Lucina was describing and for a few moments I breathed more easily. Then I asked whether Sheila had talked to anybody about her problems with Alan.

'I don't think so. She kept a lot to herself. She may have talked to her friend Sylvia, but I don't think so. None of Alan and Sheila's circle knew what she was going through. D'you remember Mrs Day?'

I did, of course. Gwen and Arthur Day were an older couple from the village who'd befriended my parents. Gwen worked for Alan, painting plates alongside Lucina in the pottery. She and Arthur were conventional Gloucestershire people, but they liked Alan and Sheila and, if they found their lifestyle unorthodox, they kept their feelings to themselves. I remember Mrs Day as a beloved elder, someone whose goodness was above question.

'Mrs Day realized there were difficulties,' Lucina went on. 'She said something to me once, in the pottery.'

I could just see it. Mrs Day with her neat white hair and kind face. She must have come upon Sheila in the kitchen in a state of distress and, when she returned to the pottery, let slip something indiscreet to young Lucina, as they stood side by side at the work bench.

'Sheila was practically having a breakdown while I was at Hawkley,' Lucina went on. 'It's devastating for any woman to be deceived; and when you're pregnant, it's even worse.'

'And she wasn't painting, was she?'

'I don't remember Sheila doing any art work at all during that period. I can't remember her even picking up a pencil to do a drawing. She didn't have a space to work; whereas *he* had the whole pottery.'

'Did Sheila make pots while you were there?'

'No, no, Sheila wasn't a potter. She didn't get her hands in the clay.'

*

At some point in 1957, Alan took a teaching job at Kingston Art School. This meant he was away in London for half of every week, leaving Sheila to cope alone with baby, toddler, pottery and garden, all without a car. To make matters worse, he started a new affair with a married woman. I'm not sure at what point Sheila learned of this; if she didn't know the facts to begin with, she will have sensed Alan's distractedness. But the affair was not the only difficulty: money was very tight, and the commuting gradually became too much for Alan. A crisis point came when, driving home down the A40 at the end of a long day's teaching, he fell asleep at the wheel and the car hit a tree. Alan wasn't badly hurt, but the incident served to underline to my parents that their living arrangements were not sustainable.

Sheila struggled to think straight through the fog of hurt, her still untreated thyroid disorder and the demands of motherhood. Many years later, she told me it would have been better if she'd opted to stay in Gloucestershire with Anna and me, leaving Alan free to pursue the life he wanted in London. But at the point where the decision had to be made, she wasn't ready to give up on her marriage. She still loved Alan, she felt divorce would entail intense shame and she had no means to earn a living. She knew that life in the city wouldn't suit her, especially now she was a mother. Leaving the natural beauty of Gloucestershire would be painful; but she couldn't face the alternative. Alan, for his part, was ready for change. He'd grown bored of the repetitive processes involved in producing pottery to sell, and was now more interested in making sculpture. For him, too, it would be a wrench to leave Hawkley, but he had a mistress and many friends in London and he thrived on the high energy of city life.

Early in 1959, my parents sold Hawkley and bought a house in Putney, in south west London.

*

For me, the departure from Hawkley was traumatic. I've never forgotten the anguish I felt on that grey December morning in 1959 when my sister and I were taken to Stroud railway station by our parents and handed into the care of Sylvia Lauder. Nobody troubled to explain where we were going nor why – at least, not in language I understood – nor when we would all be reunited. I remember being lifted onto a huge, noisy and frightening train and sitting with my feet dangling from the seats, staring at Sylvia in bewildered panic. Perhaps my sister understood what was happening; I did not.

But it wasn't just the ill-thought-out manner of our departure which troubled me. To be wrenched away from the idyllic corner of the woods which I loved and knew as home was devastating. It left me with a sense of exile which has lasted to this day.

PART FIVE

FEBRUARY 2019

It was a cold, grey, February afternoon. Dad wore a grey fleece hat draped over his bald pate, giving him the look of a mediaeval Italian elder in a painting by Piero de la Francesca. I felt a flicker of admiration: it was something of a feat to achieve such style when bedridden.

He looked at me sharply, the pupils of his brown eyes very dark. 'Are they starting to arrive?' His tone rose a notch as the look in his eyes became a glare.

I hesitated, unsure how to reply, then glanced towards the fire, which burned sluggishly in the grate.

'No,' I replied. 'Linda's in the kitchen and I'm sitting here with you. There's nobody else in the house.' Linda was the third carer.

A look of confusion spread across Dad's features, as I cast around for how to reassure him. 'Nothing on today,' I added in the most soothing voice I could manage. It wasn't uncommon for Dad to become convinced that he was having an exhibition of his work in the house and garden. Remembering a strategy which Linda sometimes used, I rummaged for the desk diary on the shelving beside the bed. Linda would show Dad a blank page, and tell him today was a day for resting. But the diary wasn't in its usual place.

'Christ knows if we've got enough chairs,' Dad went on. 'Have you counted?'

I decided to change tack. 'We've got lots,' I replied, nodding and smiling.

'Have you counted *them?'*

'Yes,' I lied. 'We've got thirty… How many people are you expecting?' This was unkind of me, for even the simplest of questions made Dad feel stressed, and he rarely knew the answer.

'Don't know,' he said, shaking his head slowly from side to side with an air of failure. 'Thirty, forty.' He sighed deeply. 'How many people are out there now?'

'Out where?'

'In the garden, in the living room!' He was starting to shout.

Now it was my turn to sigh. 'It's not today, Dad,' I repeated. 'Today's an easy day. Nobody's coming…' Should I pretend there was an event planned for another day, I wondered? Recognition for his work was the thing Dad craved above all else. He wanted the house and garden to be crammed with people wandering from sculpture to sculpture, speechless with admiration.

'Well when is it, then?'

'End of next week,' I blurted out. 'Friday. You've got ten days to get ready.'

'By myself?' his tone turned to one of astonishment mixed with rage. 'Aren't you going to help me?'

I stood up. 'Not if you shout at me.' I walked towards the window which gave onto the front garden, careful not to fully turn my back, for that would enflame Dad further. In this mood he inhabited the mindset of an emperor, and my status as his youngest daughter became that of a serf. 'If you talk to me nicely,' I added after a moment, 'then yes, of course I'll help you.' I glanced from Dad to the yellowing winter grass around the pond. Behind it, near the fence, I could just make out the twisting form of a bronze sculpture on a plinth. Dad's brows were puckered in annoyance, but he made no reply. Should I wait, I asked myself, and see if I could get the conversation onto something more agreeable? No, came my inner voice, don't risk your afternoon being ruined. Bad-tempered exchanges with Dad in patriarchal mode still had the power to knock me off course. I picked up my bag and slung it over my shoulder. 'I've got to go now,' I told him in a softer tone, stepping back toward the bed. 'Remember, it's not today. Today's an easy day, a rest day.'

Chapter 12
The Studio

WHEN WE ARRIVED IN PUTNEY in December 1959, the house was barely habitable. There was no heating, no floor or sink in the new open plan kitchen and no bathtub in the bathroom. Alan planned to do most of the renovation work himself, but lack of money obliged him to prioritize the top two floors, which were to be rented out to lodgers, over our living quarters on the ground floor.

Sheila hated the chaos, the noise, the dust and the fact that Alan was now in overdrive, working eighteen hour days, often in a state of furious agitation. She was still suffering from her hyperactive thyroid symptoms and in January 1960 went down with a bout of bronchitis. Alan refused to accept that she was ill, until he had no choice: in early spring, the thyroid problem was finally diagnosed and she went into St Stephens hospital in Fulham for treatment.

Sheila's stay in hospital was short, but the treatment failed and a summer of hell lay ahead. Dee was diagnosed with diverticulitis and was herself admitted to St Stephens, obliging Sheila to take on the running of her house in Fulham, where several rooms were rented out. Matters became much worse when Bum had another heart attack and had to join Dee in hospital. Sheila spent the late summer running between her children, her mother, her father and their house.

I have a dim memory of those months, although I was not yet three and a half. Bum, who knew full well that he was dying, pleaded with Sheila to bring him whisky. She used to purchase a quarter bottle every couple of nights and wrap it in a brown paper bag. When she arrived at the hospital, Bum got her to draw the curtain round his bed while he took a few swigs. Then, after checking that the nurses weren't looking, she would slip the bottle into his bedside locker.

Sheila felt no qualms about the whisky. She knew where Bum was heading, and wanted to ease his passage as much as possible. She arrived home from the hospital at my bedtime, thin, haggard and distraught, the large handbag in which she'd concealed the bottle dangling from her bony shoulder.

Bum died in St Stephens on 26 September and was buried in October. I was too young to understand what was happening, but I remember being driven into Putney Vale cemetery with Anna and Sheila in a slow procession behind the hearse. When we clambered out beside the chapel, the air was cold and smelled of autumn and a crowd of elderly strangers dressed in drab colours stood waiting for us in silence. Inside the chapel, Anna and I sat through the ceremony on a hard pew, breathing in a fog of sadness.

*

While Sheila was dealing with her parents' illnesses and getting my sister and me into nursery school, Alan was painting the top floors of the house and advertising for lodgers. Soon a stream of intriguing strangers, some from Africa and others from Ireland, shared our front door and our telephone. Smart in their work clothes, they waved at five-year-old Anna and three-year-old me as they made their way up the stairs in the evenings. One day we set up a little table inside the front door and tried to sell them knick-knacks: dandelions from the lawn in a jam jar, boiled sweets from Dee which we didn't like and fragments of china we'd dug up in the garden. I remember a tall, bemused African man in a grey overcoat stooping to peer at the items on offer.

Our house was on a corner plot, its large garden screened from the side road by a high brick wall. Now that the lodgers were in, Alan turned his attention to creating a studio for himself in the square coach house at the bottom of the garden. It had once accommodated a couple of brewers' horses and their trailer, in the days when barrels of beer were delivered to London pubs by horse power.

Scraps of straw and chaff lay on the dirt floor, and the air smelled sweetly of horse dung . Alan loved the horsey smell, which reminded him of his childhood summers riding on the South Downs; but he was single-minded about his plans. He unscrewed the manger from the wall and placed it on the terrace, where it became a novel and dangerous plaything. We would clamber in, causing the curved aluminium bars to rock on the paving slabs, threatening to crush our small fingers.

Next Alan laid a concrete floor and fitted a stove, which he fed with anthracite and kept going day and night in winter. Then he had an electrician install the kiln, while a couple of builders knocked down a wall and replaced it with reinforced glass from floor to ceiling, to let in light. Alan did the rest himself. Amid the racket of hammering, drilling and expletives, shelves climbed rapidly up the back wall, soon to sag under the weight of coloured liquids in jamjars, poisonous powders, rags, tools and old saucepans.

Over the next few years, Mummy left Anna and me in the studio with Daddy if she had to go out. I hated to be apart from Mummy. In my four or five years of life, our very close relationship had given me a profound appreciation of how unhappy she was, so that when she wasn't with me I felt deeply ill-at-ease. I was too young to reason: it didn't occur to me, for example, that she might take her own life. I simply felt that I should be there, beside her, at all times, like a bodyguard. Daddy made it clear that he resented my fierce attachment to Mummy and when I was left in his charge, while she went I knew not where, I got the feeling he'd quite like it if she didn't return.

One afternoon when Mummy ushered us through the creaking stable door onto the rough concrete studio floor, the first thing I saw was Daddy standing at a tripod in his beige boiler suit. It had once been white but was now ingrained with pink smears and brown grit from the red clay he sculpted in. I stood on the threshold, breathing in a strong musty smell, similar to the odour of damp soil, but with a cold, chalky character: the special smell of Daddy's world.

Anxious as to what mood he was in, I peered past Daddy into the huge, cavernous space, where strange forms draped in opaque plastic towered on tripods at the height of an adult. Soon I felt a tickling at the back of my throat, for every shelf and every work surface was covered with a layer of fine, pink-brown dust.

Daddy never wanted to stop what he was doing for more than a few seconds, so as soon as Mummy had gone he threw little aprons over our heads, tied them round our waists and set us up at a low table with a lump of clay apiece.

Then he returned to the sculpture he was working on. The space between us was filled with the billowing voice of a famous soprano singing on the radio and conversation was not an option. If I needed something, I might tentatively call out 'Daddy…' but as often as not he didn't respond. I wouldn't get up from my seat and approach him, because I knew, in the way that children do, that my presence was only tolerable to him if I didn't make demands.

It was autumn and, long before Mummy reappeared, the floor to ceiling windows turned black. When at last she pushed open the outer door, weary-looking but at least physically in one piece, I dropped the creature I was making, ran towards her and threw my arms around her legs. She was home; all was well.

I still have several tiny cats, a bed complete with blanket and pillow and a figure of an old man which I made during those episodes of forced creativity – all carefully dried, fired and glazed by Daddy.

Chapter 13
Anna Romano

ANNA ROMANO, OUR CLEANER, was short and sturdy. She moved about the house with an energetic brusqueness which made light of having to carry a hoover up the stairs or a basket of washing out to the garden – tasks with which Sheila struggled.

Sheila's pencil drawing of Anna is unnerving in its honesty. It was done at speed and is all the stronger for that. There's nothing flattering in the way she depicted the tousled black hair, thrown up in a hasty top knot first thing in the morning while Anna was getting her young son ready to hurry out the door. The pencil marks are thick and dark, made with a soft 6B pencil. Shading on the side of the neck and under the chin suggests a film of dark facial hair growing on Anna's golden skin.

Beneath the vigorous black arches of her eyebrows, Anna's large eyes, clumsily rimmed with eyeliner, convey a world-weariness that is unexpected in a woman in her twenties. Or is it just fatigue? The eyelids are puffy and a furrow of dark shadow descends below the right eye. Life was tough for this young Italian migrant, trying to survive in the London of the early 1960s.

In the drawing, Anna's face is full, the nose suggested with a few tentative marks which leave the viewer uncertain as to its exact shape. It's not important because our eyes are drawn irresistibly to the mouth, which tells all. It's a wide, generous mouth, consonant with the fullness of the cheeks. Sheila's pencil has accentuated the deep V in the centre of the upper lip.

The corners are indicated with a short, deft mark on either side, at a downward angle so slight that it's almost imperceptible. It's just enough to create the impression that Anna is distinctly

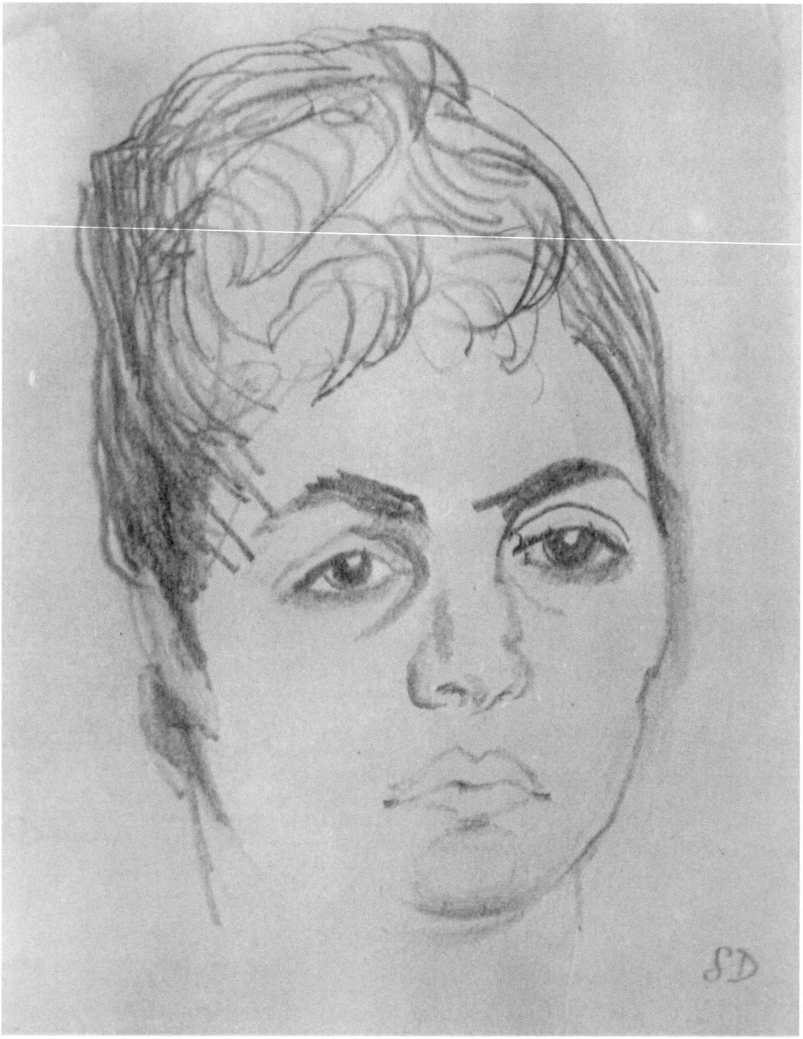

Anna Romano, c. 1961

unimpressed with life. The father of her child, a Nigerian, has disappeared, leaving her to bring him up alone; she's working too hard and not sleeping enough; and life in London's not as great as once she dreamed it would be. The two corner marks are echoed by another in the same tone, at the point where the lips meet, just below the right nostril. Anna's lost in thought, her lips a fraction open.

While Anna cleaned our house and drank coffee with Sheila, I played with her son, often in the garden. On the summer's day when Sheila did the drawing, we sat opposite each other, stark naked, in a cast iron bathtub which Dad had left on the terrace, under the sheltering branches of a plane tree. It contained an inch-deep layer of damp soil. Happy in each other's company, we were busy making mud pies to line up on the paving stones.

In the house, Sheila put down her pencil, took a swig of coffee and stretched her arms above her head. 'Thank you, Anna,' she said, 'I enjoyed that.'

Anna turned her eyes on her boss. 'Finished?' she asked. 'Can I see it?'

'It's nothing special,' Sheila handed Anna the drawing book. 'I'm horribly out of practice.'

Anna studied the sketch with a look of mild astonishment. 'But it's lovely, Sheila. I never knew I looked like that. Very nice.' She glanced at Sheila with a searching look. 'You should draw more often.'

She was right, of course; Sheila should have drawn or painted every day. But at that moment in her life, she was lost. Still plagued by her hyper-active thyroid, she spent her days caring for us children, running the house, visiting Gaga and wondering whether she should leave her marriage.

Chapter 14
Orange Sun in a Mauve Sky

SHAPED WITH A PALETTE KNIFE, a blackish orange sphere hangs in a mauve sky. At the outer edges of the sphere, the mauve darkens into purple and a series of fine knife marks creates the impression that, by the force with which it's spinning, the sky has propelled the sun into an orbit around the earth. Further from the sphere, the sky's paler, but still mauve: the paint slapped on with confidence, using a broader knife. Where the sky meets land, it's in the form of a dull, flat green field, half bordered with a privet hedge.

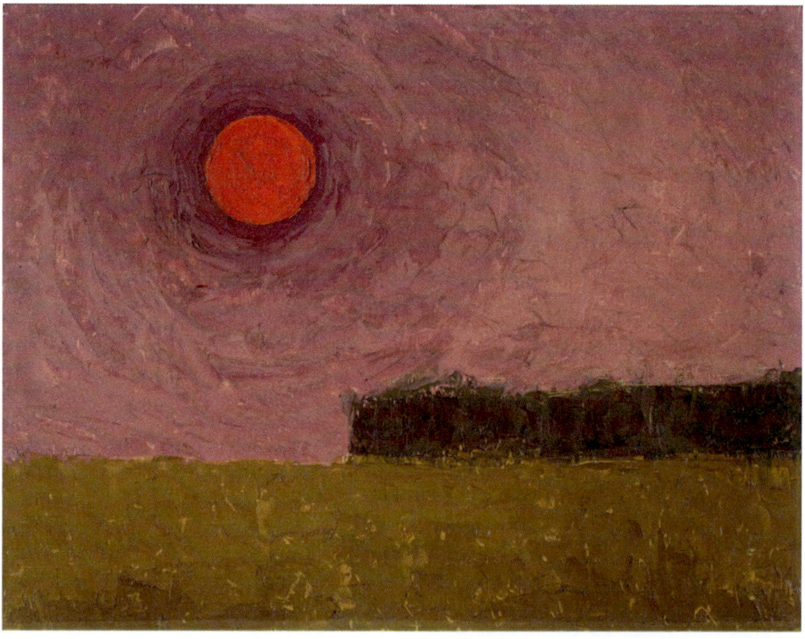

Orange Sun in Mauve Sky, c. 1950

Orange Sun in a Mauve Sky hung on the living room wall during our years in London. I was in the habit of lying on the divan under the bay window when I was tired, and I must have spent many a minute gazing at its burning intensity. I knew it as one of Mummy's paintings from the era before I'd arrived in her life. As such it intrigued me powerfully; but I don't remember asking her when she painted it, where the flat green field was, and what had made the sky so very mauve. Instead I enjoyed the warm sensation I felt in my stomach when I gazed at that burning sphere, which equated to a wild, rebellious hope. The painting spoke to me of an unknown time when Mummy was full of energy, and fearless to the point that she could slap whatever colour she chose onto a board and swirl it about with a knife till she got the effect she wanted. That wasn't the Mummy I saw lying on the sofa on Saturday afternoons, sobbing silently into the cushions, while Daddy stomped about on the bare boards.

The other work I remember clearly from our living room was Daddy's sculpture of my cat. The real cat was a slim and slinky tabby with white paws and an exceptionally sweet nature: even Daddy adored her. I'd named her 'Pussy', but Daddy thought 'Gladys' suited her better. It annoyed me that he should question my choice of name, but I liked seeing him stroke her with his broad, clay-calloused hands, when he found her lying in the sun on the terrace.

At some point during his early adventures into sculpture, Daddy made a cat stretched out on its side, modelled on Pussy, although he coloured it with a dark glaze and polished it with boot black. The sculpture went down well with me and Anna, and soon it had pride of place in an alcove in the wall beside our kitchen table. We would stand stroking the tummy with our little hands and marveling at how Daddy had recreated the texture of Pussy's fur, and the characteristic way she liked to stretch out her front legs, resting one paw on top of the other.

The tail, too, fascinated us, trailing behind her back legs as if she might at any moment flick it in annoyance.

*

In September 1961 I was sent to join my sister at Hotham Road primary school, a red brick Victorian edifice just one block from our house. In those days, Putney was poor and my parents had deliberately chosen a school where we would mix with local children whose backgrounds were completely different from our own. There were Jamaicans, Nigerians, Greeks, Ghanaians and white South Africans, along with a lot of children from working class English families.

I was still in the Infants part of the school and learning to read when it dawned on Sheila there must be a reason why Anna and I were reluctant to invite our school friends home for tea. When she questioned us, we explained that we couldn't risk them seeing our home-made crockery, for fear of ridicule. In the hands of a young child, the plates Daddy had made at Hawkley were very heavy. He'd used coarse red clay and the texture on the unglazed side was like the surface of a ploughed field. Neither did we want our friends to see the home-made brown bread we lived on, also made by Daddy, who kneaded the dough with the same vigour with which he kneaded clay. We feared the scorn of our little friends, to whom 'bread' meant Mother's Pride.

The day after this conversation, Sheila walked down to Woolworths in Putney High Street and bought a set of blue and white striped china plates and mugs. She hid them at the back of the cupboard, explaining that they would only be used when we had friends home for tea, and that this could only happen on days when Daddy wasn't around. Thrilled with the plates and excited by the need for secrecy, we accepted the rules without question.

Our clothes were chosen for us from bin bags of cast-offs supplied by Daddy's salaried friends. Given the choice, I would have wanted to wear red and pink, or the colours in *Orange Sun in a Mauve Sky*. But, under Alan's influence, Sheila selected only items in what she called 'earth' colours – beiges and browns and olive greens. On just one occasion, she ignored the bin bags and bought me a brand new dress, for Christmas. She hung it by the tree, shrouded in a sheet of coloured tissue, and I eyed it longingly while waiting for Christmas morning to arrive. But when at last I was allowed to tear off the paper, my excitement was demolished in an instant: it was a dull shift in beige and muted brown.

Just once there was a brief moment of rebellion, where Anna and I joined forces. It happened in December 1962, when I was five and she seven. We'd each been given the grand sum of two and sixpence to spend on Christmas shopping. To us, this was an astonishing windfall. But instead of buying presents for our parents and grandmother, as intended, we marched down to Woolworths – just the two of us – and used the money to purchase pink nylon Alice bands with bows. We both knew, without the shadow of a doubt, that our parents would consider them 'appalling'. Despite that, I'm proud to say, we didn't hesitate. I've never forgotten the glee I felt when I saw my grinning face in the bathroom mirror, framed by pink nylon.

*

Our lives revolved around Mummy, while Daddy spent his days in the studio at the bottom of the garden. He sometimes appeared in the house unexpectedly for a few minutes with an air of impatience ('where do you keep the Vim, Sheila? I've run out,' or 'Got any milk?'). At these moments I would watch him warily for signs of an imminent outburst of temper.

Mostly I could tell, from Daddy's body language, that he was in a hurry and hadn't come to talk to any of us, least of all me. I knew I meant less to him than Anna did and I dealt with that by clinging ever more tightly to Mummy. But that didn't stop me wishing he would spend time with us. I harboured a private hope that one day, if I tried very hard, I could get him to notice me and see that I had things to say for myself. I wasn't as compliant or pretty as Anna, but surely I deserved a little bit of his attention?

One grey and drizzly autumn afternoon in 1963, Daddy burst into our living room in his clay-smeared overalls with an excited look on his face. He greeted Mummy with unusual warmth and filled the electric kettle at the sink, while regaling her with the details of something good that had just happened. 'I think this calls for a celebration, don't you?' he ended, glancing at me and Anna with a mischievous look. A moment later he grabbed his wallet and marched out. I heard the front door slam and assumed that was the end of another flying visit. But three minutes later the key turned in the lock, and in he burst again, this time clutching a box of Mr Kipling's chocolate cupcakes. He'd been over the road to Mr Gleeson, whose grocery shop was opposite our garden wall.

Oh delight! Anna and I leapt up from where we'd been sitting on the floor by the stove and ran to our chairs at the kitchen table. By now Mummy was setting out four cups and saucers and four little plates, so she must have known what Daddy was planning.

'I've warmed the pot,' she told him, gesturing at the big brown earthenware teapot on the kitchen counter. She knew better than to make the tea, because Daddy would only drink loose leaf tea and he liked a mixture of Indian with China. If Mummy put the different teas in the pot herself, she was likely to get the proportions wrong. Or the amount of hot water. Or something else.

When we were all sitting round the table, Daddy grinned at me and Anna. 'Well girls, whaddya know, they're going to show my head of … !'

He was referring to a portrait sculpture which had been accepted for the Royal Academy Summer Exhibition. We smiled up at Daddy, glad to see him happy but wondering how long it would be before he opened the box with the cupcakes.

Sheila poured the tea: Daddy's first, then hers, then she glanced at Anna. 'D'you want tea darling, if I make it very milky?' But Anna shook her head. Sheila went to the sink and made two glasses of Ribena.

And now the big moment arrived. With the grin still on his face, Daddy tore open the cardboard box with his clay-ingrained fingers and shook out the cupcakes onto the table. Each one sat in its own case of pleated greaseproof paper and was crowned on the top with a layer of sugary chocolate icing. Daddy passed one to Anna, one to me and one to Sheila. Then he took the last one, peeled off the paper and set it down on his plate.

This wasn't the first time we'd had cupcakes as a treat, and Anna and I had devised a special method for making the pleasure last as long as possible. The trick was to lift the layer of sugary icing right off the cake, and lay it upside down on your plate. You could then gaze at it longingly while you chewed your way through the very dull and not very chocolatey sponge cake, delaying the moment of oral delight so as to make it all the more wonderful when it came.

On this occasion Daddy watched me lever off the icing with an air midway between amusement and disdain. Luckily, Anna was doing the same thing, although she did it more quickly than me and without getting as many crumbs on the table. I held my breath, but the circle of icing broke in two just as I lowered it onto my plate. Disappointed, I glanced at Mummy, but her eyes were on Daddy. She was smiling and I knew that what mattered to her was not the mess on the table, but the fact that he was here, and for once we were having a family tea. And then I looked at Daddy, who was stirring sugar into his cup, *still* grinning. An unfamiliar sense of happiness spread through me.

Looking back, I realise how profoundly disabled Mummy, Anna and I felt on a daily basis by Daddy's absence. During all those hours and days when we barely saw him, we operated like a three-legged animal which had lost its fourth leg to a grievous injury. On that special afternoon, eating cupcakes in his upbeat presence, our fortunes had momentarily improved and we felt complete.

Chapter 15
Rejection Slips

I KNEW THAT SOMETHING was gravely wrong between my parents, but I didn't understand what it was. They often rowed in front of me, but when old friends were present they kept up a semblance of 'normal' family life.

On Sundays we had a big roast lunch, often with Tim and Bridget Gibbs and their three children, sometimes at our house, sometimes at theirs. Alan instituted a competition to see who could produce a Sunday roast big enough to feed four adults and five children for the smallest amount of money. His favourite solution was a cut called 'scrag end of neck', which he bought from Sid, our butcher in the Lower Richmond Road. Sid was a tall man with bulging, spam-like cheeks, a bald, shiny head and a navy and white striped apron stretched tightly over his large stomach. While Sid sharpened his knives and chatted with Daddy, I breathed in the acrid smell of blood and drew patterns in the sawdust on the floor of his shop with my toes.

The cooking of lunch was a time of high stress, whether it was Mummy or Daddy in charge; but, once the friends arrived, the meal itself was fun. Daddy loved to debate and was only too happy to have an audience for his firmly held views on subjects such as the Aldermaston marches ('marvelous'), comprehensive education ('marvelous'), art education ('in need of radical reform'), the nuclear arms race ('appalling') and the struggle against apartheid in South Africa ('inspiring').

South Africa was a painful subject for Sheila. Bay had divorced his first wife and re-married Ivy, a white Kenyan. After some years farming with her in Kenya, he wrote to Sheila that the Mau Mau independence movement's attacks on white farmers had made

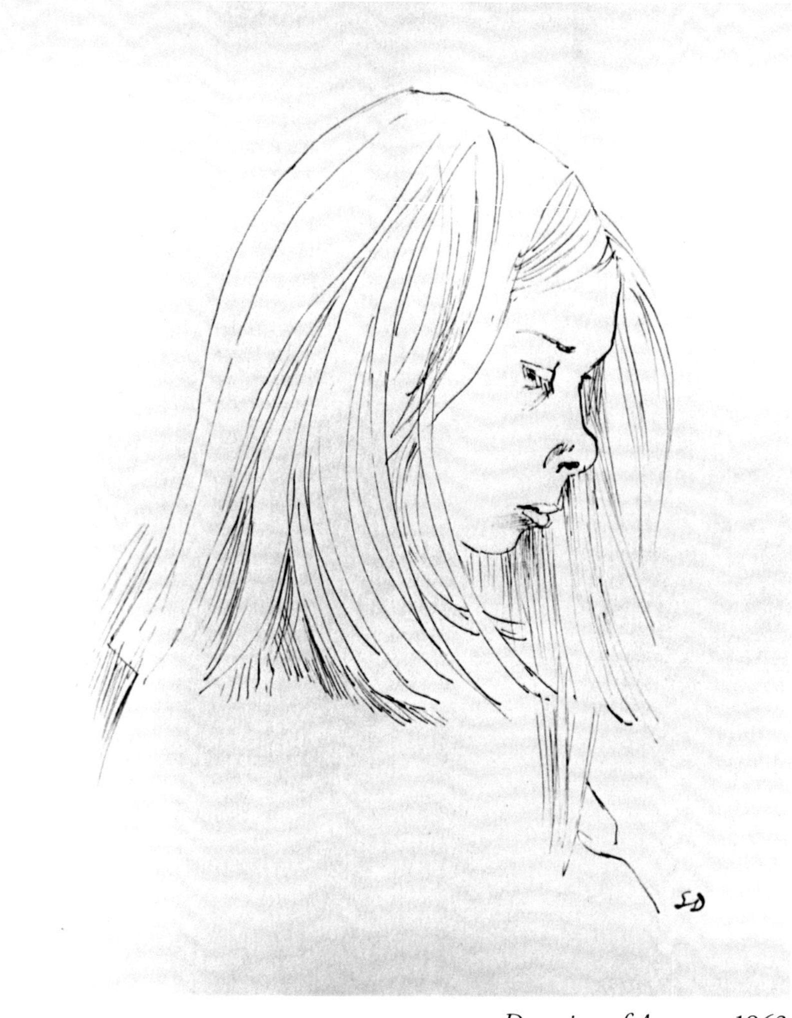

Drawing of Anna, c. 1963

their lives impossible[1]. In 1961 he packed his new family, their possessions and a couple of rifles into a lorry and made the trek south to Pietermaritsburg in apartheid South Africa, where they bought a piece of land and built a house. Sheila was strongly opposed to apartheid and disapproved of her brother's sense of entitlement to live in Africa as a white man; but she didn't want him to come to harm.

The Gibbs family had a place in Somerset, to which we were often invited: a whitewashed stone cottage in a clearing at the bottom of a long, mysterious track. I loved it from my first visit, when I was barely five years old. There were echoes of Hawkley in the way the place looked and smelled: the dripping, lichen-spangled trees along the track as we bumped along in our ancient Hillman van, the woodsmoke wafting from the chimney when we reached the clearing, the low, drystone walls that sheltered the front terrace of the cottage like a pair of protective arms and the moss and tiny flowers that grew in the cracks.

William, Chloe, Anna and I passed our days playing in the woods beyond the clearing, scrambling down into the fern-choked channel of a former canal, then hauling each other back up to race between the trees, tripping over the rusting remnants of a past, industrial age. Sheila and Bridget were indoors with Rosie[2] the baby, making beds and preparing lunch while Daddy and Tim sat on the terrace, drinking coffee, smoking cigarettes and discussing the difficulties they were having getting their work shown in London galleries.

When it rained, Tim retreated to his studio, a wooden structure on the grassy bank above the cottage. One very wet day, Sheila and I put on our mackintoshes and climbed the slippery bank to take Tim a sandwich for his lunch.

---

1 Bay won't have acknowledged the legitimacy of the Mau Mau's claim to their homeland.

2 Rose Gibbs is now an established artist and writer.

When we stepped through the studio door, scattering raindrops onto the chipboard floor, the smell of oil paint filled our noses. Tim was perched on a stool in front of a heavy wooden easel, paintbrush in hand, narrowing his gaze at a spot on the canvas. He was a tall, handsome, olive-skinned man, who always dressed in baggy cords.

'Hello there!' he exclaimed, taking in Sheila's arrival with a look of delight. 'How lovely to see you!' He had to shout to make himself heard above the hammering of the rain on the roof.

'We're not here to disturb you.' Sheila smiled back. 'Just wanted to catch a glimpse of the man at work…'

'You're not disturbing me!' He put down his paintbrush, took a step towards her and kissed her on both cheeks.

I could tell, from the way he looked at her, that Tim had a special feeling for Mummy. That made me happy: here was a man who appreciated her warmth and beauty, like my daddy should have done.

*

In the early 1960s, Alan took a night job as an operator at the international telephone exchange, using his French and Italian to put through calls. When we came home from school that winter, he was on his way to work and we spent the dark evening hours in the living room with Sheila, drifting from the kitchen table to the sofa and back again.

Over supper, we told her about school and she told us how she'd spent her day. If she'd had a letter from Bay, there might be photos of the cousins we'd never met, dressed in old fashioned frocks in a parched, flat landscape; or she might tell us an anecdote about Gaga, who'd recovered her health and was enjoying a busy social life based around her church.

One evening, after swallowing her last mouthful of corned beef and mashed potatos, Mummy pushed back her chair and got to her feet. I stared at her across the kitchen table, wondering what was up.

'Right,' she said, in a voice tight with tension, 'I've got to get a move on. If I don't get these forms filled in tonight, I'll miss the deadline.' Glancing at the chaos of plates and pans that littered the table, she went on, 'Put your plates by the sink, please, I'll wash up later.' With that she marched to the living room door and we heard her on the stairs.

Anna looked at me, then poked me in the arm. 'Come on, Tonky,' she said firmly. 'Mummy needs the table.' Anna was eight, and I knew better than to argue.

Slowly I scraped my chair backwards across the wooden floor and picked up my dirty plate.

I was standing on tiptoes, pushing the plate to the back of the counter, when Mummy reappeared with some paper forms and a pen and ink drawing of Anna in a frame. 'Thanks, darlings,' she muttered, placing the drawing on a chair. Then she wedged the forms under one arm, went to the sink, wrung out a dishcloth and wiped the table clean. A moment later she sat down and spread out the forms. I wondered if she'd forgotten we were in the room, and glanced round for reassurance from Anna. But my sister had retreated to the sofa and lay with her legs trailing over the arm, engrossed in her library book.

'These blasted rules,' Mummy muttered. '"*All works which are not accepted for exhibition must be collected between 10am and 4pm on Thursday 16th November.*" Which I can't do, because I've got a hospital appointment!' Her felt tip pen made scratching noises as it travelled across the paper. When her hand stopped moving, she picked up another sheet of paper and I saw her lips forming words. '"*The decision of the selection panel,*"' she quoted, '"*shall be final and no correspondence can be entered into.*" Humphh!' Mummy stood up, placed the form in a corner of the table, picked up the drawing and looked at it intently. Anna's long fair hair fell to her shoulders in sharp points. Seen in profile like this, her nose turned up at the end and she had a sulky look. Mummy turned to me. 'Fetch me a duster, darling. From the cupboard under the sink.'

The duster I found was less than clean, which had Mummy muttering again. She got up and opened the double doors at the back of the kitchen which gave onto the balcony, letting in a rush of cold air. After she'd shaken out the duster, she came back to the table and polished the glass in the frame till it shone. For an instant her eyes lit up. 'My Annakins. Not sure I really want to part with you… But ten guineas is ten guineas. You could both have new shoes…'

Now she fetched a roll of brown paper and wrapped the drawing very carefully, with a sheet of cardboard over the glass. She wound white string around the package, crossed the two ends and turned it over. Then she asked me to place my finger at the point where the strings met and press down firmly. To do this I had to stand very close to her, breathing in her sweet-sweaty smell, and concentrate hard . I was good with my hands but my fingers were still small – I was only six. I stood very still, pressing for all I was worth and trying to stop the string wriggling away from under my fingertip. At last the knot was tied. Mummy picked up the package and tested the string. 'It's a bit on the loose side,' she murmured to herself, 'but it'll do.' Then she turned to me. 'Thankyou, love. And now, go and put your nightie on, I'll be with you in a minute.'

*

In the spring of 1965, Sheila was admitted to hospital for a further attempt to treat her overactive thyroid, which continued to produce unpleasant symptoms such as sweating, anxiety and trouble sleeping. This time she had to consume a drink of radioactive iodine, in conditions of isolation, which she endured without support. Sylvia Lauder wrote to her afterwards:

> 'What an incredibly brave girl you are! It all sounds so nightmarish, food thrust through the door, no human contact. I wonder you didn't go bonkers. I really hope it's done the trick and that you will now flourish exceedingly.'

The drink reduced the activity of Sheila's thyroid gland, resulting – as was common in those days – in it becoming underactive. This produced symptoms of weight gain and lethargy, which were eventually stabilised with medication. But it would be some years before Sheila flourished.

Chapter 16
The Ragged Man

BY THE EARLY AUTUMN OF 1963, things had become so bad between my parents that they agreed Alan would move out. By now he was teaching part time at an art school in Romford, Essex, and could afford to rent an attic room in the home of some local friends. During the day, when he wasn't teaching, he continued to work in the studio. He came into the house for meals cooked by Sheila, sometimes eating with us, sometimes alone; but at night he left and returned to his attic.

It was a desperate time for Sheila, who felt abandoned and betrayed. She was left with the lion's share of responsibility for us children; and she had to live with the knowledge that Alan was now free to enjoy himself with his married woman lover whenever he chose – not to mention the stream of female students she saw walking through the garden, towards the studio.

Our house had a big bay window at the front, from which there was a clear view into the assembly hall of the Church school opposite, about which we knew nothing. One day when I was under the weather I spent several hours lying on the divan bed beneath the window, staring at the street. Sitting on the pavement opposite, with his back resting against the wall of the school, was a bearded man in ragged clothing, clutching a bottle. I'd never seen him before and his appearance frightened me.

When it was almost time to pick up my sister from school, Mummy announced we had to go to the shop over the road. Mr Gleeson sold everything from Kelloggs cornflakes to faggots, cheese, bread and milk and we shopped there on a daily basis. When Mummy had bought half a pound of butter, instead of walking directly to school down our side of the road to fetch my sister, she led me across the road towards the Church school, which meant we had to walk right past the man on the pavement. I tugged at her hand, but she refused to hurry. Not only that; she greeted the man as we passed.

The following day, when I looked out of the window, the man was still there. It was a grey, winter Saturday and it was drizzling. We didn't have plans for anything that day and I felt bored and listless. Mummy lit the stove and asked Anna if she fancied toast and dripping. Anna always fancied toast and dripping, which I couldn't eat because it made me queasy. So Mummy made a big stack of toast from a soft white cottage loaf. She brought it over to the stove with the dripping from last Sunday's roast, and some jam for me, and we sat on the floor, crunching our way through the slices.

Anna and Mummy both liked singing, and they were very fond of The Beatles. When she'd finished eating, Anna asked Mummy if she knew the words to "Eleanor Rigby". Mummy did, of course – she could memorise any poem at the drop of a hat. She smiled at Anna and began to sing

> Ah look at all the lonely people
> Eleanor Rigby
> Picks up the rice in the church where a wedding
>   has been
> Lives in a dream
> Waits at the window
> Wearing the face that she keeps in a jar by the door
> Who is it for?

It wasn't the easiest of tunes, but within a few bars Anna was singing along with Mummy, hitting all the right notes. At eight she already had a beautiful singing voice.

When they moved on to Penny Lane, I tried to join in. It was less sad than Eleanor Rigby and I was feeling left out.

Penny Lane is in my ears and in my eyes
There beneath...

Anna stopped mid-line and frowned at me.

'Shut up, Tonky,' she pleaded. 'You're completely out of tune.'

I clamped my jaw shut and wrapped my arms tightly round my knees, glaring at Anna and glancing at Mummy in the hope that she would come to my defence. But Mummy acted as if she hadn't heard and they started again and went on till the end of the song. Then she stacked the crumby plates, got up and went to the sink.

Later that day, when I was sitting on the divan drawing a picture, and Anna was lying on the sofa reading her book, Mummy put on her coat and shoes and said she was going out for a moment. It was still raining and through the window I watched her open the garden gate. A moment later, to my astonishment, she was crouching on the pavement opposite, speaking with the ragged man. Then she was coming back up the garden path and the man was walking beside her, dragging one of his feet, as if it didn't work properly. I wondered how he would manage the steps up to our front door; but in another moment I heard voices in the hall. Next thing I knew he was sitting at our kitchen table, dripping water onto the floor from his wet clothes and talking slowly with Mummy, who was filling the kettle. A strong smell of tobacco mixed with something dark and grimy wafted towards me. I couldn't understand much of what the man was saying, but Mummy told me later that was because he was Irish, from County Mayo. She said she'd been feeling lonely that day and when she saw him through the window it had dawned on her that he was probably feeling the same way.

Chapter 17
The Electricity Bill

AFTER DADDY MOVED OUT, our lodgers were moved into the basement and we inhabited the ground and upper floors of the house. I shared a bedroom on the first floor with Anna, where we slept in bunk beds. That winter, I had trouble getting off to sleep and often, when I could hear my sister's breathing become slow and even, I would slip out of bed and pad downstairs in my nightie. The doors in our house, which in 1960 Daddy had spent days sanding and varnishing, had beautiful porcelain door knobs; but the one on the living room door was coming loose. One night, as I turned the knob as gently as I could, my eyes landed on Mummy's back. She was seated at the desk in the far corner of the living room, between the glowing coals of the stove and the dark red brocade of the floor to ceiling curtains, her head inclined at an angle as her writing hand moved deliberately across a sheet of paper. At the other end of the room, the kitchen was in darkness. The only illumination came from a tall and spindly standard lamp with a metal base and a scorched purple shade which cast a pool of yellow light onto the desk.

I stood for a second and studied Mummy's shoulder blades, trying to assess whether she'd been crying. No, I thought, not this time. Then I walked softly towards her, trying to avoid the splintery places where Daddy's attempts to join old floorboards together had gone badly. Mummy had wanted a carpet in this part of the room, but he'd insisted on a bare floor.

Now Mummy put down her pen and swiveled in her seat, one eyebrow raised. She was trying to look stern, but I could tell she was pleased to see me.

'I can't sleep,' I muttered, by way of explanation. Then I trotted towards her and threw my arms around her neck.

'My darling,' she murmured, pulling me onto her lap and holding me tight. We sat like that for a long moment, each deeply comforted by the presence of the other. When at last she loosened her arms, I slithered to the floor and stared at the papers on the desk. They were long narrow sheets and the script consisted of boxes, pound signs and numbers. On some the ink was black; on others, red. Mummy's cheque book lay open, her felt pen resting against a wad of counterfoils.

'The bills,' she said, by way of explanation.

I picked up the one nearest to me, which was headed 'London Electricity Board'. 'Why's it in red?'

Mummy looked at me. 'We're late paying. Final demand. Daddy told me he'd paid it, but he hadn't.'

I felt a sense of constriction across my forehead, almost the beginnings of a headache. 'So… what happens if Daddy doesn't pay?' I could tell it was going to be bad.

'It's allright, darling, I'm going to pay it myself. I was just writing out the cheque when you came in.' She picked up her pen and started to write on a fresh, pristine cheque. 'I was just totting up how much I've got left in my account. I don't want it to bounce…'

I stood at her elbow, following the swirls and dashes of her elegant handwriting. She formed each letter with the same care she would have employed in a drawing. If I paid very close attention to what she was doing, I hoped, that might somehow ensure that the bank would honour the cheque.

'If you don't pay,' I ventured in a small voice, 'what do they do?' I only half wanted to know. It hadn't escaped me that there was a second red-inked bill in the pile.

Mummy hesitated. Then she put down her pen, tore the cheque from the counterfoil and waved it in the air to dry the ink. 'They can cut off the supply. But don't worry, darling,

I'll put this in the letterbox first thing in the morning and phone them to say it's in the post.' She put the cheque into the envelope and held it out it to me. 'Would you like to lick the sticky strip?'

*

With Daddy no longer living with us, Sheila made a strenuous effort to find a job. If only she'd passed her Camberwell diploma, art school teaching would have been open to her; but that door was firmly, frustratingly, closed. By now she was seeing a psychoanalyst, who suggested she work as an art therapist and began to refer patients to her on a private basis. On the strength of this, Sheila approached the Cassel psychiatric hospital, who passed her details to Springfield hospital in Tooting. Without an art therapy qualification, she could only work as an assistant. She was taken on as a part time Occupational Therapy Helper in May 1966.

Sheila was shocked by the condition of the in-patients she met at Springfield, many of whom were so heavily sedated that they couldn't find the motivation to lift a paintbrush. There was one man, however, Paul, who showed great enthusiasm and some aptitude for painting. Sheila paid him a lot of attention and became very interested in his predicament; sometimes she spoke to us about him over supper. One day I came home from school to find her on the phone in the hall. She was standing up and her cheeks were flushed with anger.

'How dare they tear up his work, without asking him if he wanted to keep it? Or asking *me*, for that matter?'

I couldn't hear the reply. A moment later she continued:

'Paul has real talent. And, hardly surprisingly in the circumstances, very little confidence. If the nurses are allowed to destroy his work, can't you see how damaging that will be for him?'

I tiptoed past her into the living room. I didn't know what a psychiatric hospital was, but I felt proud of Mummy for standing up for her favourite student.

Chapter 18
In a Class of our own

IN 1965 I WAS EIGHT YEARS OLD and trying hard to make sense of my family and how we fitted into the world. Daddy had started taking Anna and me away on long weekends without Mummy, to stay with his Oxford friends who lived in Sussex. One was a banker, another a picture restorer married to a 'gentleman' farmer. They lived in large houses with extensive gardens and their children had the self confidence which comes with money and private education. The boys had shiny new bikes, and one family had their own ponies grazing in a meadow behind the house.

We were received with great kindness but there was also pity – partly because we were away without our mum, about whom Daddy's friends questioned him in lowered tones, but also because our rusting van made funny noises and when they took us to the beach, our towels were threadbare. The best asset Anna and I had was our long, straight hair – my sister's ash blond, mine golden brown.

It was clear to me that these people lived in a different world from us. And yet, when I watched Daddy holding forth about one subject or another at their dining tables, he seemed entirely confident he belonged among them.

Back in Putney, my puzzling continued. Although my parents were different from Daddy's Sussex friends, they were even *more* different from the parents of the kids I met at school. Mummy and Daddy were 'well spoken' and lived in a world where art mattered above all else, whereas my classmates' parents ran shops or worked as cleaners. The parents of my close friend Stephanie were teachers, but their working class London accents signified a gulf between us.

And then there was Gaga, whose accent was really quite posh. She lived in one large room in her tall house on the Fulham-Kensington border, but it was furnished with mahogany antiques and she went on holiday to country hotels – something we never did. And twice she'd taken Anna and me to see *The Sound of Music*, live, with Julie Andrews, in a theatre where the seats were covered in red velvet plush.

One evening when Daddy came in from the studio to eat supper with us, I asked my parents what social class we belonged to. We were sitting at the kitchen table.

'I mean,' I explained, 'are we middle class or working class?' Those were the only two I'd heard of.

'Us?' Mummy replied, glancing at Daddy with a look of complicity. 'I'd say we're neither. We're artists, darling.' I picked up a tinge of pride in her voice. 'We're in a class of our own.'

I stared at her. 'What, just us?'

'Us and other artists. People who paint or sculpt or play music… or act or write plays.'

'And books?' I'd already decided I wanted to be a writer.

Mummy smiled. 'Yes sure, a writer is a kind of artist.' She glanced again at Daddy, who was stirring sugar into black coffee and watching me with an air of amusement.

Although she didn't intend it this way, I found Sheila's assertion that we were in a 'class of our own' an isolating and confusing message. For if we were neither middle nor working class, I told my eight-year-old self, we must belong to a very small and rarefied group of people. In which case, were we doomed to spend our lives feeling like misfits, except on the relatively rare occasions when we hung out with fellow artists? I certainly felt a misfit among the working class kids at school, and would only feel marginally better a couple of years later when my parents moved me to a church school in more affluent Roehampton. Here the children spoke like me but their fathers had professional jobs and new cars with smoothly-purring engines. I made a few friends;

but my father's clay-smeared clothing and rattling old van at the school gate caused me acute embarrassment.

I swallowed Sheila's statement whole, and for the rest of my childhood I lived under the delusion that I was not a middle class child; I even half believed her subtle message that being from a family of artists made me special. I would be well into my twenties before I understood that nothing could diminish the social status accorded to my parents on the basis of their accents, regardless of their meagre incomes.

What my parents didn't tell me, possibly because it wasn't something they thought about much, was how difficult it had been for members of their generation who *weren't* from middle or upper class families to become artists. Much later it would dawn on me that it's one thing to grow up in comfort and reject your family's money and values in order to paint or sculpt, as they had done; but quite another to grow up in poverty and choose to become an artist.

And my parents were never *really* poor; they were simply less well off than many of their friends. My mother had made her choices knowing she could turn to her parents in hard times; and my father's family had offered him a job in the family business, which he chose to turn down.

Chapter 19
Martin

MARTIN'S DARK BROWN EYES gaze at me with an intensity which I find unnerving. The irises are huge, set in clear whites which seem all the brighter for the burnt ochre Sheila used on the eyelids and the burnt umber at the temple. The thin black eyebrows rise in a sharp, defiant arch above each eye, tracing the line of the forehead. Here is a striking young man of dark complexion, with looks to melt the heart of the coolest teenage girl; and yet he's haunted by a dark foreboding, which Sheila nailed with some brilliance.

The portrait was the product of a long conversation between Martin and Sheila, in which he unburdened himself on a weekly basis. Sheila both painted and listened: the artist-cum-therapist. Martin's dream was to become a theatre director, but it seemed an impossible fantasy. He was applying for a post as an assistant stage manager with the Royal Shakespeare Company (RSC), he told her, but didn't believe he was 'good enough' for such a job.

I find it difficult to unlock my gaze from those insistent eyes, which brim with self doubt and a desperate need to be heard. The painting has always engendered a level of fear in me, but I'm determined to grasp how Sheila pulled it off, in the studio she set up in a small back bedroom in 1967. She'd recently been accepted as a member of the Contemporary Portrait Society, which had given her more confidence in her abilities.

Peering at the surface of the canvas, I see that slicks of brownish-pink paint, laid on with the palette knife, give form to the lean cheeks and long nose. When I move close to the canvas, the pink sits strangely with the burnt umber marks at the temple, abutting

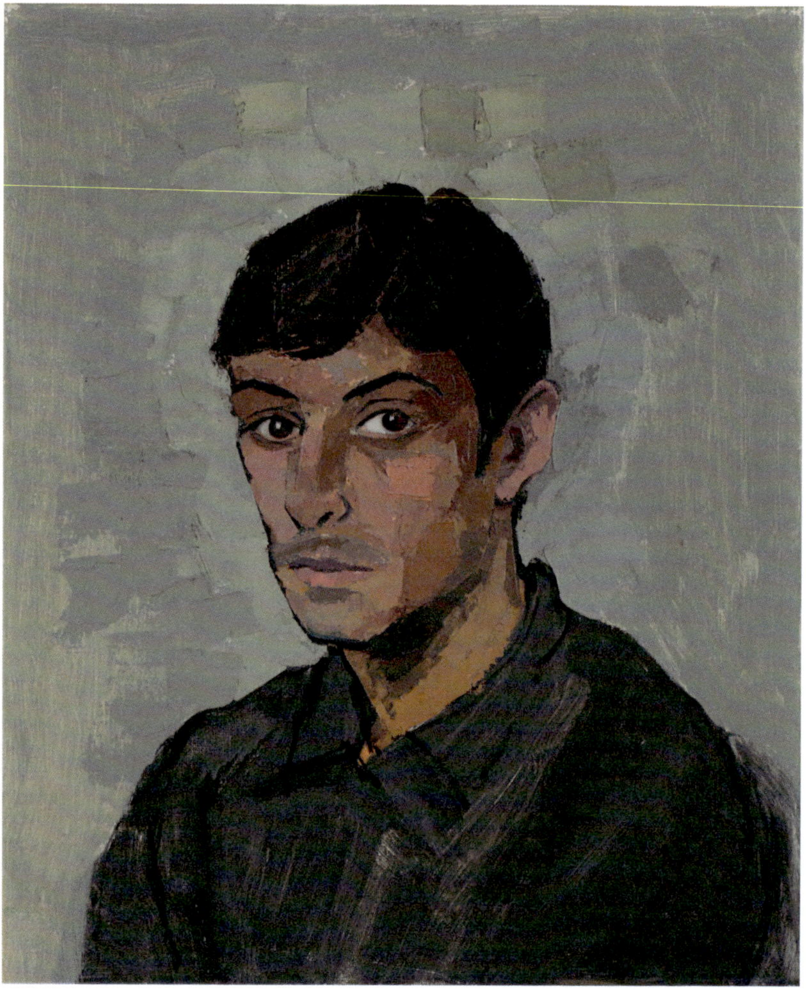

Martin Scott, 1967

Martin's trim black hair, and the dark olive green of the jaw and neck; but from a distance the effect is compelling.

Martin's looks had indeed melted the hearts of Melanie, his step-daughter, and Anna, her school friend. They were twelve in the summer of 1967, and thrilled to be taken on jaunts by twenty three-year-old Martin, who was newly married to Melanie's mum Ros. Ros was an actor in her late thirties; she'd first met Sheila in the school playground a couple of years earlier and they'd discovered that as artists and lone mothers they had a lot in common.

Sheila never got to finish the portrait of Martin; but the viewer barely registers the sketchy parts, so strong is the portrayal of the face and neck. The brush marks on Martin's grey shirt are thin in places, an under-layer of paint to which Sheila intended to return. Thick palette-knife slabs of a luscious grey-blue surround the head, and one does not notice how they peter out into hasty brush marks at the edges of the canvas. There were to be more sittings; Martin and Sheila enjoyed each other's company; neither of them was in a hurry.

I have only a hazy memory of the weeks when Sheila was painting Martin. It was summer and Daddy took Anna and me away on more than one trip. We went to Sussex to stay with his posh friends and we went camping in Devon with his long term girlfriend Wendy, to whom we'd now been introduced. A wordless, paralyzing fear built up in me before each trip. Daddy's temper continued to terrify me, and I knew that if I missed Mummy too much and cried at bedtime, he would get irritated. The thing I liked about the trips was that we always went to the countryside; but I felt bad about leaving Mummy all alone in our tall, sad house, when I knew she'd rather be in the country too.

After one of the trips we arrived home on a hot August afternoon to find Mummy in the hall saying goodbye to Martin. She'd been working on his portrait, she told me as she hugged me, and I noticed an unfamiliar gleam of satisfaction in her eyes. 'It's going well, I think,' she added.

A few days later, Martin told Sheila he'd been offered the post with the RSC. His initial reaction was to assume the RSC had made a mistake; but they hadn't and in early September he moved to Stratford on Avon to take up the job, leaving Ros and Melanie in London. Sheila put the painting aside, thinking she'd finish it one weekend when he was back.

Martin drove to Stratford in a sports car which he'd recently acquired by selling Ros' Fiat without her permission. Two weeks later, he called her to say he was coming to London for the weekend. But on the Thursday evening he took some friends for a ride in the car and crashed it. One of the passengers died at the scene and Martin sustained multiple head injuries. These led, five days later, to his death.

I have a dim memory of the acute distress that ricocheted between Ros, Melanie, Sheila and Anna in the wake of this terrible event. To Anna and Sheila, Martin had been important; to Ros and Mel, he'd been everything. Our world already had a tendency to darkness. Now it grew darker, though for me the sense of loss was not acute. Martin had been an intriguing stranger who got on well with Mummy and whose spirit she'd captured with uncanny force in the painting.

Chapter 20
Change

BY NOW MY SISTER WAS SETTLED at secondary school and I was in my final year at primary school. Urged on by the psychoanalyst she'd been seeing for several years, Sheila was seriously thinking of making a real break with Dad. She wanted to live in the country, but knew she needed to be within easy reach of London, so that we could see him regularly and she could submit her work to exhibitions. She began to look at schools and houses in West Sussex.

One afternoon that spring, unaware of the embryonic plan, I came home from school in my pleated skirt and red blazer with my cello on my back. Mummy was alone in the kitchen and I could tell from the look on her face that something was up. As she helped me out of the straps of the cello case and kissed me on the cheek, I wondered what it was.

'T,' she said, 'I've got something to tell you.'

I laid the cello down beside the sofa and went to stand in front of her.

'I can't carry on like this,' she said slowly. 'I've got to leave.'

'Leave?' I gasped, thinking for a terrible moment that she was going to abandon me. 'Can't I come with you?'

Mummy pulled me towards her and held me tight. 'Yes of course, I wouldn't dream of going without you! And Gaga's coming too. Not to live with us, but she'll be nearby.'

A tear rolled down my cheek and sank into Mummy's polo neck jersey. I nestled my head into her bosom, which smelled of Lux flakes.

'I've got to get away from Daddy,' she went on. 'The situation's killing me.'

The words sliced through me. I knew things were very bad, but it hadn't occurred to me that she might die.

'I'm thinking of buying a house in the country.'

I pulled back my head and stared up at her, struggling to make the transition from the terrifying idea of Mummy dying back into the present moment. She was gazing at me calmly and she looked fully alive.

'I've seen a place I like to the south of Chichester,' she went on. 'It's one half of a farmhouse, surrounded by fields.'

For a few more moments I tried to digest the enormity of what she was telling me. Then the words 'farmhouse' and 'fields' began to register and my quaking heart leapt upwards. Ever since leaving Hawkley, I'd dreamed of going back to live in the country. A farmhouse of our own sounded like a dream come true. I squeezed my arms tightly around Mummy's rib cage. She would feel much better in Sussex, far away from Daddy and his girlfriend, and we could spend lots of time outdoors.

Mummy released me and we stood staring at each other.

'You look pleased, T,' she said slowly.

I jiggled up and down on the spot as her serious expression began to soften.

'When, Mummy?' I demanded. 'When are we going?'

PART SIX

APRIL 2019

I stood outside Dad's door, mug of tea in hand, trying to guage his position in the bed through the stained glass panel in the door. According to Christian, Dad had had a rough night, waking at four and six and seven and calling out; now, after the rigours of his bed-bath, he'd fallen into a deep sleep. It was two in the afternoon.

I pressed my shoulder against the door and watched it slowly swing open. Dad lay on his back with the duvet pulled up to his chin and his favourite brown and gold paisley blanket spread over the top. His breathing was slow and deep. I took a step onto the carpet, pushed the door shut behind me – very softly – and tiptoed round the foot of the bed. I had no wish to wake him; I would just sit with him for twenty minutes while I drank my tea.

Dad's left eye was closed; his right one open but unseeing. As his chest rose and fell beneath the bedding, I picked up a faint whiff of after-shave mixed with that sweet, musty smell I knew so well. It was a strong, man's odour which I remembered from childhood as something that had lurked in trunks and suitcases. If I opened the wooden chest where Dad stored his wool blankets from the war, it would waft into the air, mingled with the smell of mothballs. I'd mentioned it once, a few years back, thinking Dad must know he had his own, special smell; but he took it the wrong way and went into a huff.

The grey fleece hat was slipping onto the pillow, leaving the bald top of Dad's head exposed. I remembered what it used to feel like when I sat on his shoulders, aged about two, my little hands resting on his forehead, feeling the horizontal ridges of flesh above his worry lines. Dad held my ankles as he strode along country paths in Somerset or Gloucestershire, negotiating clumps of nettles and patches of mud with the confidence of a man who loved to be outdoors. Sometimes the weakness in his legs caused him to stumble, and curse, but he never fell while I was on his shoulders.

The colours in Dad's skin had altered since those distant days; there were patches of blue on his forehead and pale brown age spots; but the shape of his head remained unchanged. Today his breathing was silent. Suddenly anxious, I studied the subtle movements of his chest as it rose and fell under the duvet. He was fine, I told myself, Christian would have noticed if something was wrong. I thought of the countless times I'd observed Mum while she slept in her last years, mistaking the pallor in her face as a sign that death was imminent. Half an hour later she'd be struggling out of bed and making for the kitchen, the kettle and the biscuit tin, telling me to lie on the sofa while she made a pot of tea.

It was different, of course, with Dad. His muscular wasting condition had weakened his torso to the point where he could no longer stand. A less bloody-minded character would have succumbed to a wheelchair decades earlier, but Dad had kept going, seeking help from every alternative health practitioner he could find, practising yoga and swimming three times a week. The way he'd dealt with his disability had long filled me with admiration. No self pity, no complaining; just adapting his life-style, changing his diet and carrying on regardless. When he reached his sixties, Dad's legs had started to give way from time to time and he'd developed the knack of flipping into yogic relaxation at a second's notice, so that when he hit the floor, or the pavement, he was almost never injured. He would roll over, slowly sit up, and wave away anybody who tried to help him.

According to Anna, a doctor whom Dad had seen in London some years back had pronounced him to have the healthiest internal organs he'd ever come across in a man in his eighties. Perhaps it was all the raw food he'd eaten as a young man, she joked, or the single-minded pursuit of art…

I put down my mug and let my eyes wander around the room, over the portrait heads and small sculptures displayed on every surface.

I loved the way the light streamed in from the two front windows and fell in bars across the oak floor. And now a happy thought dawned in my mind: after all the years of conflict and anger, I'd reached the point where I felt comfortable with Dad. That was the last thing I'd ever expected.

Chapter 21
Sefter Granary

SEFTER GRANARY WAS THE NAME of the whitewashed half farmhouse in West Sussex which Sheila moved us to in September 1968. Five miles to the south of Chichester, our new home lay in a flat, marshy landscape of nurseries and agricultural land between the city and the sea, a couple of miles inland from Pagham Harbour.

I'm not sure how much thought Sheila gave to the practicalities of life at Sefter before she bought it. She'd checked out the local secondary schools in the previous few weeks and found one she could live with. What she hadn't properly considered was whether my thirteen-year-old sister, already a London teenager and very close to Dad, could be expected to adapt to life in the depths of the country. Nor had she worked out how, as a lone parent on a low income, she was going to run a dilapidated house with an acre of land.

The salt waters of Pagham Harbour flooded the fields around Sefter from time to time. A tiny brown river, Pagham Rife, passed within metres of our back garden and meandered slowly sea-ward through beds of grey-green rushes which smelled of silt and cow dung. In the harbour itself, sea birds and water birds inhabited the mud flats left by the retreating tide. They took off soundlessly in groups and veered at sharp angles high above, watched by camouflage-clad men with giant cameras.

I can see how Sheila's lack of forethought came about. At that moment in time, she was like an injured animal, wanting to slink off into the undergrowth to nurse her wounds in private. I think it took every ounce of her strength to make the break from London and find a new home. I remember her telling me how, after viewing Sefter for the first time, she wandered into the water meadows behind the house. The land was so choked with tall reeds that walking was difficult, but to a painter weary of spirit who'd spent eight unhappy years in a city, the strong sea light, the huge open sky and the terns wheeling overhead were very appealing. She squatted down on a tussock of coarse grass, closed her eyes and listened to the sound of the wind in the reeds. 'Sefter for Sheila', she heard them whisper, 'Sefter for Sheila'. She walked back to her car, drove to the nearest phone box, rang the agent and made an offer.

A pair of rusting iron gates stood open at the entrance to our new driveway. Bordered by a flowerbed on the left and a parade of staddle stones on the right, it curved round the side of the house and finished in a gravel yard by the back door.

We had the western end of the farmhouse, the other half being home to an elderly woman we rarely saw. In our half there were four bedrooms and two living rooms, one of which had double doors opening onto a sunny front garden. Our upstairs windows looked south over a wheat field to a line of bungalows and tiny houses with pointed roofs known as Nyetimber, the white walls of which were often set aglow by the sharp sea light. Bognor Regis was less than three miles distant.

Anna and I were sent to Chichester High School for Girls. On our way home in the afternoons, the school bus dropped us on the main road, a hundred yards from the house. Dressed in green blazers and pleated skirts, we walked up a pot-holed farm track to our gates. The track continued another fifty yards to two farm workers' cottages, a rusting metal barn and a cluster of half-ruined buildings.

For Anna, the move to Sefter was problematic from the start. She'd not wanted to leave London and felt she had little in common with the girls she met at the new school. For me, by contrast, Sefter was an outdoor adventure in an intriguing new landscape; and I was eleven, so changing school was a necessity.

Although we'd lived in London most of our lives, Anna and I were at ease in the countryside. On our trips with Dad, he'd often dragged us on walks of epic length and we'd learned to close gates behind us, skirt round cows with calves and take our litter home. On warm evenings that first autumn at Sefter, Sheila let us roam the fields near the house. The biggest one, a quarter of a mile in length, was planted with maize for cattle feed. When we ventured in, I was fascinated by the pinkish brown, dusty soil, the shiny, almost plastic texture of the maize leaves and the giant cobs of pale corn in their silky, hairy cocoons. As the weeks went by, the plants outgrew us in height and we took to pressing deeper and deeper into the field.

One unforgettable evening, we'd led a new school friend into the heart of the crop when we heard a distant, mechanical roar. At first it sounded far away, but as we listened, the sound grew louder and louder and we realized that the combine harvester was on its way towards us. 'Quick!' Anna shouted. 'Run!' Gripped by panic, the three of us joined hands and raced towards the hedge, tripping on broken stalks in the closely planted rows and scratching our bare legs till they bled. When we reached the edge of the field we squatted, shaking, against the trunk of an oak. Fifty yards away, the huge red beast of a machine charged in a billowing cloud of pale brown dust through the spot where we'd been standing.

Sheila spent our first winter trying to sort out the inside of the house with the help of Mr Daniels, a kind, semi-retired local builder. He was short and grey-haired with a large tummy encased in a dark brown jersey. He used to turn up in the evenings, when Sheila was cooking supper and we were doing our homework. He'd spend a couple of hours putting up shelves and painting walls, while Sheila brought him mugs of tea. I recall the warmth and gentleness with which he said her name, in his rural Sussex accent. 'She-i-la? I don't want to worry you, love, but this 'ere brickwork's crumblin'...' or 'You've got damp comin' through the bathroom wall, She-i-la, see that grey patch? No good me tilin' over that…'

The first few months at Sefter tested Sheila, but she loved being in the country and her walks along the sea wall at Pagham Harbour, observing the silver-grey water, the cocoa-coloured mud and the plover and oystercatchers busy in the sky overhead gave her a sense of space to match her new, separated woman freedom. In February of 1969, just five months after we arrived, she set up her heavy studio easel in the living room with the double doors, dusted off her wooden palette and began to paint. Over the next two years she would produce five of her best portraits.

The first one was *Gaga in a Grey Blue Dress*. My grandmother had bought herself a small house in the back streets of Chichester, planted its tiny garden with climbing roses, and found a bridge circle by joining the local church. She was busy and contented, but made time to come to Sefter for the sittings.

*

I jumped down from the cream and green school bus and scrambled onto the verge, anticipating the whooshing sound and the gust of diesel-smelling air as the driver accelerated away towards Nyetimber. Dust stung my eyes and I clutched a fence post for balance. Mummy had dinned it into me that I mustn't cross the road until I'd checked for traffic in both directions. It was still winter and the air was cold on my bare knees. I waited while a car whizzed past and then I marched as fast as I could across the road and onto our track. I loved that first moment of feeling the grit and dried mud under my lace-ups: now I was safe, and in two minutes I'd be home.

The strap of my heavy satchel dug into my shoulder as I circled between the rain-filled potholes, breathing in the smell of cow dung. Fluffy twirls of Old Man's Beard clung to the hedgerow, the relics of last year's flowers. Up ahead, a light burned in our living room window and by the farm buildings, the tractor was reversing with a load of silage in its forks. Now a sticky sweet smell replaced the wafts of cow dung, reminding me of the molasses Daddy used to put in his home made bread. But it was too upsetting to think of Daddy. I broke into a run through our iron gates, past the staddle stones and in at the back door.

The first thing I saw on the kitchen table was a plate with three buns, their icing shiny white, lined up in a row. One for me, one for Anna and one for Mummy. But where was she? I dumped my satchel on a chair. From behind the living room door came a murmur of voices. Then I remembered: Gaga was here today, for her portrait. Mummy had told me this morning. So how were three buns going to be divided between four of us? Anna would be home on the next bus. I pushed open the door. Mummy was sitting at her big wooden easel in the paint-smeared smock she wore to work, her eyes narrowed and her lips pouting in frustration.

'It's still not right,' I heard her mutter. 'Damnit!' Then she looked up. 'Teresa! Hello, darling!'

'Hello, Mummy.' I took a step into the room. Gaga was sitting very still on a wooden kitchen chair, looking like she dare not move. 'Hello, Gaga.' I wasn't sure what to do. Should I kiss my granny's powdered cheek, as I normally would? Or should I tiptoe back out, so as not to disturb them. What would I do about the buns? And why hadn't they finished? Mummy wasn't usually working when I got home from school.

'It's allright, darling.' Mummy laid her palette on the table with a sigh. 'We've done enough for one day, and the light's fading fast. Time for tea. Say hello to Gaga, darling. And to me.'

I wanted to go to Mummy first, but politeness sent me to Gaga.

'Hello!' she cried, her face lighting up as I stepped forward. 'How lovely to see you! And don't you look smart in your uniform!' I didn't like to kiss wrinkled skin, but I couldn't hurt my granny's feelings so I bent down and brushed her cheek with my lips.

Then I went to Mummy and gave her a hug. If we'd been alone I'd have sat down on her lap and nestled my head into her neck, but it didn't feel right to do that in front of Gaga. The air round Mummy smelled of turpentine. I glanced briefly at the canvas, then forced myself to look away. This was only the third sitting and she wasn't happy with what she'd done today.

'Those iced buns,' I began.

'I don't want one,' Mummy cut in. 'One for Anna, one for you and one for Gaga.'

Phew, I thought, although I only half believed her about not wanting one. 'Come on, let's put the kettle on.' I was ravenous and tea would be more of a palaver with Gaga here. We'd have to have cups and saucers instead of mugs, for a start. I took Mummy by the hand and pulled her out of her chair.

Once we were seated round the table in the kitchen, Gaga wanted to know about school. I told her I liked both my English teachers, the history teacher was scary but everybody laughed at her behind her back and I'd come top in a maths test.

'What a clever girl you are!' Gaga exclaimed. I squirmed with pride. Privately I suspected the maths result was a mistake: I'd never been good at maths in London. But I wasn't going to say so. I smiled sweetly and took a large bite of bun.

Through the glass panels in the kitchen door, the sky was turning black. Mummy got up and put on her coat and wellies, ready to meet Anna off the bus.

'Offer Gaga some more tea,' she told me, 'I'll be back in five minutes… unless the bus is late.'

I glanced at Gaga, wondering if Mummy was going to drive her home, leaving me and my sister alone in the dark. Mummy must have read my mind.

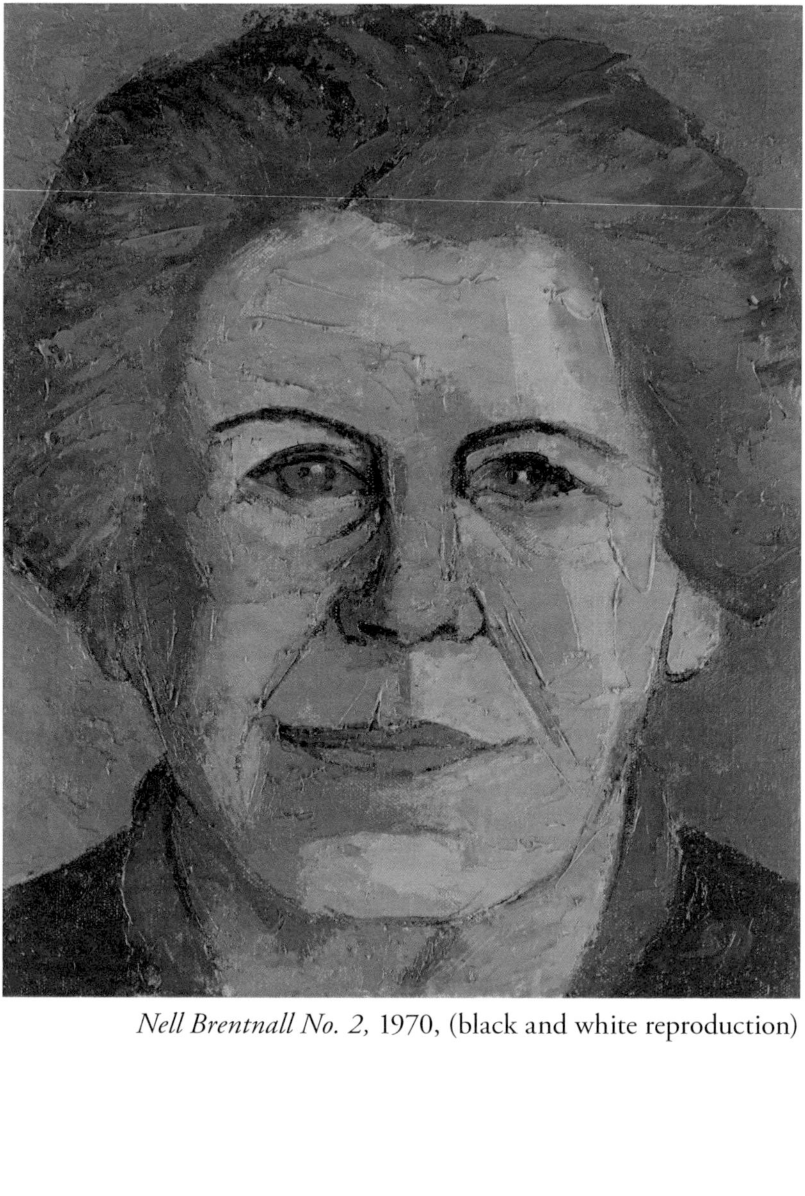

Nell Brentnall No. 2, 1970, (black and white reproduction)

'Don't worry, darling, Gaga's staying the night.' She tugged affectionately at my pony tail, then picked up the torch and walked out the door.

Good, I thought, so we'll be four tonight, with somebody sleeping in every bedroom. Sometimes, after dark, I didn't like that flimsy back door. Mummy locked it before she went to bed, but I had scary thoughts about what would happen if an angry man were to turn up and try to force his way in.

*

Before Gaga's portrait was finished, her friend Nell Brentnall commissioned Sheila to produce two portraits of herself as presents for her adult son and daughter. Sheila quoted a relatively modest price. She would be free to start the painting in the Easter holidays, while my sister was on a school French exchange and I was with Dad; Nell could come to stay at Sefter for the sittings.

I have black and white photographs of both Sheila's portraits of Nell. The first and larger of the two, a head and shoulders painting, is more conventional than the second and, to my eye, less interesting[1]. Nell's sturdy, handsome strength is apparent in the firmness of her jaw and the breadth of her shoulders, but she gazes at the viewer with a diffident expression, as if she's worried that they'll find her wanting. Produced with a combination of palette knife and brush work, it's an honest, unflattering depiction of a woman of seventy who's feeling uneasy. The courage Nell had to summon to allow herself to be looked at closely is evident in the taut muscles of her face; she doesn't appear to be enjoying the experience.

The second portrait was painted a year later in April 1970 and again Nell came to stay at Sefter for the sittings. Rejecting the idea of a second canvas of the same size as the first one, she persuaded a

---

1 The first portrait can be seen at www.sheiladenning.com

reluctant Sheila to work very small on this occasion. Ironically, the result is a painting in which the chin and hair push at the edges of the canvas with a fierce energy. It's one of Sheila's strongest portraits. The paint is thick, mostly laid on with the knife, and this time Nell comes over as an earthy, warm and powerful woman. The impression of power is achieved through the generous slabs of paint with which Sheila conveys the planes of the chin, the upper lip, the cheeks and forehead. There's a confidence in the gaze which makes the painting altogether different from the first portrait. Nell is feisty and engaging – a woman who knows who she is, and is no longer afraid to be seen.

*

In the spring of 1969, at the end of our first winter at Sefter, the size of the garden became a problem. Dad used to visit for the weekend once a month. One Sunday evening, as he was leaving, he commented on the weeds that were taking over the long flower bed bordering the drive. I felt Mum wince – it wasn't as if she hadn't noticed. A month later, nettles a metre tall tickled the bonnet of the car as we drove up the drive. The sight depressed us and in Sheila it produced a sense of panic, as it dawned on her that she'd taken on far more garden than she could ever cope with. After some weeks of worry, Mr Daniels came to the rescue by introducing Sheila to a teenage girl from Nyetimber who wanted grazing for her twelve-month-old grey gelding. Sheila had the back garden fenced and turned into a paddock, which became home to the improbably named and mesmerisingly graceful 'Beau Geste'.

At one stroke the problem of grass cutting was solved and I acquired a local friend. Susie's background couldn't have been more different from mine – she'd left school at fifteen and worked full time in her parents' grocery store – but I was pony-mad and willing to play the admiring young apprentice.

That summer, when we came home from school, Sheila drove my sister and me through the bungalows to the beach, passing miniature palms, clumps of waving bamboo and ageing residents dressed in pastel colours, who ambled slowly with tiny dogs on leads. The shingle beach was lined with wooden huts and invariably deserted; it shelved steeply towards the pinky-brown water. Sheila would bring a rug from the car and spread it on the warm pebbles, while my sister and I tore off our clothes and hurtled into the sea. We both loved the water; and for my sister, our trips to the beach provided some meagre compensation for a move that had thrown her life into disarray.

By now Sheila was getting to know the men in the farm cottages, one of whom was the tenant farmer of the local fields. As the summer holidays approached, she persuaded him to lend her a small paddock. Anna, now 14, was going away with friends. Knowing how much I loved riding, Sheila hired a piebald pony named Pinto from a local stables. He was small, stocky and good-natured. Urged on by Susie, I rode him round the paddock for five blissful weeks, learning to canter and jump and ride bareback. When I dismounted at dusk, I used to throw my arms round his neck and bury my face in his oily mane, enjoying the feel of his muscly body next to mine and breathing in his sweet smell of dung mixed with grass cuttings. Those were my happiest days since leaving Hawkley.

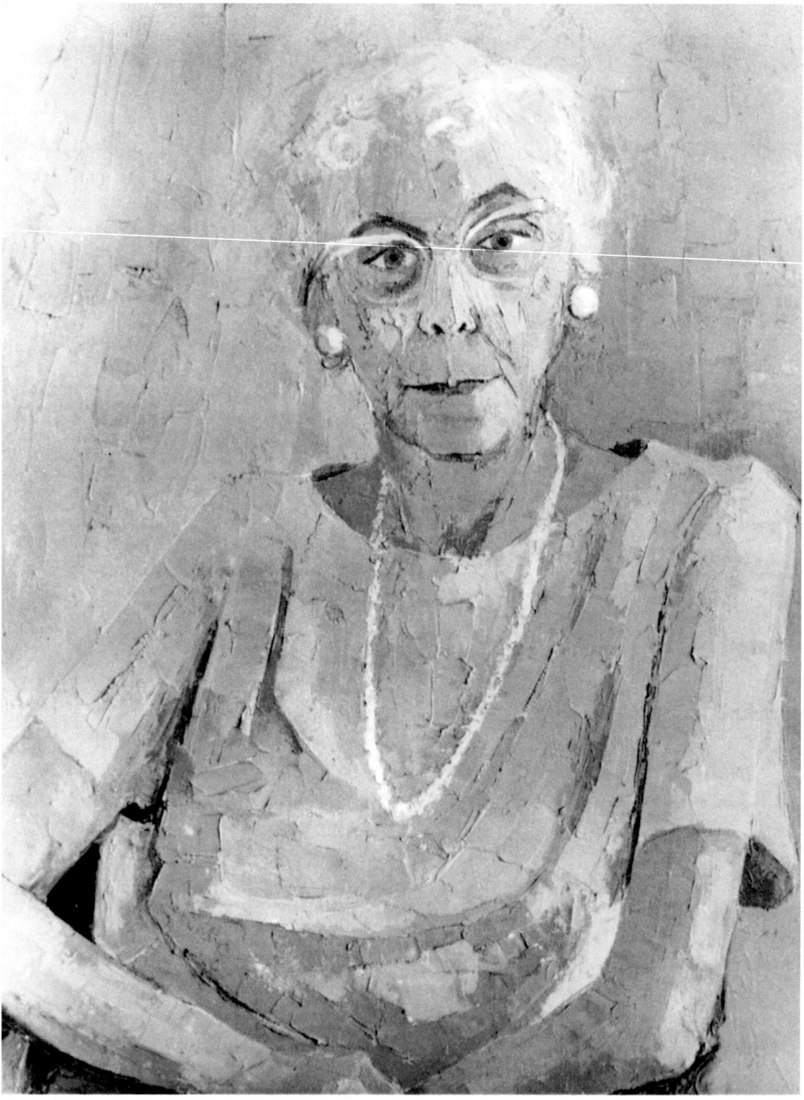

Professor Jo Chandler, 1969, (black and white reproduction)

Chapter 22
Professor Jo Chandler

EARLY IN 1969, while working on the portrait of Gaga and negotiating fees with Nell Brentnall, Sheila received a letter from Dr Mel Marshak, her former psychoanalyst. Mel enclosed some photos of a friend of hers, a tall, thin, bespectacled woman whom she described as a professor at San Jose State University in California. The friend would be staying with Mel at her country cottage near Midhurst later that summer and Mel was hoping to commission Sheila to paint her. Would she please state her price?

The friend, who remained nameless, had a lean, intelligent but unassuming expression, which Sheila warmed to. It was clear she was important to Mel, but Sheila didn't know how she fitted into Mel's life.

Sheila quoted a low fee but warned that she would need quite a number of sittings. Mel replied, enclosing more photographs of her friend:

> '...though I have not told her anything about it, I'm sure we can 'organize' her sufficiently to give you the sittings you need. I think I prefer her without the spectacles, but I suppose you'll have to determine that for yourself. Let me know... if you feel she would be, from your point of view, a good 'subject'.'

Sheila was confident that the woman in the photographs would be interesting to paint and in late August she received an invitation to meet her at Mel's cottage. She now learned that the woman's name was Professor Josephine Chandler, 'Jo' to her friends; she was six foot tall with short white hair, long limbs and a long neck. In her height and slim frame, she was of similar

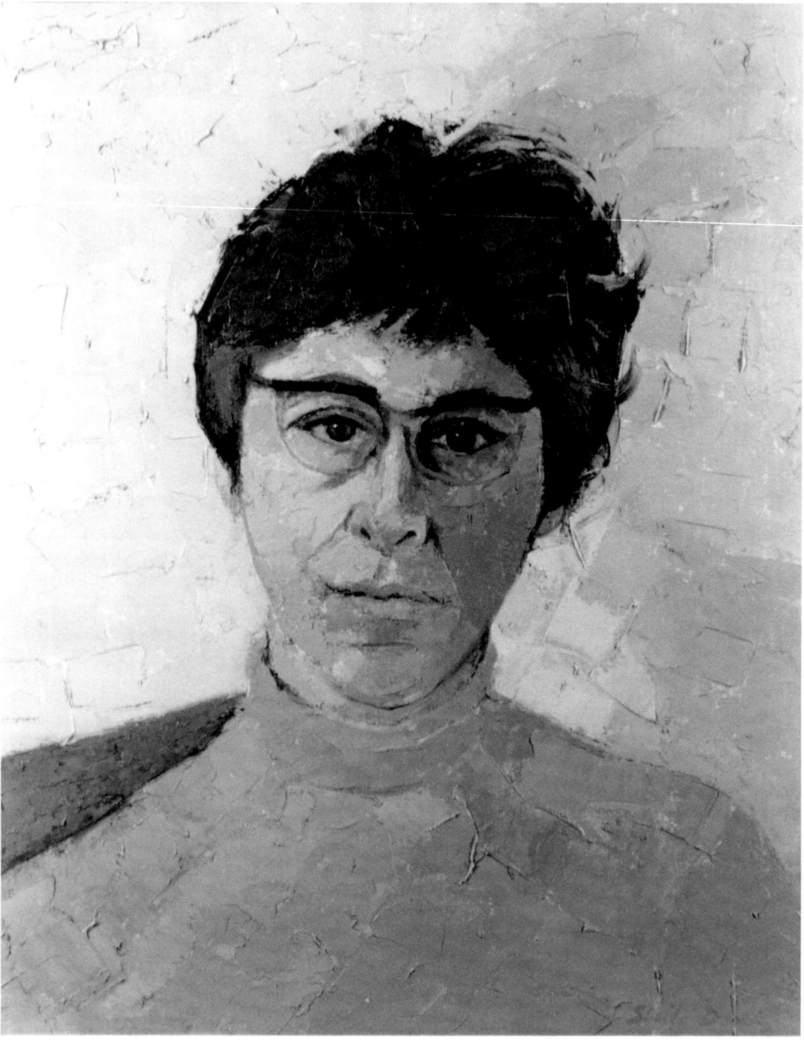

Dr Mel Marshak, 1970, (black and white reproduction)

body type to Sheila, but she lacked Sheila's grace and physical self confidence.

'I don't like being looked at,' Jo confided in her Californian accent during the first sitting, a couple of days later. 'Never have liked it. I'm too tall, there's no two ways about it.'

Not being one to impose herself on other people, Sheila enquired whether Jo would prefer to abandon the portrait sittings.

'I'll do it, Sheila,' Jo replied with a half smile. 'I'll do it for Mel; she's set it up, I guess it's important to her. But don't be offended if I don't look at it, will you?'

The sittings took place in a back room at Mel's cottage, with Sheila driving over every morning and returning home in the afternoons. Hoping that music might help to distract Jo from the discomfort of being looked at, Sheila borrowed a tape player. At Mel's request she was working on a bigger scale than usual, with a canvas measuring 24 by 18 inches (60cm by 45cm). That meant she could fit in Jo's head, shoulders, torso and arms. She put on much of the paint with her palette knives, building it up layer upon layer.

Mid-way through the sixth or seventh sitting, during a break, Sheila left the room to use the toilet. When she returned, she was taken aback to find Jo standing in front of the canvas, scrutinizing the work. She tiptoed out again and made tea in the kitchen. When she carried the mugs into the room, she saw a look of surprise on Jo's features.

Slightly nervous, Sheila raised one eyebrow. 'Well?'

Jo shook her head. 'It's a very funny thing, Sheila, a very funny thing. I know I said I wouldn't look at it, but curiosity got the better of me. And d'you know what? I don't mind it at all! In fact, when I look at what you've done, I quite like myself!'

To my eye, Sheila's portrait of Jo Chandler is the best she ever painted. I never met Jo so cannot say whether or not it's like her; but as a painting, I find it riveting. Jo sits quietly in her chair, her left shoulder higher than the right, and her left eyebrow raised quizzically beneath the spectacles. Her long, thin arms emerge awkwardly from the sleeves of her summer dress: she's clearly a gangling figure and Sheila hasn't sought to hide it. But the astute look captured in the eyes is so impressive that it lends both face and body a lanky beauty. Jo has an unusually long upper lip stretching above her wide mouth. Her expression is very focused, as if she's looking intently at Sheila, determined to take an active role in the process of being painted.

There's a richness in the way Sheila has applied the paint, all over the canvas. I love the way she's conveyed the pale fabric of the dress with small, palette knife-shaped squares of paint. It's a loose-fitting, comfortable frock of the kind my grandmother wore, high-necked, designed to hide rather than show off the body. A string of white beads hangs down from Jo's neck in a sharp V, subtly distracting the viewer from the shapelessness of the frock.

Sheila kept a file of notes for every portrait commission. In the one for Jo I found a letter sent from California a few months after the portrait was completed.

> 'The portrait… has been the object of much interest and admiration. It is now framed and hung. One of my friends the other day said of it 'It's *you*, Jo! How do artists do it?'

*

By now Sheila was working on a portrait of Dr Marshak herself, again working mainly with a palette knife.

For me at twelve, the sight of this portrait on my mother's easel crystallised the facial appearance of the woman I knew had helped her find the strength to leave my father. Dr Marshak had short, dark, slightly wild hair, black-framed glasses and shoulders that sloped sharply beneath a dreary polo neck sweater. The face was small and feminine, the chin pointed, the eyes dark. The expression was one of empathy combined with intense interest, as if Mel was a person who listened not only to the words people said but also for all the other cues, from body language, to smell, to the meaning of their silences.[1]

At that age I found the idea of Dr Marshak a little frightening. I didn't understand what psychoanalysis was, but I knew that without Dr Marshak doing whatever she did in her consulting room, Mummy wouldn't have succeeded in escaping from the torment of her life in London and I wouldn't have spent my thirteenth summer cantering round a field on Pinto.

When, a few years later, Dr Marshak commissioned Sheila to paint her partner, Marion Grimaldi, Sheila put a record 42 hours into the portrait[2]. The result was a big, bold painting which at first sight was impressive; but after looking at it closely following Sheila's death I had some reservations. I liked the sense of space around the head and shoulders which resulted from the use of a large canvas measuring 26 inches by 20 (65cm x 50cm). Marion appeared as a tall, attractive woman, with a chic haircut and an air of confidence; her strong presence held the viewer's attention. Square marks made with the palette knife described the wall behind the head and Marion's plunge-neck blouse. But I was bothered by a disparity in the eyes: one was dark, focussed and utterly convincing, while the other was paler and less focussed. I was also unsure about the expression. Sheila painted Marion's mouth

---

1 In an obituary of Dr Marshak in the *Journal of Analytical Psychology*, dated 1 February 2011, I found the following: '... [she] possessed a keen sense of humour, an ability to play within the analytic material, and she often provided an embodied sense of how the analyst's love could impact the analytic situation... She was endowed with a great intellect, a rigorous analytic attitude, and a richness of spirit rivalled by few.'(*The Journal of Analytical Psychology*, 2011, 56, 151) (tinyurl.com/JAP2011-DrMarshak, accessed 28.8.2020)

2 The portrait can be seen at www.sheiladenning.com

and facial muscles in a polite, rather tight smile – something she had almost never done before. Possibly that's what Dr Marshak wanted; for me the smile undermined the remarkable strength in Marion's bearing.

*

Old friends visited us at Sefter from time to time; but in general Sheila's was a solitary existence, bordering on the reclusive. The one friend she made locally was Eric Mellon, a potter who lived in Bognor Regis with his artist wife. Eric had studied illustration at Central School of Art after the war and was making a name for himself painting nude figures onto his own stoneware and experimenting with ash glazes.[3] He had red cheeks, a long beard and a warm, humorous manner; I liked him from the first time I came home to find him sitting in our kitchen. There were dribbles of glaze on his trousers and as he listened to Sheila talking about the portrait she was working on, he wore an expression of engaged concentration – the same look I'd seen on the faces of so many of my parents' artist friends. I felt a sharp pang for my absent Dad and the world we'd left behind in London. Life in Sussex provided ample contact with nature, but very little with kindred spirits.

Sheila felt lonely at times, but our new life suited her. She needed peace and quiet and was happiest living close to nature. It wasn't good for her career in that she couldn't easily pursue contacts at London galleries or attend private views; but in just two years she'd produced more paintings than in the previous eight. She continued to submit work to national exhibitions, but was realistic about what could be achieved whilst my sister and I remained at home, and clear that her wellbeing was more important than public recognition.

3 Eric Mellon, 1925–2014, ceramic artist.

On the middle weekend between Dad's monthly visits, my sister and I went to London to see him. We travelled by train after school on Friday evenings and returned late on Sunday afternoons.

Dad had kept the studio when our old house was sold and bought himself a new, smaller house round the corner. South and West London were buzzing with the high energy and optimism of the late 1960s and Dad was fired up about the fringe theatres that were opening around the city, the rock concerts in Hyde Park and the tales of Woodstock[4] which floated across the Atlantic. He approved of flower power and the ethos of free love; he liked the explosion of self expression in the way people dressed and wore their hair; and he thought it great that old social mores were being cast out in favour of a freer lifestyle.

When we arrived on Friday nights, tired and a bit apprehensive, Dad would dish up supper in his kitchen and reel off a list of ideas he had for how to spend the weekend. Portobello market on Saturday morning, followed by coffee with the Gibbses or the Vulliamys who lived round the corner; then a stroll down High Street Kensington, where we'd spend an hour at Kensington Market, the emporium of hippy stalls selling Afghan coats, incense, candles and Alpaca jerseys. Dad took us to Biba[5] too – I was keen on fashion and once in a while my saved pocket money would cover the cost of a pair of stripy tights or a purple T shirt. Then home for a bite to eat – 'you can have a short rest, girls, if you're tired' – and quickly out again to see a fringe show or a modern dance troupe. Dad had no insight into how exhausting it was for us as young girls in the throes of puberty to cram so much

4 Woodstock was a music festival held in August 1969 in New York, which became a defining moment for the flower power generation. Performers included Jimi Hendrix, The Who, Sly and the Family Stone and Crosby, Stills and Nash.

5 Barbara Hulanicki created the fashion label Biba and opened her first store in High Street Kensington in 1969.

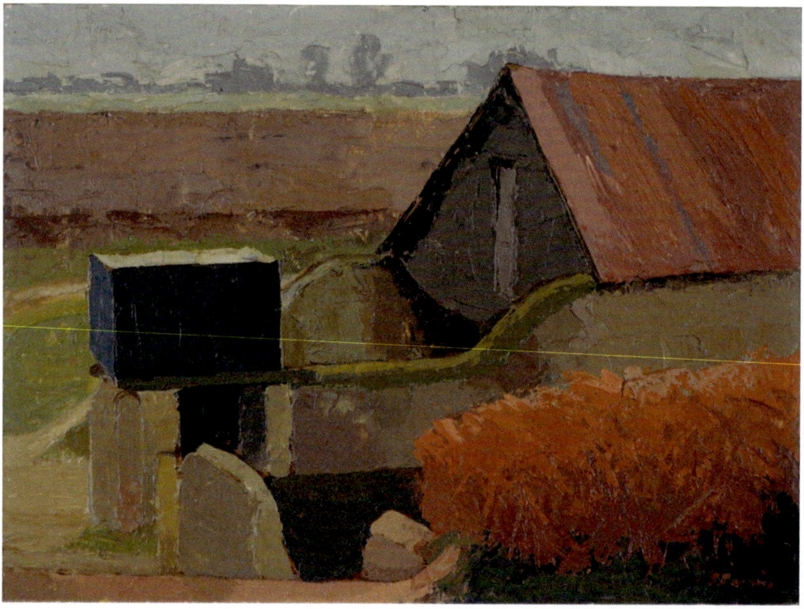

Farm buildings, Sefter, c. 1969

into a weekend, leaving no space for the difficult emotions which seeing him threw up for us and no time to do our homework.

On Sundays, Dad cooked us a roast lunch before driving us to Victoria station. While I rushed around the flat packing my scattered possessions into my bag, delicious smells of roasting meat drifted up the half flight of stairs from the kitchen. I often noticed that Dad's facial muscles were starting to sag and his shoulders were sinking. I took these signs as a warning to be careful what I said, for he would soon become snappy and morose. After this had happened a few times, I deduced that Dad found it hard to say goodbye.

On the way home in the train in the gathering dusk, I wondered what Mummy had been up to all weekend. I glanced across the pullman at Anna, who was busy doing her French homework. Always afraid we might miss our stop, I carefully monitored the passing stations: the unfamiliar urban skylines of Dorking and Horsham, then beautiful and tiny Amberley in the middle of the

Downs, followed by water meadows with the scary river Arun snaking through them, the dark silhouette of Arundel castle, then Barnham, then a lot of rattling as we approached Chichester and shot past the end of Gaga's back garden. It was dark by now and I was very tired. At last we were scrambling out of the train in Chichester with our carrier bags and coats; and there was Mummy, a tall, lone figure in a white anorak, ready to drive us back to Sefter.

On one such Sunday evening, I opened the living room door and saw a new landscape on Mummy's easel. With the passing of time Sheila had grown fond of the dilapidated farm buildings she looked out on from her bedroom window and while we were in London she'd painted them. It was a small work on hardboard in which she recorded the relationships between the reddish brown of the rusting asbestos roofs, the duller brown of the ploughed field behind and the orange of the beech hedge in the foreground. She included the dull grey oil tank, coated with a layer of pale green moss. The thing I liked best was the way she'd painted the horizon. In this case it was the bungalows of Nyetimber: buildings of no inherent charm, but by marking their existence in thick grey paint, against a grey-green sky, Sheila endowed them with a certain beauty; and the marks carried the eye back and back, so that the viewer was in no doubt about the mile or more of distance involved.

*

Sheila's worst headache at Sefter was being short of money. Her earnings from portrait commissions were small and in 1970 she set about searching for part time teaching work. She wrote to the Workers' Educational Association and the Evening Institutes which ran art classes for the public in some of the smaller West Sussex towns. The responses she received were friendly, but it was a couple of years before she was offered any work.

On Sunday lunchtimes when I wasn't with Dad in London, I worked in a local pub washing glasses. It was hard work, and the pot-bellied publican barely acknowledged my existence. After I'd been there a few weeks, Sheila told me she'd taken a job as a cleaner. My stomach turned over. It was excruciating to think of her being treated like I was treated, and I knew she'd be hopeless at the job. Hard physical work had never been her thing and I doubted she knew how to make a bathroom basin shine, or how to polish furniture. Happily the job didn't last and Sheila found a better way to alleviate her money problems by providing bed and board for a young French language *assistante* at our school. Marie Françoise Cau was a petite, Gauloise-smoking, twenty-one-year-old student from Toulouse. She was pretty with dark brown eyes and curly hair and she seemed at home with us from the first day, switching happily from English to French and back, appreciating the Irish stew which was Sheila's *piece de resistance* and allowing me to sit on the end of her bed and chat for hours at a time.

But money remained a major problem. Although Dad didn't dispute his obligation to make maintenance payments to Mum he rarely sent what she called the 'housekeeping' on time, with the result that she was constantly on the edge of debt. Some of Dad's cheques arrived unsigned; others bounced when presented to the bank.

Mum wrote to him frequently, pleading for money. Many of the letters were couched in polite, almost apologetic terms – whether because she genuinely felt for her ex-husband's plight as an artist who had not achieved commercial success, or because she felt he was more likely to pay up if she approached him in this vein, I do not know. She must have been aware of the active social and cultural life he was enjoying in London, while she could barely buy sufficient food. As a canny child I could not fail to compare what I saw on my visits to Dad with Mum's daily struggle to make ends meet. The contrast filled me with a painful, burning fury.

There may have been another reason for the tone of Sheila's letters. Although physically she'd left Alan in 1968, Sheila's emotional separation from him would take her several decades. It was not made any easier by the fact that, when he came to Sefter for his monthly visits, rather than going away for the weekend, Sheila often remained. In later life, she claimed that her motive had been to make things as 'normal' as possible for us children, but this wasn't the whole story. She was driven by a lingering desire to see Alan herself.

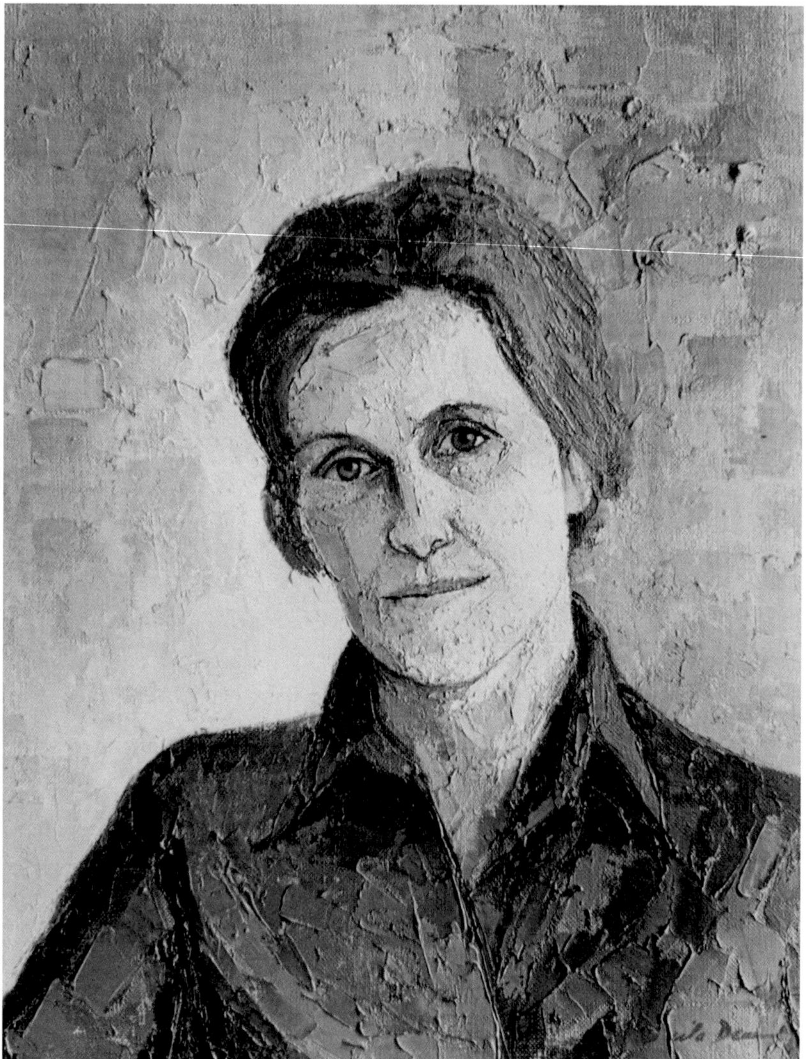

Françoise, 1972, (black and white reproduction)

Chapter 23
Françoise

SHEILA'S PAINTING WAS GOING from strength to strength, but my sister felt isolated living in the country and Sheila decided that we must move again. At the beginning of the summer holidays in 1971, just before Anna and I set off for France with Dad, Sheila told us she was toying with the idea of returning to London. After we'd gone she realized that London house prices were too high and her bad memories too raw. Besides, she could hardly abandon Gaga, who was now 78 and very settled in her new life. Once Sefter was sold, Sheila decided it would have to be Chichester.

A small, conservative cathedral city, Chichester was the county town of West Sussex, home to council offices and local grandees. Its inner core was stiff with historic buildings, many of them beautiful, constructed around an ancient market cross with streets striking off to north, south, west and east. High city walls wide enough to walk along separated the old part of town from its newer and expanding suburbs. It was on the far side of the walls, in a non-descript 1930s street, that Sheila found a small semi which would become our new home.

There was just one shop in the street, a curious place with mostly empty shelves and a strong smell of tobacco. The only items on sale were cigarettes and plain biscuits and the unsmiling, elderly shopkeeper wore a cotton pinafore over her clothes. A cloud of white hair billowed round her face like cotton wool, with a streak of bright yellow rising vertically from the centre of her forehead. If you let your eyes descend in a straight line from the streak towards the shop counter, you invariably arrived at a smouldering Players Number Six, wedged between the gnarled and freckled joints of her fingers.

One day in the summer of 1972, my sister's new boyfriend arrived from Reading. He'd forgotten our house number, so he went into the shop to ask if they knew us. The shopkeeper fixed him with a cold stare. 'The divorced woman with the two girls?' she demanded – 'the ones who wear long skirts? Number twenty three.' She spoke, he said, with a snarl, as if nothing could be more distasteful to her than Sheila's status as a divorcee and our colourful, hippy-style clothing.

*

Sheila's portrait of Françoise caught her in reflective mood, her head tilted to one side, her eyes sad, her mouth slightly tense. This is not how I remember Françoise, who was the mother of my best friend Madeleine and something of a beauty. Françoise had stylish blond hair and a glint in her eyes which let me know that secretly she found the antics of her wild older children amusing.

Madeleine was feisty and funny, good at art and a natural rebel. She was the second of five, all of whom were fluent in their mother's native French. The number of children and their bilingual upbringing made the family stick out in Chichester, despite the fact that Madeleine's English father, Michael, had a big job in the local administration. But it was more than that. Try as Françoise would to play the role of an English housewife, the French-ness could not be masked and it was clear that, deep down, she felt like a fish out of water. Sheila was soon on friendly terms with both Françoise and Michael.

Madeleine used to take me off to play in wasteland half a mile from her parents' spacious 'sixties new-build. When we ran back to the house, exhausted, Françoise would be perched on a stool waiting for us, with a large, English-style tea laid out on the kitchen table. I would chat and eat easily enough until the older brother walked in, his white school shirt open at the neck and his green and black tie dangling from his shoulders. He was devastatingly handsome and from that point on my words formed into knots and stuck in my pubescent throat.

Michael commissioned the portrait of Françoise in 1972, having already bought a still life from Sheila. Her note records that the finished painting was the work of nineteen sittings, double the amount of time Sheila expended on most other portraits. I suspect that a lot of the time was spent in conversation, with Françoise confiding how sorely she missed France. Sheila missed France too and understood Françoise's feelings only too well.

Françoise's unhappiness comes through in the portrait. The short, blond hair is flatter and less chic than I remember it. The collar of the blouse is stiff and pointed. The gaze is distant. The straight line of the mouth and slight jutting of the chin communicate a sense of resignation, marring the sparkling beauty I remember. Whatever intimate disclosures to Sheila preceded the painting of the eyes, the woman who emerges on the canvas isn't thinking about anyone or anything in her immediate surroundings. She's drifting far away, perhaps dreaming of her student days in Paris, or her family in Grenoble, whom she only sees once a year.

I was surprised when I read Michael's comments in a letter he wrote to Sheila that summer. By then he'd changed job and the family had moved to another part of the country, taking my lovely friend Madeleine with them.

'We've chosen a v. traditional but quite simple gilt frame for the portrait, and something attractive for the other painting – they ought to look v. well… We've never really agreed a fee for the portrait, but here is a guesstimated one. Do please tell me if it's a hopelessly modest sum. We are terribly pleased with the result.'

The 'modest sum' was substantially over the fee Sheila had quoted; but Michael's words leave me wondering whether he simply couldn't afford to register the unhappiness in his wife's eyes.

*

I struggled at school after Madeleine left Chichester. I was good at academic work, but socially I felt at sea. There were other girls I liked, but none as adventurous as the friend I'd lost. Solace came, in time, in the form of a new activity. I was a competent dressmaker and Dad bought me a second hand Singer sewing machine for my fifteenth birthday. I saved up my pocket money for a copy of Vogue magazine and spent hours studying the fashion photographs, looking for ideas and making drawings. Then I started to trawl Chichester's charity shops for old velvet curtains and lengths of cheap fabric, which I dyed with Dylon in an old washing up bowl. At first I used existing paper patterns to cut the fabric, but before long I was making my own out of newspaper. The whole process, from initial idea to finished garment, filled me with energy and excitement.

On a typical Saturday, aged 15, I'd be out early looking for fabric. If I found, say, an Indian cotton bedspread going for a song, I'd rush home and spend the afternoon turning it into a flowing maxi skirt while listening to *Jethro Tull* or *The Incredible String Band* on Sheila's record player – the lyrics inaudible above the thundering of the Singer as I sewed the darts and seams. Then I'd whip off my jeans, step into the skirt and rush to admire myself in the full length mirror on the landing. Once I was happy with my creation I'd slap on some cheap eye make-up, give Mum an excuse as to why I didn't want supper, and hurry to The White Horse in North Street. Here, propping up the bar as we sipped martinis, my classmates and I would chat up the local talent. There was always a party in an outlying village, and we were on the lookout for a lad with a car who was willing to drive us there.

I had no clue, in those days, as to the misery and worry my partying caused Sheila. She told me later how she spent Saturday nights lying in bed, wide awake, waiting for a phone call that never came. She had no idea where I was or when to expect me home. When finally I slammed the front door shut behind me at

1am she would meet me on the stairs in her dressing gown, her face pale with exhaustion and fury.

*

My sister and I met Penelope Dimond at Chichester Youth Theatre, a group of teenagers who put on productions in a local community centre. Penny was slightly younger than Anna, a flamboyant figure with long dark hair and large brown eyes, who rouged her cheeks like a clown and painted her lips dark red. She dressed every day in long flowing skirts, as if she were playing a part in a Chekovian drama.

The Youth Theatre soon became the focus of our out-of-school lives and Penny our closest friend. Unlike many of our well-heeled class mates, who were driven to school in brand new cars by their stay-at-home mothers, Penny was clearly one of us. She lived in a large, chilly house in the north of the city with parents who were living separate lives and, financially, almost as broke as ours. Penny disliked school intensely, got herself into trouble, and by the age of fifteen had persuaded her mum to let her leave. The one and only thing she wanted to do was to act.

Penny was soon a regular visitor to our house. She got on well with Sheila, who intrigued her as the first flesh-and-blood artist she'd ever met. Sheila, for her part, was very struck by our new friend's kohl-ringed eyes and her thick dark hair. A few months after Penny left school, Sheila persuaded her to sit for her portrait.

I was out at school while Sheila painted Penny. Years later, Penny told me that the sittings began only days after she split up with her first ever boyfriend. She sat quietly in the studio at Orchard Avenue, brooding on her feelings of loss while Sheila squinted at her, measuring the distance between her nose and upper lip with her outstretched thumb. Sheila was meticulous in her approach, Penny said, and insisted that her model sit stock still. They took breaks mid-morning for coffee and chocolate biscuits, but Penny

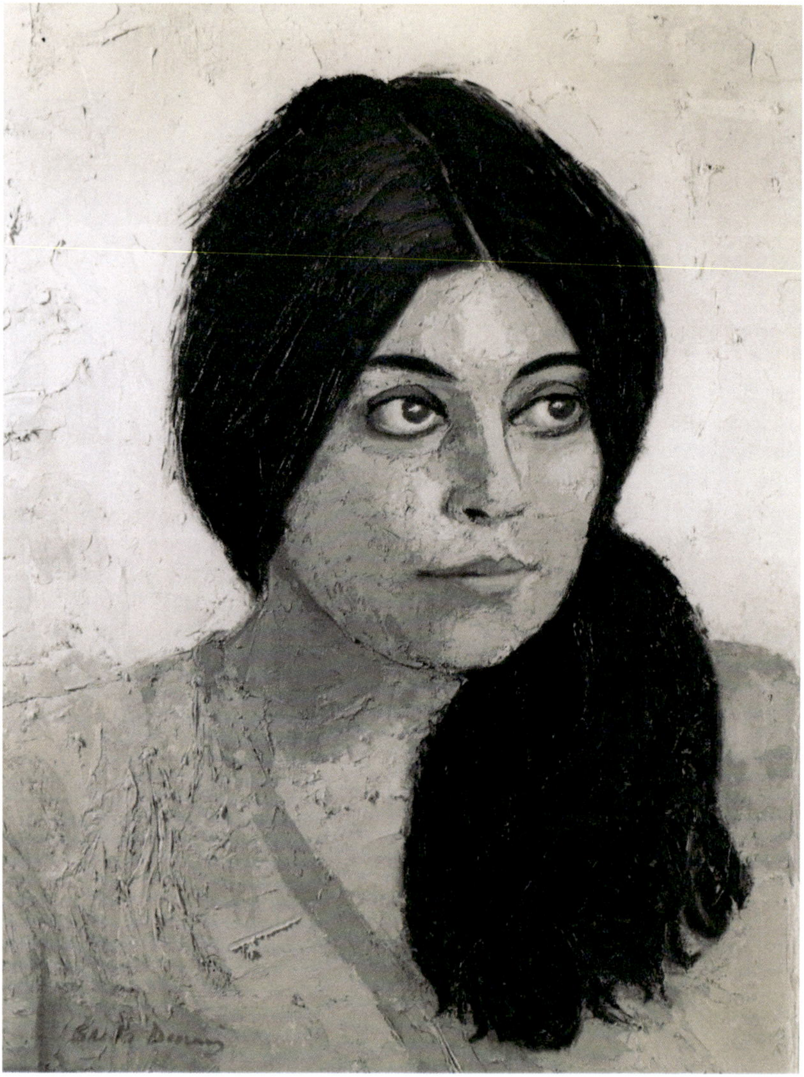

Penny Dimond, 1973, (black and white reproduction)

was too much in awe of Sheila to divulge the truth about her broken heart.

When I visited Penny in her London flat in 2019, she told me that, at 17, she'd found Sheila a little formidable. One day during a break in the sitting, when they were standing in the kitchen with their mugs of coffee, she noticed an unpleasant smell coming from a pan simmering on the stove.

'It was a really vile smell. I said to Sheila, "What's that?" And she said, "Oh, it's lights, for the cats." She lifted the lid to show me and I saw these weird grey-brown lumps, boiling away, looking absolutely disgusting!'

'Then she said "It's good for them, you know, it's proper food. I get it from the butcher. What do you give your cats, Penny?" I said "Oh, you know, the normal stuff, Whiskas or Kitty Kat." And she said "Oh, no" – in a tone of shock and disapproval – "I don't buy tinned cat food, certainly not. I go to the butcher's Penny, and I buy lights." I'd never heard of "lights", so I said "What are they?" And she replied "The leftovers, the lungs, the bits nobody wants…"' Penny threw back her head and let out a peel of laughter. 'Your lovely mum was *so* disapproving of the fact my cats had that awful tinned stuff!'

Looking at the portrait now, I'm convinced that Sheila failed to pick up what Penny was going through when she painted it. What she saw was a lovely young girl. Penny sits with her hair falling over her left shoulder, her gaze focussed on a spot in the distance. The eyes are huge and beautiful, as Penny's real eyes were, with or without the kohl; and the mouth is wide and pretty, the lips firmly pressed together. It's the face of a girl who knows who she is and what she wants to be and is determined to find her way.

Penny's parents bought the painting and it hung on her mother's wall until her death, thirty years later. Today it lives high on a wall in Penny's flat. She won't have it at eye level because, every time she looks at the picture, she remembers that moment of heartbreak in 1973.

Chapter 24
Georges

THE PLAQUE ON THE WALL beside the painting read *Le Tricheur* (The Cheat), 1636–1638. The artist, Georges de la Tour, wasn't named because the entire exhibition was devoted to his work. This was what had brought Mum and me to Paris, a trip financed by Sheila's income from a new teaching job she'd acquired.

I stood stock still, drinking in the burnt orange of the seated woman's bodice, my fingertips tingling as I anticipated what that deep pile velvet would feel like to the touch. My eyes skimmed over the pale neck and face, drawn upwards by the crimson headdress: a felt cap with sharp, irregular points, out of which a collection of extravagant red and orange plumes erupted in a graceful curve.

Mum was standing very still just a few inches from me, in her grey-blue silk shirt and pale summer trousers. She acknowledged my glance with a quick smile as her eyebrows shot towards her hair line. 'Astonishing,' she murmured. 'Just astonishing.'

'Yes,' I whispered.

My gaze switched to the intent expression of the young servant woman in the saffron-coloured turban and blue dress. She stood with her head in profile to the viewer, her body arched forwards, clutching the neck of a straw-covered wine carafe in her left hand and a delicate, V-shaped glass in her right. The glass was full of dark pink wine, but the servant's gaze was fixed on the hand of cards held by the young nobleman in the foreground, to the right. He was studying his playing cards with an air of naïve calm, gorgeous in red trousers and orange-plumed cap, oblivious to the malign intent of his fellow players. As if deliberately ignoring the nobleman, the seated woman had clamped her gaze on an older-looking man who lounged casually in the foreground on the left-hand side of the painting. He wore a mustard-coloured coat with a black sash and his elbow rested on the table with the cards in his right hand displayed for all to see. But this was a deliberate ruse: behind his back, visible only to the viewer, his left hand revealed the Ace of Clubs.

I'd seen a lot of paintings for a girl of 15, but never anything as riveting as this. I glanced at Mum again. 'You can just feel the tension between them all, can't you?'

'De la Tour was way ahead of his time, a real psychologist.'

For a long moment we stood very close together, drinking in the colour, the shapes, the four heads and torsoes arranged so deftly in relation to each other and pushing at the edges of the canvas. The wall behind the figures was in darkness, but a bright light fell on the table, entering the painting at the servant woman's shoulder, its source unclear. The soft cheeks of the over-dressed nobleman and the canny expressions of the three who were setting out to cheat him held our attention with compelling power. Here, trapped in the canvas, was a moment from the past so vivid that it might as well be happening live before our eyes.

At last Mum stepped away. Exhausted, I followed her to the next painting, slipping my arm through hers. We'd arrived the night before and I was still tired from the long journey by boat and train. In front of us a turbaned woman sat on a stool, illuminated by the light of a single candle perched on a chair beside her. A loose robe fell open to reveal her bare belly and the backs of her hands, pressed together at the knuckles, as if she were trying to grind the life out of something.

'A flea!' Mum muttered. 'Just like chez *Madame*!' We were staying in a cheap hotel near the Gard du Nord, and she'd woken to find two red welts on her ankle and another on her neck. She'd mentioned it to the landlady on our way out, but Madame had shaken her head and said it wasn't possible.

'How d'you know?' I demanded.

Mum gestured at the plaque on the wall, which read '*La Femme a la Puce*, The Flea Catcher'.

I giggled. 'Are your bites still bothering you?' I rested my head on her bony shoulder. 'Poor Mum,' I yawned. 'I'm hungry. Can we go outside and eat our lunch?'

We emerged from the *Orangerie* into the bright sunshine of the *Jardin des Tuileries*. Ever well organized when it came to food, and knowing I'd be forced to use my French if I went alone, Mum had sent me to a *boulangerie* and an *epicerie* that morning with a ten franc note. I'd enjoyed it. I wasn't shy about speaking and it gave me a thrill when people understood me.

Now we followed a woman with a large chignon and a tiny dog along a series of neat gravel paths until we found an empty bench. While Mum undid the buttons of her shirt to let the sun get to her neck, I opened my shoulder bag and took out a baguette, a wedge of camembert, a cucumber and some slices of saucisson.

'Well done, darling, this looks *magnifique*.' She sighed in satisfaction. 'What a morning. First a feast of De la Tour, and now a proper French picnic.' She reached out her hand and stroked my cheek. 'I'm so glad you're with me, darling.'

'So am I.' I tore a hunk off the baguette and passed the rest to her, scattering flakes of crust over the wooden slats of the bench. We only had three days, because on Friday I was catching the train to Carcasonne, to join Dad and a couple of his female students. I wasn't too sure what I felt about that, but I'd not been given a choice in the matter. My sister, now 18, was away all summer and Mum would be going home to an empty house, for another tedious August in Chichester.

Chapter 25
Jamie

SHEILA'S NEW TEACHING JOB had come about with the help of Eric Mellon. For some years Eric had taught at Brighton Tech, less than an hour's drive from Chichester. His recommendation of Sheila as a tutor had led to her acquiring two evening classes there.

Sheila had relatives in Brighton, from Bum's side of the family. Aunt Vere, now a widow, lived a life of luxury in a pent-house apartment in Kemp Town. Ten minutes' away in a cheaper area, Vere's older sister Kaye, a spinster with a well-developed sense of humour, had taken up painting late in life. Unlike Vere, Kaye spoke with an Irish accent and dressed in large hats and long raincoats. She'd converted the ground floor of her house into a studio and found a local artist to teach a class there once a week, attended by a small group of friends.

Now that she was working in Brighton, Sheila became a regular visitor to her two aunts. They were both interesting characters in their different ways and she felt connected, through them, to Bum and to Ireland. When the teacher of Kaye's painting class moved away, Sheila agreed to take it over.

*

In 1975, Sheila received an enquiry which led to the trickiest challenge she would ever face as a portrait painter. It came from one Surgeon Captain Godfrey Milton-Thompson, who was Professor of Naval Medicine at the Royal Naval Hospital in Haslar, Portsmouth. Sheila's name had been given to him by Alan's friend Joy Woolley, now a well-established picture restorer. The professor was looking for an artist to produce an oil painting

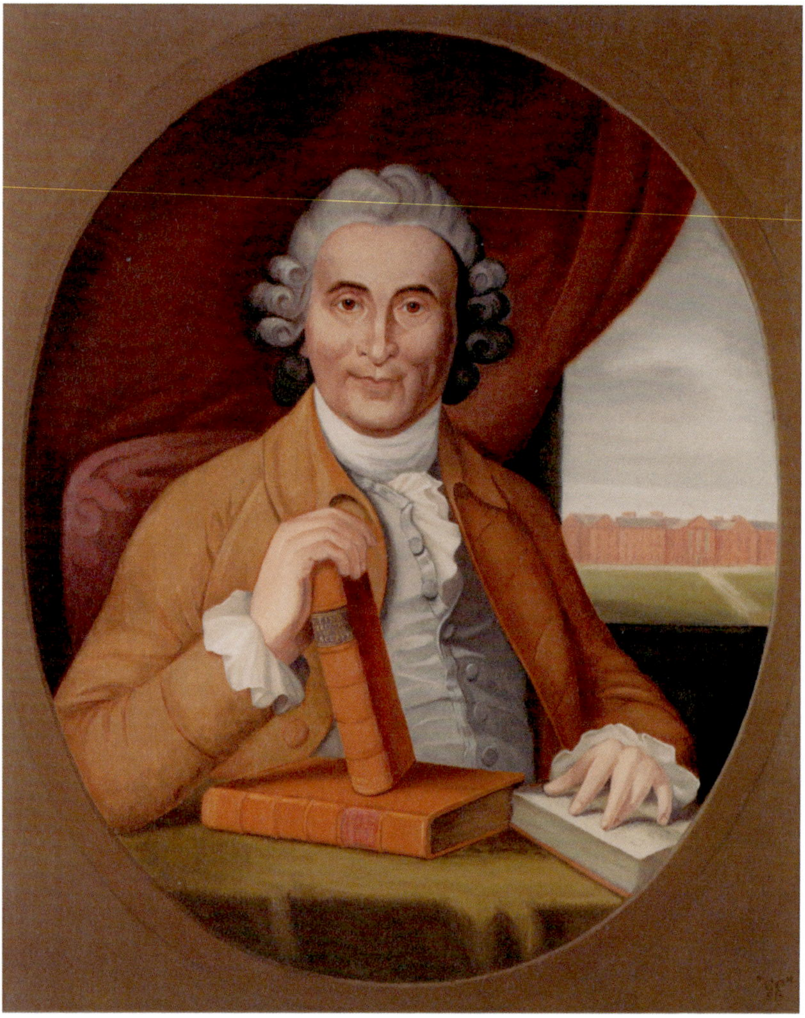

Dr James Lind, 1978

of Dr James Lind, an eighteenth century naval surgeon, from a black and white engraving based on a much earlier portrait in oils. The new work was to be hung in the medical mess at Haslar, in celebration of Dr Lind's unparalleled achievement in discovering the cause of scurvy. This, as Sheila later wrote:

> 'had been responsible for the deaths of more men [in the eighteenth century] than had all the battles with the French and Spanish fleets. He experimented with control groups and came to believe that the root cause of the disease was the lack of oranges, lemons and green food in the sailors' diet. These conclusions he published in his celebrated book *A Treatise of the Scurvy*, in 1754. Forty years afterwards, in 1795, an order was issued by the Admiralty to supply the Navy with lemon-juice.'

Sheila was a great believer in the possibilities of improving health through diet, and Dr Lind's achievement appealed to her. She learned that the portrait in oils painted in his lifetime by Sir George Chalmers had been lost; all that remained was the engraving by I. Wright.

After meeting with Professor Milton-Thompson several times and undertaking extensive research into Dr Lind and Sir George Chalmers, Sheila agreed to take on the commission. There was then a correspondence about whether the new portrait should exactly mirror the engraving, in which the be-wigged Dr Lind sat by an open window with copies of his three books; or whether it should be limited to the face. Sheila eventually advised against the latter and it was agreed that she would reproduce the painting as it appeared in the oval-shaped engraving, but in colour, with a painted frame around the oval. A substantial fee was agreed.

Sheila threw herself into the project, as is clear from the note she wrote in 1977, describing how she went about it:

'After Easter, started (Troubles!) Did 2 preliminary cartoons, freehand.

'May '77. Took them over and hung them up in Mess for size. Decided on larger one. Went into eighteenth century twill canvas a bit but found from R and C [Russell and Chapple[1]] that it is no longer made.

'Ordered canvas to be specially made from W and N [Windsor and Newton] as not standard size. Canvas made on very warped stretcher so I sent it back and they replaced it.

'Tried projecting slide but this technique was much too crude. Squared up carefully into 64 rectangles (8 x 8) and drew in charcoal. Measured within frame rebate of 5/16".

'Then, colour pattern. Anchors were flesh colours, wig, leather books, and landscape, and neck band, and shirt frills. His eyes always seemed dark brown to me, and his colouring slightly sandy – he was Scottish.

'So I felt colour of curtain behind was in a sense his aura, and after trying various schemes, the one which emphasized his eyes seemed best. Then jacket and books as one, grey waistcoat for cool and to echo wig – chair is touch of Libran urbanity and slight femininity. Colours worked out on oil paper, then put onto canvas as underpainting. Numerous visits to National Portrait Gallery, (National Gallery) and Tate to study eighteenth century colours and techniques. Only giants painted freely then, of which GC (George Chalmers) is not one. 'Chalmers' perspective not too good in books and this showed up in large so cheated a bit.'

1 Russell and Chapple are an old-established supplier of artist's materials, as are Windsor and Newton.

Sheila found a description of the original portrait in a book, which she summarized in a note as follows:

> 'His expression is good-natured and he looks intelligent, with a look of Scottish shrewdness. The corners of his mouth and the look in his eyes suggest he was a tolerant chap with a good sense of humour.'

By the time the portrait was complete, in late 1977, Sheila and Dr Lind were on very friendly terms. She even referred to him as 'Jamie' in a letter to Alan in September 1977, written after one of his weekend visits.

> '...it was nice to have your help... with Jamie (LIND) – I have taken it in and think I can apply it...'

The commitment and hard work which Sheila put into this painting is plain to see in the result, which is nothing short of superb. At the time, aged twenty, I couldn't quite grasp why she was engaging with such passion in what I thought was essentially an exercise in copying an existing painting, for what to me seemed a profoundly dull bunch of people in the Royal Navy. It is only now, reading through the file in which she kept the correspondence about the commission, that I see how she turned the project into an exercise in learning about eighteenth century portrait painting. The fact that Bum had worked as a naval surgeon in World War I may have contributed to Sheila's enthusiasm. But above all, I think she took a liking to Dr Lind himself, based on what she read about his personality, the sharp-witted warmth of his demeanour in the engraving and his undoubted brilliance in designing a diet-based solution to the problem of scurvy.

The finished painting of Dr Lind was presented to the medical mess on 17 February 1978, at an evening event with a special supper, presided over by Surgeon Vice-Admiral Sir James Watt, who was retiring as director of the Royal Navy Medical Service.

Sheila was invited to attend, with guests of her choice. She brought with her Gaga, who was now eighty five, and Joy Woolley. I recall a certain amount of agony in the days prior to the presentation. The painting was finished, and framed, but it had not yet been seen by either Professor Milton-Thompson or Sir James Watt. And in addition to Sheila's anxiety about whether these men would like the results of her hard work, there was the difficult question of what she should wear. The photographs of the event show her standing beside Sir James in a full length, long-sleeved off-white evening gown. They're both gazing up at the portrait which hangs very high on the wall of the mess. A curtain hangs to one side, and beneath the painting an elaborate flower arrangement sits on a table. Sheila looks a little uncertain, while Sir James is grinning from ear to ear.

In Sheila's files I found a printed programme for the presentation. The names of Sir James Watt, Professor Milton-Thompson and James Lind were set out clearly in large type face, surrounded by stern black lines. Even the author of the flower arrangement was named; but Sheila received not a mention. Sheila was cross about this at the time, but even more cross when, a year later, Joy Woolley collected the painting for varnishing – at the Navy's request – and saw that the plaque attached to the frame *also* failed to give her name. Joy was so angry that she wrote to Professor Milton-Thompson:

> 'I do hope you will not think I am being very interfering if I say how surprised I was to see no mention of the artist in the plaque – nor even of the derivation – (Chalmers). This is very unusual, and of course the painter of a picture is of great interest to viewers, and especially in this instance where an 18th century picture has a 1978 date on it – art historians, and even people interested in this portrait will be annoyed not to see the name of either Sheila Denning nor Chalmers – after some

> years you may have moved on and in time the history of this painting will be a puzzle. I do think, also, that Sheila Denning fulfilled this commission more than adequately, in fact I think it is the most extraordinarily good painting and I believe she did a lot of research and thought before and during painting…'

Eight years would pass before the navy had a new plaque made with Sheila's name on it.

Chapter 26
Veronica

VERONICA MAY was one of Sheila's most devoted friends. In Sheila's pastel portrait of her, Veronica sits reading, three-quarter face, in a comfortable chair with a dark red cushion wedged behind her shoulders. She's wearing an orange beret, a bright yellow scarf and an orange-yellow skirt. Knowing Veronica's habits, she'll have bought them all at once, in one of those Chichester charity shops where volunteers lovingly grouped the women's clothes by colour rather than size. The portrait conveys a serene image of a woman absorbed in a book; but it doesn't capture much of Veronica's unique personality. Unlike in any of Sheila's other portraits, the face is partially covered by the beret and the downward gaze prevents us from seeing Veronica's eyes.

Sheila almost never worked in pastels. It's possible her unfamiliarity with the medium affected her approach, but I wonder whether Veronica, who was quite a private woman, simply didn't want to be seen too clearly.

Veronica was twelve years younger than Sheila. In the drawing her hair is a thick, reddish brown and her sun-tanned skin suggests a woman in her late forties or early fifties. Possibly she'd just come back from Greece, where she went every summer, alone, for six weeks at a stretch.

On her visits to Greece, Veronica was a working artist. She spent her days prowling around little-visited ancient sites, making drawings in pen and ink. A single drawing might take her several days; she carefully considered each mark, to suggest the subtle beauty of rock, foliage and gnarled trees.

Back home, Veronica taught art at Chichester College of Further Education. She worked long hours, poured her earnings into her mortgage and found little, if any, time to draw. There was no alternative, she maintained, given her working class background. Born in the north of England, Veronica had been sent out to work full time in a shop from the age of sixteen. She'd had to fight to study art at night school, after which she became a teacher. She never married and had no children.

Some time after Sheila's death I visited Veronica in the care home where she now lived. It was a warm day and she cut a diminutive, agile figure in a turquoise T shirt and white cotton skirt, seated in a grey armchair. She was in her late eighties now, but every bit as sharp as I remembered her. I asked her to tell me about her first meeting with Sheila, when I was a young teenager in the early 1970s. While she considered her reply, I privately admired the thick white hair which framed her face.

'The day I was introduced to your mum,' Veronica began, 'I felt, "Click, I want to get to know this woman"; but Sheila gave me the impression she didn't have time for a new friendship.' Veronica held her head on one side, bird-like, and gazed at me steadily. 'I bumped into her with your grandmother a few weeks later, at a concert at your school, and she frosted me off. I got the feeling she wasn't interested.'

This information threw me. I remembered Sheila feeling isolated in Chichester, where most of the adults she met were the parents of our school friends. The mums saw her as a dangerously good-looking divorcee: they didn't understand that husband-poaching was the last thing on her agenda. At the time I'd understood that her introduction to Veronica, a happily single woman, a fellow artist and an ex- Londoner, felt like a stroke of luck.

'Sheila was very wrapped up with her mum,' Veronica went on. 'She felt that caring for her – and you and your sister – was her main responsibility. But I wasn't taking 'no' for an answer! I thought, "OK then, I'll wait".' A triumphant smile flitted across Veronica's features.

It touched me to learn that Veronica had had to be patient in the early days of her acquaintance with Sheila, with whom, over

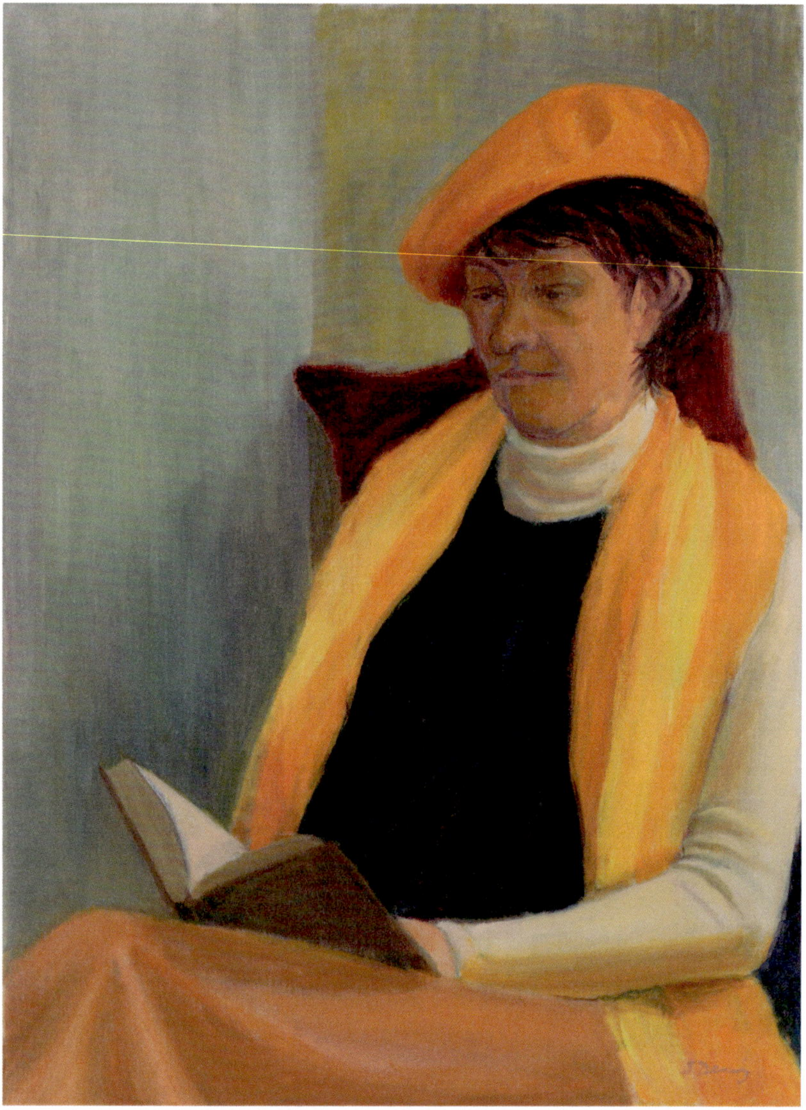

Veronica May, 1995

time, she'd formed a deep friendship. 'What was it in Sheila that you clicked with?'

Veronica hesitated, choosing her words with precision. 'The intangible. I knew we had things to talk about – not painting, other things. I was very impressed with the way she was caring for her family. I'm so much *not* like that myself: I'm very unmaternal, I never wanted to marry. I like kids, but briefly –' she waved her hand in a gesture of friendly dismissal '– they can go now. I was impressed that family was where Sheila put her energy, although she was also doing some teaching, and painting. I sensed there was a lot there… And that, one day, there would be room for me.'

'She overdid it as a mother, didn't she?' I met Veronica's gaze. 'We didn't need as much of her time as she gave us.'

'Oh, definitely, she overdid it! But that was Sheila's way.' Veronica looked at me sharply. We fell silent, and I reflected on how, in my twenties and thirties, I'd frequently wished that Sheila had prioritized her painting more when I was growing up. I was acutely aware that she'd let her family responsibilities eat into her painting life and I felt it would have been better for her, as well as for me, if she hadn't done that. Having a mother who put her career first and achieved some worldly recognition would have been a better role model – or so I thought.

'Sheila was in a different social class from me,' Veronica went on. She was a doctor's daughter.'

'Was class an issue between you?'

'Not really, no. She didn't treat me as if I was from a different class, but I saw her that way.' She sighed. 'But at a deeper level, we understood each other. And there were good things about Sheila's background, from my point of view. She knew about picnics! Sheila would ring up and invite me for a picnic supper on the downs.'

I remembered that when I phoned Sheila from London in my twenties, in summer, she'd be packing potato salad and tomatoes and ham into Gaga's picnic basket, with a bottle of water and a thermos of tea. "It's lovely here," she'd tell me, "I'm going up on the downs with Veronica."

'Sheila's picnic basket had *plates* in it,' Veronica went on ' – plates that *fitted* – to me it was like something in a fairy story. All I knew about picnics was what I'd read in Enid Blyton!'

I smiled, reflecting that the joy of picnicking was something Sheila had discovered aged twelve or thirteen, on the banks of the river Thames, after a dip in the river with her brothers and Bum. When Sheila was dripping water onto Gaga's picnic blanket and scoffing white bread with butter and strawberry jam, Veronica was a new-born baby in a town in the north of England. The probability that their paths would one day cross must have been very low; yet Veronica had come to know Mum almost as well as me and my sister knew her.

*

In the spring of 1978, after being paid for the portrait of Lind, Sheila considered whether she could treat herself to a holiday abroad. It wasn't an easy decision, because she knew Gaga would feel nervous while she was out of the country, but she was longing for a couple of weeks in the south of France. She was still wondering about Gaga's reaction, and feeling guilty, when she found a cheap house to rent in a village in the south west. 'Damn it all,' she said to me one night, on the phone, 'I can't sit in Chichester for ever. Gaga may live another five years!'

A week later, she persuaded Veronica and two other friends to go with her.

But the holiday was not to be. The day before Sheila was due to leave Chichester, Gaga collapsed and had a major stroke. The medics wanted to hospitalise her, but Sheila put her foot down, knowing that Gaga would not have wanted to go.

I was already in France, cycling southwards with a friend. By the time I learned what had happened and made my way to

Chichester, Anna and Dad were already there, camping out with Sheila in Gaga's house. Gaga lay in the downstairs front room, too poorly to be carried upstairs. The stroke had left her paralysed down the left side of her body and her usually serene face with its familiar wrinkles and folds of skin was now lopsided. The right eye opened intermittently, but the left one remained closed. The right leg kicked and fidgeted under the blankets, while the left one lay lifeless.

For the next ten days, Mum, Dad, Anna and I took it in turns to sit with Gaga around the clock. After some time it became apparent that she wanted to tell us something important, but she couldn't form the words. She would move the right side of her mouth, and make unintelligible sounds, while her pale blue right eye fixed us with a look of helpless distress. It was awful to see. When we ate our meals in the adjoining room, with the door ajar, we would compare notes as to what we thought she was trying to say; but none of us really knew.

In the early hours of August 6th, when I was sitting with Gaga, a strange sound began to issue from her throat. I'd read about something called the 'death rattle' and wondered if this was it. I tiptoed out of the room and woke Dad, who came to the door, listened for a moment and went to wake Sheila. A couple of hours later we were all gathered around the bed when, with a profound shudder, Gaga left us forever.

Dad stayed on for another week and a half, ostensibly to help with preparations for the funeral. I had mixed feelings about his presence in this time of such crisis for Mum, who blamed herself for Gaga's stroke and consequent demise. Instinct told me it was not exactly love that had brought Dad to her side: if he really loved her, surely he would have been with us all along, supporting her as a mother and sharing the responsibility for raising Anna and me? I wondered what was driving him – was it a taste for crisis situations, or a need to feel he still had a place in Sheila's family? Or something else?

Whatever his motives, Dad put a huge amount of work into preparing the flowers for the funeral, cutting many of them in Gaga's rose-filled garden, buying others and tying them painstakingly into bunches on a tressle table outside the back door. The colour scheme was distinctly *his*, I noted with annoyance, not one Gaga (or Sheila) would have chosen. Blackish red helleniums with dirty yellow centres and dark orange dahlias, when Gaga would have chosen smaller flowers in delicate pinks and whites. In other circumstances I might have liked Dad's choices, but not in these. I felt he was trying to hijack Gaga's death for his own purposes, at a moment when Mum was too distraught to stand in his way.

But this was not at all how Mum saw it. In a letter to Dad written after he returned to London following the funeral, she thanked him unreservedly for his support while Gaga was dying, and said what a great deal it had meant to her.

The weeks that followed were dark and difficult ones for Mum, Anna and me. I was preparing to start university that autumn and made no attempt to resume the cycling trip I'd abandoned. Instead, I whiled away the rest of the summer in Chichester. A sense of devastation hung over the three of us. We were exhausted from the nights sitting up with Gaga, from the pain of watching her decline and – surely – from the bizarre experience of briefly resuming life as a family unit.

I spent the last days of summer brooding on the absence from our lives of reliable, trustworthy menfolk. I didn't count Dad as such a man and wasn't sorry he'd gone back to London. Rather, I thought of Bay in South Africa and wondered why he hadn't come to say goodbye to his mother and support his sister; I thought of Bum, who'd left us too soon, when I was only three; and of Joe, who'd always sounded like he would have been the perfect uncle. If things had been different and he'd survived the war, surely *he* would have been with us now? I lay awake at night in my room at Orchard Avenue, with a sharp sense of loss and a bubbling anger.

Mum was tired and ragged during those weeks, struggling to stay on top of the many tasks that had to be accomplished, trying to hide her grief from me and my sister and doing her best to 'keep going', as lone mothers do. One night, I found myself furiously wishing she'd find herself a new partner. With her charm and good looks, still undiminished at the age of 58, surely by now she should have met someone – one of those strong, trustworthy men whom some of my friends had as fathers – who could provide the support she so desperately needed? But Mum had rarely shown any sign of wanting a new man, a fact which perplexed and disappointed me.

PART SEVEN

JULY 2019

I was dreading seeing Dad. On my two previous visits, he'd lost his temper and told me to get out. Today, in strong July sunshine, I'd had to cajole myself into driving down the lane to his house, calculating finely that I could leave again in 45 minutes.

Charlie was working on his laptop in the kitchen. He got up to greet me and smiled when I told him what short shrift Dad had given me last week and the week before.

'I think he's in an okay mood this afternoon,' he said slowly. 'How about I go in first and tell him you're here?'

I watched from Dad's doorway as Charlie stepped towards the bed. Dad was lying very still against a pale blue pillow, his right eye open and his left eye closed.

'Look, Alan,' Charlie began, his voice brimming with enthusiasm, 'here's your lovely daughter, come to see you!'

Emboldened by Charlie's tactic, I presented myself at the foot of the bed. To my relief Dad opened his left eye, smiled sweetly and repeated, in the manner of a dutiful child, 'My lovely daughter!'

I'd never heard him use those words before. I smiled back, moved round to the far side of the bed and sat down on the old office chair, as Charlie backed out of the room.

For a few moments we stared at each other, both unsure what to say. The rims of Dad's eyes were red and his cheeks were very pale, but he seemed relatively alert. 'I thought I'd just pop in to say hello,' I told him, 'before I go back to work.'

'Good,' he replied in a weak, husky voice. 'Good to see you.' He cast his gaze around the room, as if searching for something. Then he looked right at me. 'What are you working on?'

The question took me by surprise. 'I'm writing a book about Sheila,' I replied. 'A memoir, of sorts.' There was a risk, I knew, that the response would be one of jealousy: why was I writing about her, and not him? But dementia did funny things to people's attitudes and I was curious to see what he would say.

Dad's gaze settled on my face, a trace of anxiety in his eyes. 'About her life?' he asked slowly.

'Her life, and her painting.' I sat quietly, waiting for him to digest the information. At the window behind the bed, a profusion of yellow-green leaves pressed against the glass, bright in the summer light.

A full minute went by. Then the look of anxiety on Dad's face intensified and he cleared his throat. 'Is it revealing?' he asked.

'Yes,' I replied, giving way to a powerful urge to be real with him. How, I wondered, could a man with dementia appreciate that a memoir about his ex-wife might be revealing?

Another minute went by. I sat very still, glancing from Dad to the clock on the wall beside the door. The sharp focus in his eyes had gone and he seemed lost in thought. Then he cleared his throat again and turned his face towards me. 'Does it upset you?'

'Sometimes it does.' This was the truth: I'd wept many times as I read the Denning family letters, especially the ones about Joe. And I'd raged and wept as I delved into events at Hawkley. 'But that's ok,' I added fiercely, 'it's all part of the process.'

A few moments passed. Then I asked, 'Did Mum ever talk to you about her brother Joe, the one who died in the war?'

His expression was blank. 'No.'

'Or Bay, who emigrated to Africa?'

'No.'

For a couple of long minutes, we lapsed into silence. Then Dad spoke again. 'Is it very *revealing?'*

Now I wasn't sure what to say. Revealing about what? I sat back in the chair. How could Dad, who spent most of his time in a largely fanciful mental world, step out of his dementia when it suited him, in order to discuss something important? 'Yes, and no,' I said slowly.

'There are things I've left out...' A life of ninety five years could scarcely be fitted into three hundred pages. And besides, there were things which simply didn't belong in the public domain.

There was a very long pause, and then I asked if he thought about Sheila from time to time. I couldn't stop myself hoping he would say that he did.

'No,' he replied. 'But… I don't feel very proud of that.' He stared at the ceiling and I could tell that he was chewing the inside of his mouth, something he did when he felt uneasy. After another long pause he spoke again. 'I'd like to read some of it.'

'Okay. But I never show anyone what I'm writing till it's finished. Then you can read it.'

'It's quite a sad subject to take on,' he added a moment later.

I bridled. 'Her life wasn't all sad! Her childhood was happy, especially when she lived at Frampton. And in Sussex, she was reasonably happy; she produced a lot of portraits there.'

Dad fell silent; but a minute later he asked, 'Is it going to be published soon?

'No, no, it'll take me years to finish it.'

A look of relief spread across his face. 'It's sad she's not here now, to enjoy life.'

After yet another long silence, he turned to me again. 'Are you staying the night?'

'No Dad, I live close by, I can be home in half an hour.' We'd had this conversation many times, but Dad never remembered where I lived. 'And now,' I added gently, 'I must leave you in peace and get back to work.' I bent down and squeezed his hand by way of farewell.

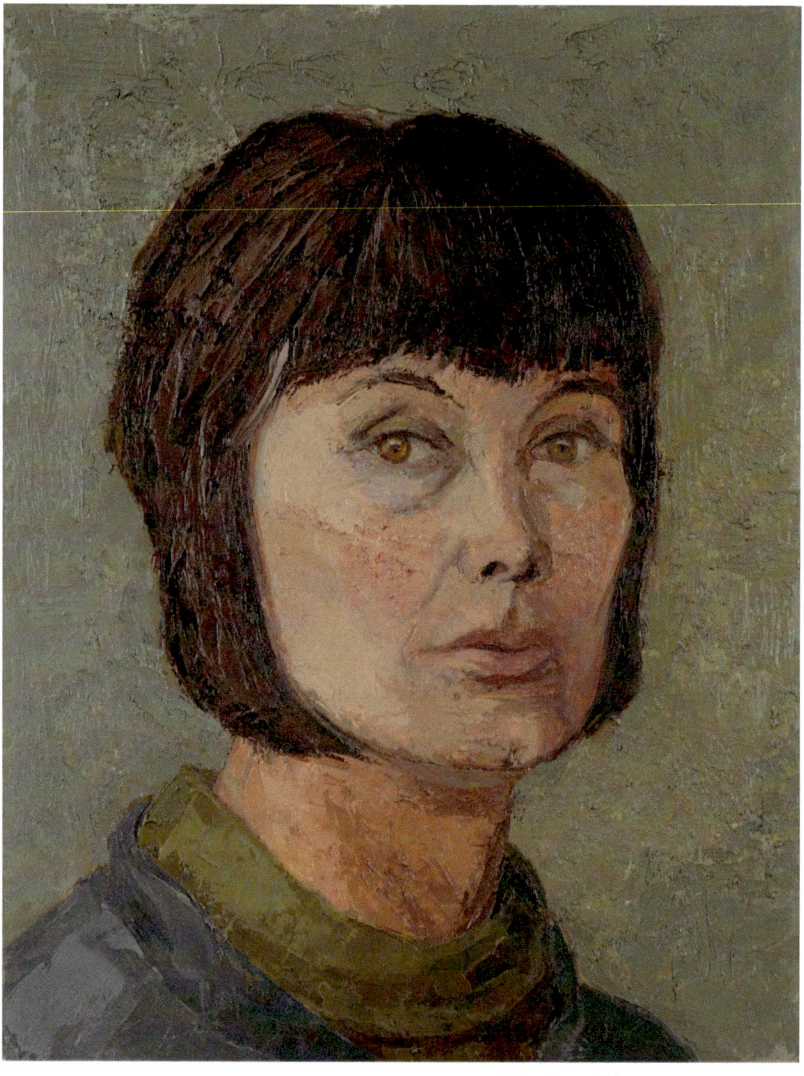

Sheila, self-portrait, c. 1979

Chapter 27
Self Portrait in a Green Turtle Neck

ONE DAY IN 1979, while I was away at university, Sheila set up a series of mirrors in her studio at Orchard Avenue to paint a new self portrait. Never one to be overly-generous towards herself, she worked on a Rowney hardboard panel measuring just twelve inches by sixteen. The use of the board rather than a canvas suggests that she saw this piece of work as a filler, something she would toss off between commissions. It never acquired a frame.

Ironically, this is one of Sheila's best portraits. I have it propped in front of me as I write. Here's my mum, aged 59, taking a long, cool look at herself. There's bravery in what she's doing. She's placed herself three-quarter face against a sage green wall. The fabric of her turtle neck top, a dull, olive green, sits quietly against the bronze skin of her throat. A grey-blue painting smock covers her shoulders in the bottom corners of the painting. The paint is thick and generous, laid on partly with a palette knife, partly with brushes. There's an oily, rich quality to the surfaces. The dark brown hair is carved with deep, satisfying knife-grooves.

As for the face, it's so uncannily like Mum that I can only gaze for a few seconds, before turning away. Everything about it is *her*. Those are her prominent cheekbones, the tanned skin mottled subtly with tiny dabs of red, indicating that she no longer has the skin of a young woman. Those are her arched eyebrows, her grey-eye-shadowed eyelids, her thin, faintly lilac skin beneath the lower lids; those are her wide open amber eyes; her small nose, her long upper lip ending in the full mouth. The lips are slightly parted, the expression serious. I glance from the eyes to the mouth and back, trying to put what I see into words. It's the face of a strong woman who knows her own worth; but in the eyes there's still a hint of sorrow, disappointment, even anger. Just a hint, but it's there. To me, her eyes say: 'here I am, still able-bodied, still good-looking; but nobody wants me, do they?'

Mum's eyes are focussed on a far-off point beyond my left shoulder. But as I gaze, her pupils swivel and she stares straight at me.

A wave of nausea hits my stomach. So she's still here, watching me, while I write about her. She knows that I'm spreading out the secrets of her life for all to see.

I've wrestled with a sense of guilt about this since day one. When we discussed the idea of my writing a book about her before her death, Sheila was clear she didn't want me to write about her personal life, *at all*; just about her life as a painter. At that point neither of us realized that I would find it impossible to separate the two.

I force myself to look at her.

How could I have made sense of your life, Mum, without delving into your relationship with Dad? I did try, at the beginning, but I didn't see a way to do it. Sheila the painter can't be detached from Sheila the hurt and angry woman. And how would I have explained why you barely painted between 1951 and 1969?

Still looking her in the eye, I take a deep breath, for I've got something more difficult to say.

I've been working on this book for two years, mother, and gradually I've grasped that I'm doing it as much *for me* as for you. I need to understand who you were and why you lived the life you did, so that I can disentangle myself from your long arms and let you go.

Chapter 28
Dear Alan, Dear Sheila

IN THE SUMMER OF 2019, Dad was still with us, mainly drifting in a world of his own. At this point Anna, who was to be his sole executor, started to go through his papers. Once or twice a week she would spend a long afternoon sitting beside him in the old office chair, trawling through his home-made filing system while he slept. Buried among old bank statements, she found numerous letters from Mum to Dad and a handful from him to her. She stuffed them into two envelope files and gave them to me.

On a rainy evening in August, slightly anxious as to what I might discover, I settled on the sofa and opened the first file. The sight of my mother's handwriting on so many folded sheets of letter paper caused my eyes to sting. So she'd written Dad a great many letters over the years, and he'd kept the lot.

It took me a long time to sort Mum's letters by date order, ranging as they did from the mid 1970s to the late 1980s. Some were in envelopes with postmarks, others were loose. Some of the sheets were dog-eared, as if they'd been read over and over; others were smooth, making me wonder if they'd been read at all.

I was expecting the subject of money to feature prominently, but I was wrong. By 1976, apparently, Mum had moved on from the strain of her years as a lone parent, demonstrating an ability to forgive and forget which both astonished and worried me. Her letters were written in a tone of warmth and friendship, as if Alan were a very dear old friend, or even a temporarily absent partner, rather than the ex-husband whose behaviour had caused her so much unhappiness.

Every few weeks, I gleaned, in the period after I left home, my parents had spent the weekend together, sometimes in Sussex and sometimes in London. And in between times, they'd spoken on the phone and written to each other. In Mum's letters, the recurring themes were the trials and tribulations of her life as a working artist and her desire to know how Dad was getting on with his creative work. My parents also commiserated with each other when their work got rejected by galleries.

Sheila wrote in May 1976:

> 'Thank you very much for the nice weekend. I wasn't looking forward much to fetching all my throw-outs back, and felt quite out of sorts on Friday (– baffled, as well as angry.)
>
> But there's a sense of order, and beauty, about your house that is very soothing. And it seemed to do me good. Thank you.'

Sheila often described moments in her painting life. In February 1977, she wrote:

> 'Isn't it unaccountable one's capacity to work? Yesterday, Monday, though I was in there at 9am I couldn't do anything, so it seemed – it was a terrible struggle against matter, though I stuck it for 6 hours (minus a prolonged lunch break). Today, all the conditions being the same, it just flowed and I felt it could hardly go wrong! – I suppose there was one condition different, now I think of it – yesterday I couldn't get warm and today was mild.'

I pictured Sheila in her front-room studio at Orchard Avenue, rationing herself to one bar of the electric fire, on a freezing February day. She was earning a small amount from teaching and portrait commissions and beginning to exhibit still lives and landscapes, but she had to manage her resources extremely carefully to avoid getting into debt.

Later that year, after another visit to Alan, she wrote:

> 'It was very nice to see you…
>
> It's been murky dark here ever since I got back and has hardly stopped raining. Difficult to paint. I couldn't do anything to my big painting yesterday, I just couldn't see it – so had to do something else in almost monochrome. Finished – in 2 mornings – I'm getting quicker.'

Alan disapproved of Sheila's slow, deliberate style of painting (although he often admired the results, as I eventually discovered). In his letters, he sometimes urged her to try working faster. And during their weekend *tête-à-têtes*, he encouraged her to relax more. Hence she wrote in the summer of 1978, after another visit to London:

> 'I've been lazy! Although I got home at 3, I decided I needed an early tea in the garden and a rest, and I lay there in the sun until I decided it was time to go and have another tea with Veronica, after which it was far too late to start painting, of course. So I'm going to get up early and start in the morning.'

Alan's wartime injury had been compounded by a muscular wasting condition and handling large sculptures was now very difficult for him. Determined to keep going as an artist, he started to draw and paint for the first time in his life, confronting a long-held conviction that he simply could not draw. Each time Sheila visited him in London, Alan asked her to look at his work. She was invariably warm, admiring and encouraging in her response and continued to talk about what he'd shown her when she wrote the next letter:

> 'I've been thinking about your paintings, and you. I was really very impressed with them. There seem to be lots of real *painterly* qualities in them, which I find

astonishing in someone who has spent so many years in other arts which don't require quite the same qualities – ie composition, colour sense, and *Drawing* ability!!! What made the strongest impression on me I think was the charcoal drawing which is unlike any drawing of yours I have ever seen before and seemed to have great strength and a positive masculine aggression, if you can understand the word in a favourable sense. Good luck! Press on – it's all very exciting!'

To one of her letters, Sheila pinned two pages of technical advice, in response to a request from Alan.

> 'Brushes. Oils.
> Winsor & Newton and Rowneys probably equally good, though I prefer W & N… I wouldn't buy student's quality – "educational" – and I would keep off nylon, personally. Best is hog bristle or, for small brushes, sable. (but specify sable oil brushes, ie long-handled and short bristled.)
> 'One has also the choice of shape, flat or round. Most people use flat now, but in the past round were used and I'm trying to use them now sometimes (for my 18th century portrait?) and find them nice. You have to experiment to see which suits you best.'

Alan frequently travelled in Europe. In August 1977 he borrowed a friend's house in Florence, writing to Sheila:

> 'I've done 13 paintings now – 7 "large"… and 6 small. Not v. much, I suppose, given that I'm doing v. little else. But I've learned a lot at each go, I *think*. Anyway, painting outdoors hasn't any bogies for me now. A polythene bag for 4 tubes (a red, a blue a yellow and a white!) turps, oil, 3 brushes, a paper palette and a light-as-a-feather easel and whatever it is I'm painting on.'

Alan was prolific as a painter. Some of his early work was sketchy and slight, but within a few years he was producing evocative landscapes of southern France and Gloucestershire. He had a knack of seeing the warmth in the colours of natural materials, and reproducing them convincingly. Though full of struggle, his style was loose and suggestive: he was more interested in recreating the atmosphere of a group of farm buildings or a wooded valley, than in describing it precisely.

In the autumn of 1979, Sheila's friend Margaret Holgate invited Sheila to visit Crete with her, where Margaret had worked as a volunteer after World War Two. Sheila was so taken with the island and the Cretans that on her return home she started to teach herself the Greek alphabet and enrolled in a language class. The following year she went to Greece alone, and from then on an annual visit became the high point of her year.

I was still at university and enjoyed the letters Sheila sent me, describing her adventures. I loved to think of her confidently wandering about on her own, practicing her new language and feasting on the arid landscape and ancient sites. When she came home, sun-tanned and happy, she told me tales of being ferried from one island to another by handsome boatmen who fed her grapes. I was impressed by her determination to travel as much as she could, despite being on a tight budget and lacking a companion. I wondered whether on one of her trips she might find herself a new partner.

At the time it didn't occur to me that Mum also wrote to Dad from Greece, but in one of the files I found this, written from Athens in September 1980:

> 'I'm sitting having supper on a hilly pavement...[on] the lower slope of the Acropolis...
>
> I wish I could convey to you something about being here that seems to touch my deepest feelings. It is

> a quality that I am finding in the people, and in the sculpture. Both seem to be in touch with the springs of feeling in a very simple, warm and direct way, and the expression of it and the feeling is one. I think you would feel it here. I never understood sculpture before. The relation between person and person, on the grave-stones, between man and animal, adult and child (sculpture all this) expresses such a tenderness that I am constantly moved to tears.'

*

Theatre and opera were important to my parents and Alan's visits to Chichester were scheduled to allow as many performances as could be fitted in. Sheila wrote in advance of one such visit:

> 'I have got us tickets for *A Midsummer Night's Dream* in the gardens of West Dean, on Sat night. I don't think we can come straight back to Tennessee Williams after that, do you? Perhaps Fri evg if you are thinking of coming down then. Have got *Beggar's Opera* tickets for Mon…'

Birthdays were important, too. In February 1979, Sheila spent her birthday with Alan in London, and once again he showed her his latest work.

> 'Thank you for making my birthday so nice! From the cake – to taking me out to dinner, which was sweet of you, and which I really enjoyed. I'm so glad I came – and seeing your drawings was – very moving, somehow, and a privilege. Thank you for showing them. I don't know that I could have done the same. I did get a strong feeling of movement and growth from them, and I feel you are being richly rewarded

> for the way you are persevering with your difficulties. Don't waver – press on, and I'm sure you will have made great progress soon.'

The more I read of Mum's letters, the more I was struck by the generosity, even tenderness, with which she addressed Dad. It was clear that, despite their divorce, Dad had remained the most significant adult in her life. This wasn't exactly news to me; and yet the timbre of her words shocked me. Now I understood why she'd never wanted a relationship with a new man. My understanding was confirmed when I found a letter sent by Sheila in early summer 1981, in which she invited Alan to accompany her to Greece the following September. To my relief, there was also a letter from Alan, in which he gently declined, saying he'd already arranged to go to France with the Gibbses.

In general Alan's letters, in contrast to Sheila's, contained long descriptions of the highs and lows of his working life. He rarely referred to Sheila's work. He was often frantically busy, and sometimes apologized for writing 'in a rush to catch the post'. But his tone was never cold and from time to time *he* addressed *her* with palpable affection, as in this letter written on New Year's Eve 1981:

> 'You were very sweet to me over Xmas – which was not unusual, I may say. As I sat munching the small morsel of Christmas cake I allowed myself, today, out of the huge hunk you gave me to bring back, I thought too of the birthday cake and how kind and generous and magnanimous it was of you to make it for me. I assure you I am not insensible of these things… which somehow mean a lot to me…'

Although he was not generally one to worry about other people's feelings, I suspect that Alan was plagued by a level of guilt towards Sheila: guilt about his behaviour in the past, and guilt about their present relationship, in which he clearly came off better than she

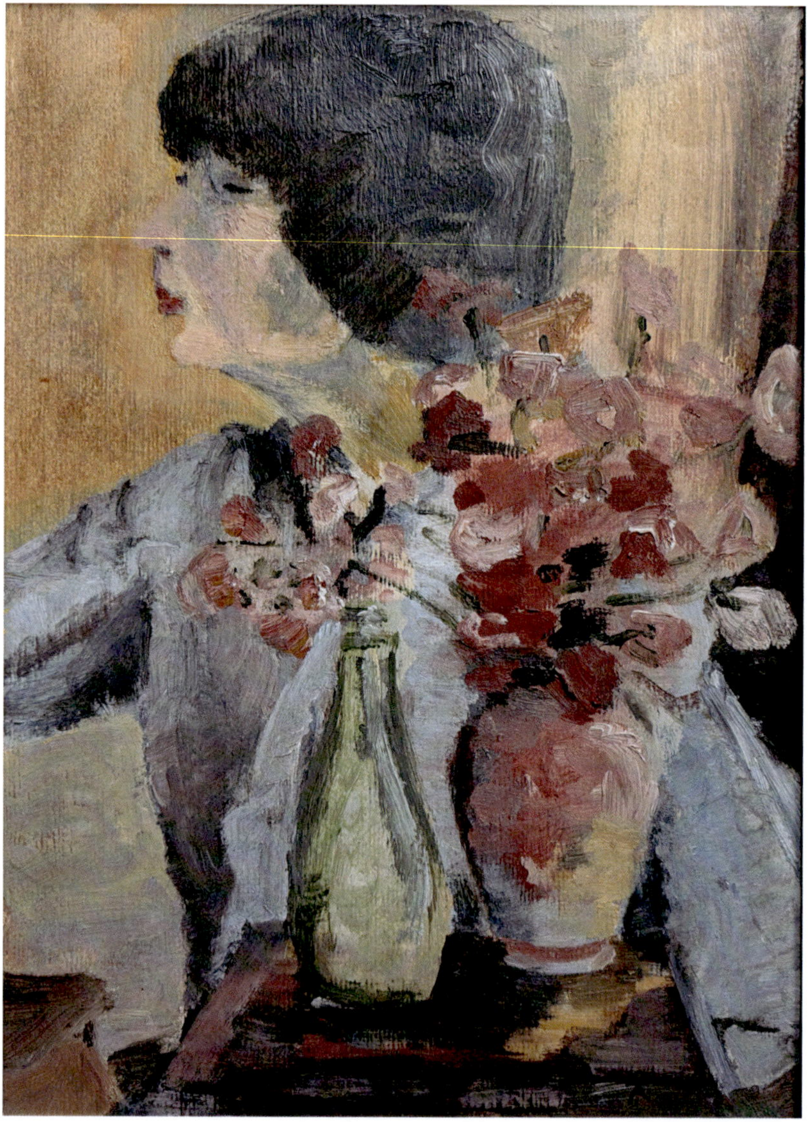

Sheila by Alan, 1983

did. He wasn't blind to the fact that he benefited from her undying care and support, while retaining absolute freedom to do as he pleased, with whomever he pleased, in between their meetings. In November 1976, one of Alan's girlfriends, an Austrian woman, gave birth to their son, naming him Philip. I'm not sure at what point Alan told Sheila about Philip's arrival; he first informed me in 1988, when I was 32 and Philip was 12. Once I'd got over the shock, I was thrilled to have a brother.

*

At some point in 1983 my parents spent a day together, painting each other simultaneously. As a slow worker, Sheila only produced an oil sketch, which she hung on her wall. She wrote to Alan shortly afterwards:

> 'Your portrait looks down on me rather unnervingly. It is more like you in daylight, rather too much so for comfort. I want another go at it.'

In the portrait which Alan painted of Sheila that day, she has her eyes narrowed and her arm outstretched, as she tries to measure some dimension of Alan's face – the length of his nose, perhaps, or the gap between his eyebrows. Her neck and shoulder are partially obscured by two vases containing flowers, yet he has perfectly captured, with his subtle colour range, my mother's unique beauty.

Chapter 29
The Unfinished Self Portrait

I WAS NOW A CRIMINAL LAWYER living and working in London, my fashion design plan long abandoned. One Friday evening in April 1992, feeling drained by a series of back-to-back court hearings, I took the train to Chichester. At Dorking station I woke abruptly when my head bumped against the filthy window pane. But soon I was dozing again, waking just in time as the train clattered into Chichester.

Mum met me on the far side of the station barrier, striking as ever despite her shapeless trousers, off-white anorak and the old silk scarf tied round her greying hair. We hugged each other tightly and set off, arm in arm, across the station car park towards Mum's white Polo. She'd nicknamed it 'Rosie' because of the pink rose petals scattered on its bonnet when she found it for sale, second hand, on the forecourt of a petrol station on the Downs. The rose petals had long since blown away and moss now grew in a furtive but determined line along the rims of the windows.

After a few years in North London in the mid 1980s, Mum had come back to Chichester and bought herself another semi. When I'd put down my bags and taken off my coat, she took me by the shoulders and steered me towards the glass panel above the front door, which flooded the hallway with light. 'Let's have a look at you,' she said. I disliked these moments of maternal scrutiny, which occurred on every visit. Mum's eyes were sharp: if she thought I looked exhausted or drawn, which invariably I did, she'd tell me so. I gazed at her in silence, waiting for what I perceived as criticism, although it wasn't intended that way.

'You're a bit thin, my darling,' she pronounced, patting my skinny arms and studying the dark shadows under my eyes. I knew I was thin; but so was she. It was our build: long and lanky, with little muscle and no flab. And with the work pressure I was under, I couldn't help being tired. I shrugged my shoulders to indicate I wanted her to release me and took a step towards the staircase. 'You're in the back bedroom,' she told me, 'the bed's made up.'

Upstairs I flopped down on the bed. The muscles of my neck were like steel cable and a tight band pressed across my forehead. My eyes wandered around the room. On the small chest of drawers, Mum had arranged a bunch of wild flowers in a jam jar – picked, no doubt, on one of her walks. She did this every time I came and the gesture always touched me, however jaded I was feeling. Mum walked a lot these days, often with Veronica, who lived in the adjoining street close to a footpath leading to open fields.

I could hear Mum moving about in the kitchen below. I must go down, I told myself. Swinging my legs over the edge of the bed I sat up, noticing the pale green light that seeped in at the window from the garden. Sheila had painted the walls a subtle, dirty pink since my last visit and hung her new landscape of Kingley Vale over the bed. My grandmother's nursing chair with its sage green velvet seat stood in the corner. For all her lack of domestic efficiency and her slender financial means, Mum was good at choosing the right colours, paintings and furniture to make a room attractive. And the house was spotlessly clean; though that, I knew, was purely thanks to Celia, Mum's cleaner.

I took off my socks and shoes and padded down the stairs to the kitchen, breathing in the smell of baked potatoes. Mum was standing at the wall-mounted electric oven. I tiptoed up behind her, wrapped my arms around her waist and rested my head on her shoulder.

'One hundred and eighty degrees,' she muttered before adding, in a louder voice, 'The bloody oven's taken to overheating!' Then she reached her hand to my cheek and stroked it. 'Lovely to see you, darling. The food's almost ready. Could you lay the table?'

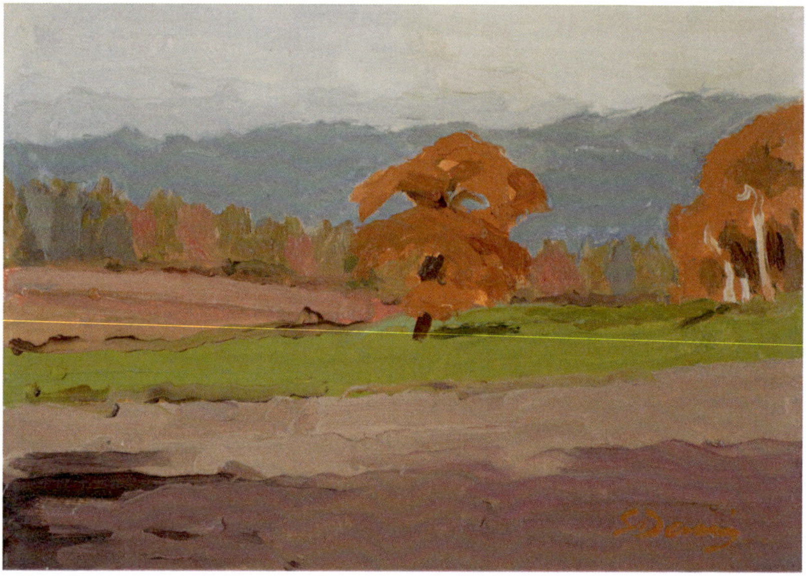

Near Kingley Vale, 1986

'Mummy,' I replied, speaking into the side of her neck, 'Sorry I was grumpy.' I drifted into the living room, where the cutlery lived in a drawer beneath the dining table.

Germaine Greer's *The Female Eunuch* lay open on a chair. I stared down at the curious image on the front cover. A naked female torso, minus head, arms and legs, hung from something like a curtain rail, with handles fixed to the hips. I felt tempted to pick up the volume and skim the table of contents, but I was half afraid to touch it. The book was akin to a power object for Mum. It seemed to crackle with the furious anger which she often expressed these days when talking about Dad. If I picked it up, my fingers would surely burn.

I glanced around the room. Here was Mum's divan under the window, draped in a white Indian bedspread and adorned with silk cushions made by my sister. The portrait of Gaga hung in an alcove. Today's *Guardian* was spread across the sofa: Mum read it almost every day.

Above the fireplace she'd hung a painting of the River Thames[1], which I liked very much. And here, on her beautiful oak bureau, a framed photo showed Bay in South Africa, lean and slightly stooped, his face half covered by a white cloth hat.

In 1987, with some reluctance, Mum had flown to South Africa to visit Bay. On her return she'd told me how uncomfortable she'd felt on his smallholding, where black servants did the toughest jobs and racist remarks went unchallenged. Bay was plagued by nostalgia for England and told Sheila he longed to spend his last years in the country of his birth. But Ivy wouldn't leave the farm and he could scarcely abandon his children and grandchildren.

'Bay's coming next month.' Mum spoke from the doorway, a tea towel hanging from her shoulder. 'Three weeks, this time.' She looked pleased.

'With Ivy?'

'No, just Bay, Ivy didn't want to come. She says she can't leave the animals, but I don't think she likes trips to England.'

'Well, that's allright then!' I smiled at Mum as she went to the fridge and brought out a bottle of wine. She would enjoy having Bay to herself. 'What are you planning?' Last time he'd come, Mum had taken him to visit their childhood haunts in Wiltshire and Gloucestershire and they'd eaten in pubs and picnicked on the banks of the Thames.

'I haven't really thought about it yet. Too busy, one way and another.' Mum unscrewed the bottle and poured us each a glass of wine.

'How come you're so busy?' I'd been in court every day that week, rushing across London on the tube from one hearing to another and prepping papers every evening, with barely time to eat or sleep; that was my idea of 'busy'.

'Life, I suppose.' Mum held up her glass. 'Cheers, darling. Let me see, what have I done this week?' She glanced around at the

1 This painting can be seen at www.sheiladenning.com

various stacks of papers on the bureau. 'Sending out the publicity for my summer landscape courses; meeting a new student who wants some one-to-one tuition; sending in a painting to the Portsmouth City Biennale. Nothing major, but I've not stopped all week. Couple of shortish walks with Veronica, who's hurt her wrist and needed some tlc; oh and I think I've finally finished the portrait of Celia.'

I held out my glass to chink it against hers. 'When you reel it off like that, it sounds like a lot.'

Mum looked faintly amused. 'I don't just sit here on my backside, darling. There's always something needs doing.' Now she rummaged in her handbag for a comb and raked it quickly through her grey bob. Her hair was thicker and better cut than mine, and she never failed to comb it before a meal.

'Perhaps you *should* sit on your backside, at least sometimes,' I replied. 'You're seventy two, no spring chicken! How did Celia turn out?' I meant the portrait, not the person.

Mum raised her eyebrows sharply. 'Celia's no spring chicken either, you know, she's my twin. It's turned out okay, I think.'

I'd only met Celia a couple of times. She was small and arthritic with whispy white hair, and I thought it unfair that she, rather than Mum, was the one who lugged the hoover round the house. Mum complained that Celia chatted too much, but after listening with sympathy for some weeks she'd leant on Celia to sit for her portrait.

Mum put down her glass and went to the kitchen. She returned with the baked potatoes and a dish of smoked mackerel, slices of lemon and a bowl of fresh watercress. 'Bit of a simple meal this evening. We'll have something more elaborate tomorrow night.'

I was barely listening, for I'd picked up a postcard with a black and white image of a carved stone frieze propped on the mantelpiece. Only one person could have sent *that* to Mum. I turned it over and, sure enough, there was Dad's indecipherable scrawl, half concealed by a French postmark. He'd sent it a week ago from the Dordogne, where he'd stopped to look round an

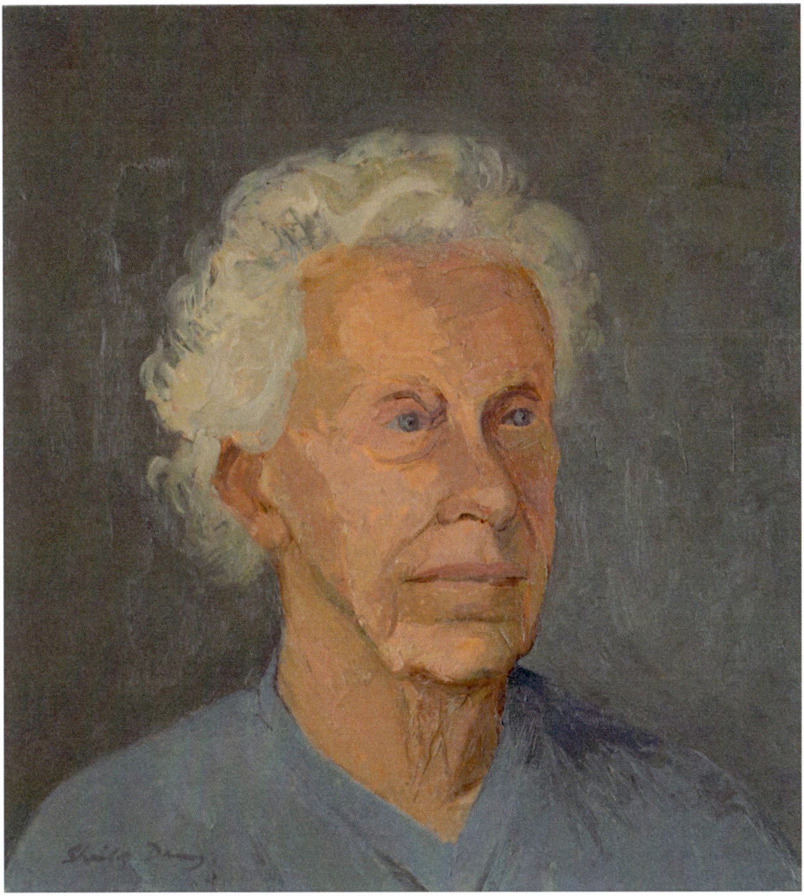

Celia, c. 1992

abbey en route to the south. Damn, I thought, does he have to rub it in that he's off to France again with… I hesitated to pronounce her name, here in Mum's living room, even inside my head. It was two years now since Dad and his new partner had hooked up, and it appeared this was not going to be a passing liaison.

I'd met the woman and liked her, but I knew Mum was still smarting from her arrival in Dad's life.

Putting the postcard back on the mantelpiece, I sat down at the table. 'This looks delicious, I like simple food.'

As we ate I asked Mum about her arthritis. A couple of years back, she'd shown me the joint of the index finger on her right hand, which was becoming knotted and painful. Fearful it might limit her dexterity for painting, Mum had gone to the library and read everything she could find on how to combat arthritis. The most helpful thing was a book which recommended the drinking of hot cider vinegar laced with honey and a diet in which aubergine, tomatoes and all red fruit were proscribed.

Mum looked at me with an expression of triumph. 'All gone! The diet worked a treat.'

'Are you still avoiding tomatoes?'

'Mostly.' She smiled. 'Once in a while, as a special treat, I go to Waitrose for those delicious organic vine tomatoes.' She put down her fork and held up her right hand. 'I'm pretty sure I'm out of the woods, what d'you think?'

I reached across the table, took hold of Mum's wrist and studied her fingers. To me they seemed as long, slim and pointed as they'd always been, the fingers of a painter. All the joints were slightly knotted, but none was bigger than the others. The back of her hand was mottled with age spots.

*

That night I slept deeply in the blissful silence of the back bedroom. In the morning, I asked Mum to show me the portrait of Celia. It was a breezy, sharp spring day and we shivered as we crossed the yard from the back door to the studio, a converted garage. It was a long, low-ceilinged room, with a back window looking onto the garden, where Mum's two apple trees were pink and white with blossom.

'This is such a lovely space to work in,' I exclaimed as we walked in.

'I know,' she replied, 'everybody says how nice it is.'

It surprised me that Mum managed to cram in four students

and a sitter for her portrait class on a Thursday morning, and five for the afternoon still life class. A metal tray with coffee mugs stood on top of the plan chest, beside an old biscuit tin I recognized from childhood.

'Still teaching two classes a week?'

'They're always pestering me to do more, but I can't face it. If I did three I'd barely get any time to paint myself. I've got several new portrait commissions lined up. And there's quite a lot of admin with teaching, fixing term dates, sorting out the money, making sure everybody's happy.'

'Advertising?'

Mum shook her head. 'I never advertise, I've always got a waiting list. I do a little flyer for the summer landscape course, that's all.'

In June each year, Mum ran a one-week course on the South Downs. She would meet her students each morning at an agreed spot, usually in West Dean village, where there were interesting downland views. The leaflet for this year's course was pinned to the back of the studio door. While she moved the portrait of Celia onto an easel in the middle of the room, I read the list of things to bring:

> 'Easel if you have one.
> Camp-stool or chair
> Painting materials, including water for acrylic
>   and water-colour painters
> Boards and clips if you need them
> A hat or cap with a brim, essential for outdoor work
> Wellies or good shoes – the grass can be damp.
> A thermos of elevenses.'

'Right, darling, Celia's ready for you. I've turned her sideways, so you get the best light.' She made for the door. 'Take your time. I'm going to make us a picnic.'

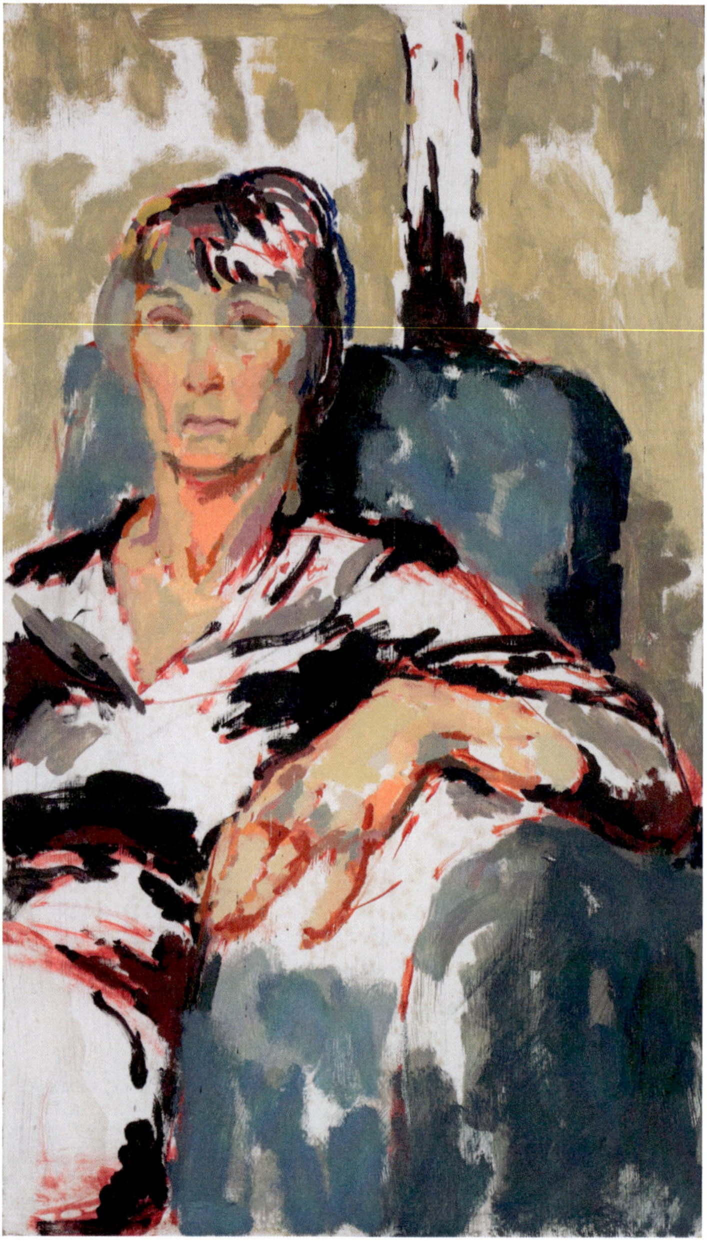

Unfinished Self-portrait, 1992

I stepped into the middle of the room and stood for several minutes in front of the portrait. It was a convincing likeness of the person I'd met, and Mum had captured the slightly ethereal quality of a woman making the transition from full physical and mental vigour towards old age; but I wasn't sure I liked it. Using her palette knives, Mum had got Celia's snow white hair rolling and crinkling around the sides of her head, and in places the sea green wall showed through, hinting that the hair was growing thin and whispy. The skin was loose and pink around the watery blue eyes, in which I read the distant, reserved gaze of a woman who didn't really like being looked at. Possibly that was exactly the expression Mum had seen on Celia's face; but the result was that I felt shut out.

My eyes dropped to the mouth, which was wide, generous and loose, as were the folds of flesh around the chin. Almost shockingly wide and loose, compared to the tight, closed look in the eyes. I tried covering the top part of the face with my hand, suspecting that the mouth and chin, seen alone, suggested a man. But I was wrong. It was a fine bit of work, I concluded; I simply didn't like it.

I turned away, intending to return to the house, until I caught sight of a self portrait I hadn't seen before. It was on Mum's heavy wooden easel, in a corner of the room where the light was less bright. I hesitated for a moment, wondering if she was ready for this painting to be looked at. But curiosity got the better of me and I went and stood in front of it.

I was immediately gripped. This was a work entirely out of character and it had a special force. Working with brushes on a narrow strip of primed hardboard – a leftover, most likely – Mum had flung down the paint at speed. It was a beginning at most, the work of no more than a single sitting. Areas of white primer remained untouched; but the painting was all the more alive for that. Mum lounged in a grey-blue high-backed armchair, her left hand extended on the arm-rest. The fresh and vigorous brushwork gave the impression of a woman who, a few seconds earlier, had flung herself into the chair in disgust, or exhaustion.

She gazed directly at the viewer – herself – with a cool, serious look in her eyes. The upper eyelids were pink, as if she'd been crying; but the overall demeanour was calm and steady, that of an older woman coming to terms with the pack of cards life had dealt her. The planes of the cheekbones and cheeks were conveyed with colour changes from ochre to brownish pink and the undulating line of the firmly closed mouth conveyed a mood of resignation. The dark line of the chin and jaw perfectly evoked Mum's remarkable beauty, above her long slim neck. She wore a black and crimson blouse which I recognized, open at her sun-tanned throat and stretched tightly over her shoulders, breasts and belly. In the bottom corner of the painting, her left thigh rose at an angle, suggesting her feet were propped on a chair in front of her.

'Bravo, Mum!' I said out loud. My spine tingled as I studied the painting for several more minutes. Then I closed the studio door behind me and crossed the yard to the house, where Mum was standing at the kitchen window, filling a flask with tea. We were going up on the Downs for a walk.

Chapter 30
A Sudden Journey South

THE PHONE WAS RINGING when I arrived home from work. It was Mum, and I could tell from her voice that something was up.

'I've had a call from Ivy, in South Africa.' She paused. 'About Bay.' Another pause.

'What is it?'

'He's got lung cancer.' Bay wasn't in hospital, because they'd caught the cancer far too late for anything to be done: he had only weeks to live. Mum wanted to see him one last time, and was about to book a flight.

'*You're going to South Africa*?' My head began to spin. 'What, *now*, before Christmas?' It was mid-December. Mum had broken her hip earlier in the year and was walking with a stick; I didn't like the idea of her taking a long-haul flight, all alone. She was almost seventy nine and seeing Bay was going to be painful.

'Can't you wait twenty four hours?' I pleaded. 'Perhaps I could come with you. I'll talk to work.'

Mum sounded surprised. 'You don't need to come with me, darling. You might not find it easy staying with Bay and Ivy'.

'Why?'

She cleared her throat. 'When I was with them in 1987, I was quite shocked by the way they live. The house is just a single storey, very dark and gloomy on the inside. They can't afford anything better: they don't even have medical insurance.'

'Isn't that essential?'

'Well, yes, you'd think so, but they don't have it. Bay says it's too expensive. He's only got a handful of cows now; he gave up the pigs some years ago.'

We boarded the plane to Durban on Boxing Day evening. Mum's newly-pinned hip bothered her in the night and I dragged myself from dreams to shuffle with her up and down the gangway. When we returned to our seats, she described the countryside around Bay's place.

'Rolling, green, with red, red earth; when I was there before it reminded me of Normandy. I went for a walk almost every day.'

'Was it safe?'

'Absolutely. The footpaths were alive with farm workers from the neighbouring farms and they'd stop and salute me in Zulu.'

'You understood?'

'Well enough. I always saluted back, and they repeated the words for me until I got them. It's a difficult language, all clicking sounds. But the Zulus are lovely, friendly people. We must definitely do some walking while we're there!'

I said nothing. I liked Mum's spirit, but I wasn't sure about the walking. In eleven years, South Africa had changed. Apartheid was over, the ANC were in power and Mandela was president. That was all to the good; but violence against white farmers was now a daily reality and we'd be white visitors on a white-owned farm.

Trevor met us at the airport. A short and smiley man in his forties, he was newly married to my cousin Jill, whom I'd last seen in Chichester twenty five years earlier. As we sped inland on a fast highway, he related car-hijacking stories. 'My company loses five vehicles a day, nationwide. Think how many vehicles they're losing in a year!' He sat hunched over the dashboard in white shirt-sleeves, shoulders almost touching his ears, with Sheila beside him.

'Colleague of mine had a lucky escape last week,' Trevor went on. 'Often they shoot the driver, this time they gave him a lift into town! The thing to do, if you should ever find yourself in that situation,' – Trevor shot me an insistent glance in the rear-view mirror – 'if you hire a car, is to co-operate *immediately*, and whatever you do, don't look at them. You keep your eyes on the ground, move very slowly and explain exactly what you're doing. These guys are jumpy as hell, one false move and they'll press the trigger.' He glanced at me again and I resolved, privately, that no way would we hire a car. 'Nice country we live in, eh-eh?' I smiled, wishing he would change the subject.

It was early afternoon when we left the highway behind. Out in the country, the sky was pale blue, the air warm and sticky. Trevor took a small road which meandered through luxuriant green meadows. Trees sheltered small farms; red-roofed bungalows stood in twos and threes.

'Almost there now,' he told us. I rested my hand on Mum's shoulder as the car turned in through an open gate-way, on which a hand-painted sign announced 'Longonot Farm'. We bumped down a grassy track lined by poplars and pulled up beside a single storey house.

A woman in shorts and a Tee shirt was walking towards us across the grass.

'Hi Sheila!' she called as we got out of the car. 'Hi, T!'

Jill stepped into Sheila's open arms and buried her face in her shoulder. 'So glad you could come!' Her voice came out half choked. She'd grown more full-figured with the passage of the years, whereas Mum had shrunk and her bones protruded through her pretty cotton clothes. I fancied her legs were swaying with fatigue. Under a fresh layer of powder her face was pale and the skin beneath her eyes had turned translucent.

'Hi T!' Jill released Mum and turned to me. Her dark hair was cut in a neat line at the nape of her neck and her cheeks were covered in freckles. 'So good to see you both. My, it's been a long time, eh-eh?' I stepped forward and hugged her, aware now of the heat of the sun on the top of my head.

Jill glanced from me to Mum. 'It'll be a bit of a shock when you see Dad,' she told us in a soft voice.

A wide timber verandah stretched the length of the house. Crammed with old chairs, milking pails and plastic buckets, it looked onto a bed of pink and yellow roses. The freshly-turned soil was a rich, red-brown, a colour almost matched by the painted wooden boards. The house itself lay long and low, built of breeze blocks with metal windows and a roof of corrugated iron. As we stepped onto the boards, a pack of dogs trotted towards us. Jill stooped to pet a border collie, which stood with its muzzle in the air, snapping at flies. A much smaller dog with a short, ginger coat sniffed around Mum's heels, its ears folded back against its head. Mum wasn't keen on dogs. I watched her face, hoping she hadn't noticed the Alsatian lolling in the shade a few feet away.

'You'll get used to them, Sheila,' Jill told her. 'We have to have them, for security.'

Inside the house, the air was cool and the light was dim, making a pleasant change from the brightness of the afternoon. In the large living room, a floor of polished quarry tiles shone through the gloom. Heavy wooden dressers lined the walls and the smell of polish mingled with the smell of dog food.

Jill led us to an open doorway. In the lighter space beyond, we saw an old wooden bed on which a threadbare blanket was draped over a pair of raised, shockingly thin knees. I nodded to Mum and Jill to go in ahead of me and turned to face the wall, where a painted leopard in a dull green savannah stared at me from a dark brown frame. Through the doorway I could hear the rasping sound of my uncle weeping. Slowly I turned my head. Jill was bending over the bed, trying to soothe him. Then he arched his back and pressed a cloth hanky to his eyes. As I caught sight of his face, my eyes filled with tears. He'd been thin the last time I saw him, but now he was skeletal.

When I entered the room a few minutes later, Mum was standing by the bed, holding Bay's hand. Colour had returned to her cheeks, together with a calm which astonished me. She stepped back for me to greet him and then she knelt on the carpet and took his hand again. Bay's head had become so thin it looked as if someone had pressed the two sides of it together with a pair of plates. His high forehead was all bone, his nose just a line, a twig, and the area around his mouth had sunk. His lips were pale and dry.

I pushed a stool towards Mum, to get her off her knees.

'Thankyou, T, ' she whispered, easing herself onto the faded velvet cushion. My gaze wandered from Bay's face to the folds of crumpled skin on his slender neck. The top button of his rumpled brown pyjama top lay open. He had my grandmother's narrow, sloping shoulders, and they seemed to have grown narrower with illness. My eyes lingered on his sun-weathered forearms, resting almost life-less on the sheet. They were two or three inches wide at the wrist and not much bigger at the elbow, the whole length of each one covered in a dense fuzz of white hair – the result, I thought, of long years working under a hot sun. The joints of the hands were knotted and bony and his fingers were long and tapered. But the thing which drew my eye the most was the point where Mum's arm and hand met Bay's: for her forearms, too, were long and thin, her skin a mottled brown. Her thumb joint was knotted, just like Bay's and her fingers were as slender and elegant as his.

A blue bottle landed on Bay's throat.

'The fly-swatter,' he whispered, and his watery blue eyes flitted from my face to a worn square of rubber attached to a piece of wire, lying on the blanket beside him. 'You be fly-swatter-in-chief,' he commanded, with a trace of his old humour. After nearly fifty years in Africa, he still spoke with an English public school accent.

Holding the flyswatter, I stood over the bed. The bedroom stretched the width of the house, with windows to front and back and a door onto the verandah. A series of faded, flower-pattern rugs covered the floor, between Bay's bed and the one opposite, which must be Ivy's. A drubbing sound drew my eye to the far corner of the room, where a fluffy white dog was eating from a bowl on the floor.

We'd been with Bay no more than fifteen minutes when a small figure walked in. I guessed this was Ivy from her age alone, for nothing about her accorded with my memory of the shapely woman in a green and white spotted dress whom I'd met as a child in London in the 1960s. Thick grey hair fell to her shoulders, framing a darkly weather-beaten face, with a prominent forehead, eyebrows and chin. Her face was as narrow as Bay's but much stronger: nothing was pressing in on it. A cloth hat of faded khaki perched on the back of her head, as organic a part of her as the cigarette which smouldered in the corner of her mouth. A frown puckered her forehead. When she spoke, her voice was thick and gruff.

'Tri-vor come to git you at the airport?' Ivy's pitch went up at the end of the sentence. Her bright green eyes moved from me to Sheila and back again. They seemed to hold a mixture of fear and shyness, and I felt sorry that we were both so tall.

I smiled. 'So kind of him. We found him without any trouble.'

'Goo-od,' Ivy replied, 'That's goo-od. She-i-la, will you have a cup of tea?' She gave full value to all the vowels in Mum's name and pronounced 'tea' like 'ti'.

*

For the next ten days, Mum and I slept in a little room beside the kitchen with two single beds, a chest of drawers and a strip of green carpet in the middle of the concrete floor. We were kept awake by the search lights which burned on the verandah, beaming a light bright enough to read by through the flimsy cotton curtains. Trevor had told me how common it was for white-owned farms to be attacked by angry, machine gun-wielding 'criminals' and some time after midnight each night I was woken by the soft pattering of feet on the wooden boards outside the window and an intermittent, throaty growl. I lay in terror with the sheet over my face, waiting for a gun to be thrust in at the open window.

Gradually the pattering became louder and faster, convincing me that all six farm dogs were racing up and down the verandah together, as an invisible enemy closed in on the house.

Mum spent her days in the living room, waiting for the opportunity to be alone with Bay. This was difficult to achieve, with relatives and well-wishers arriving every hour. They greeted Sheila with delight as the oldest surviving member of Bay's English family. Then they settled on chairs around his bed, chatting loudly while he tried to sleep. Sheila felt what Bay needed was peace and quiet, but she kept her views to herself.

Late each afternoon, Jill drove up from Pietermaritsburg to spend the night caring for her father, which she did with devotion and tenderness.

The doctor visited regularly, despite Bay's lack of insurance. He told Mum that it was too late for medical intervention to waylay the cancer and, to my surprise, she accepted it. If there was nothing to be done to prolong her brother's life, she told me one afternoon as we strolled round the garden, then the main purpose of her presence was to ease his passage towards death. Bay might have things he needed to say before he died.

Major, the border collie, was ambling behind us and Jill appeared in the doorway of a cowshed. I called out that Sheila and I were going for a walk.

'Major will make sure you don't get lost!' she replied. 'Don't go beyond the gates, mind, it's not safe.'

'Hmm,' Mum muttered as I slipped my arm through hers. 'I walked into Merrivale and back when I was here before.' We stopped to admire the flower bed outside the window of Bay's room, where pink roses bloomed beside an African lily with yellow petals and purple leaves. 'Ivy's quite a gardener, isn't she?' Mum remarked. 'Puts a lot of care into her flower beds.'

We sauntered to the line of poplars which marked the boundary. The sky was a hazy blue, the air warm with a slight breeze.

Mum turned her face to the sun and closed her eyes as her mauve blouse and blue trousers billowed around her thin frame.

A moment later she struck off up the track that led to the road. 'Come on, T,' she said, 'let's step out a bit.' I let go of her arm and quickened my pace. In half a minute we were heading for the farm gate and the road came into sight.

'Mum,' I said, 'I don't think we should go far.'

'Let's just go a little way up the lane opposite. Last time I was here, I walked there with Jill almost every day.'

'A couple of hundred yards, no more.'

We crossed the road and set off up a dirt track lined by eucalyptus trees. Here the soil was dry and orange. Behind us, a car swept slowly round a bend.

'You don't see people on foot like you used to,' Mum mused.

'Because it's dangerous.'

'I suppose so. Such a shame.'

The long, slender leaves of the eucalyptus trees twisted on their stems, flashing yellow, red and green. Soon our sandalled feet were coated in orange dust.

'Did you get any time alone with Bay, this morning?' I asked.

'I sat with him for an hour.'

'Did he talk?'

'A little. I held his hand. I told him I was ready to listen. We sat there for a bit and then he looked at me and said "Nothing to be done". He kept repeating it. "Nothing to be done".'

'Was he upset?'

'There were tears in his eyes. He didn't say more than that, but I could tell from the way he looked at me that he's glad we're here.'

'Glad *you*'re here,' I corrected her.

'No, darling, I think he feels your presence, too. The day before yesterday, when you brought in his water, he looked at both of us very hard. He looked at you and then he looked at me and then, when you'd gone, he whispered, "Sheila and Teresa".'

I squeezed Mum's arm.

'We've brought him a little bit of England,' she went on. 'Our being here is the next best thing to him being there.'

*

New Year's Eve came and went.

We were due to fly home on 6 January. The day before, after some soul searching, Mum told Bay that we would soon be leaving, and would have to say goodbye.

I slept fitfully the night before our flight. At twelve thirty I woke and lay still, listening for sounds. But I heard nothing, either from Bay's room or from the verandah. Mum's breathing was deep and regular and even the cockerels were silent.

I fell back into a deep sleep. The next time I woke, some hours later, Jill was standing in the doorway of our room.

'Sheila,' I heard her say, in a voice tinged with sweetness, 'Dad has died.' I watched Mum sit up in bed in her sleeveless cotton nightie. She rested her forehead in one hand and pushed her fringe from side to side with the other. After a few seconds I forced myself up, crossed the room, sat down behind her and wrapped my arms around her shoulders.

'It's allright, T,' she whispered, 'I was awake already.' She took my hand.

We sat in the semi-darkness without speaking, while Jill perched at the foot of the bed.

'How did he go?' Mum asked at last.

'Very peacefully, Sheila. He was coughing for a little while.'

'I heard him.'

'And then he settled down. Ivy got up, we were both sitting with him. About ten to three he started to shake, it went on for about a minute, and then he passed away.' Now that my eyes were adjusting to the half light, I saw that Jill had been crying.

'How's Ivy?' I asked her.

'Very strong.' Jill braced her arm and made a fist, meaning that

Ivy was holding back her emotions for all she was worth.

At last Mum switched on her torch and looked at her watch. It was three fifteen. 'Can we see him, Jill?'

'Of course, Sheila. Come.'

Mum threw a cardigan round her shoulders and we set off through the dark living room. The lights had gone out on the verandah and the night sky was black. When we got to Bay's doorway, we saw that someone had already covered his face with a blanket. I followed Mum into the room, grateful that she knew what to do. She went to the head of the bed and peeled the blanket back.

Only in paintings have I seen an expression of such utter exhaustion. Bay had tipped back his head, opened his mouth and gasped out the last of his life. His upper teeth were visible, very neat and small. The cheekbones were more prominent than ever, the cheeks sunken. His skin had no colour at all.

Mum gazed at her brother for several minutes. Then she stooped down and kissed his forehead.

Chapter 31
On the Lizard, Cornwall

HUNDREDS OF FEET BELOW the cliff-top garden of our borrowed bungalow, breakers laced with white spray rolled in towards the rocks. Leaving Isaac, my two-year-old, in the car to entertain his granny, I carried our bags down the sloping lawn to the back door in a frisky wind and blinding sun. As I ducked under a line of yellow cleaning rags which billowed from the washing line like miniature sails, my heart filled with delight. A three-week holiday stretched in front of us, with Tim, Isaac's dad, arriving at the weekend. Mum was exhausted from a recent house move, this time to Bradford on Avon in Wiltshire, but we were all in high spirits.

When I retraced my steps to the car, Isaac was standing on the driver's seat gripping the steering wheel for all he was worth with his pudgy little fists, while Mum provided sound effects by twisting her mouth from side to side and making screeching noises. She was shaping up as a first rate granny and Isaac loved the attention she gave him. The eighty year age gap seemed not to matter.

We ate lunch in the bright, familiar kitchen, with its old pine table and driftwood ornaments. Tired though she was, Mum listened intently to everything Isaac said and accepted the morsels of fish finger he passed her in his fingers when I wasn't looking. When I spotted the tell tale breadcrumbs on her plate and protested, she delivered one of her inimical winks. That shut me up.

After we'd finished, I helped make up her bed and left her to rest. Managing the house move by herself had used up all her strength.

Isaac and I spent the afternoon on the shingle beach below the bungalow, collecting pieces of red and yellow plastic eroded by the motion of the sea. Then we visited the old coastguard station and the gift shop on the point, with its wooden models of sail boats and light houses, before climbing back up the lane to play in the garden.

Mum slept for much of the next two days, getting up only for meals. But midway through the third morning, she emerged from her bed and walked into the kitchen in her nightie, announcing she'd recovered. I was baking a banana loaf, while Isaac opened drawers and spread items of interest over the kitchen floor.

'If you're feeling better,' I said, 'let's go out for a walk. I'll pack up some tea.'

We took the car up to the village and set off on the footpath that led across the heath to Kynance Cove. Neither Mum nor Isaac could walk very far or very fast and in an hour we were back on the fringes of the village, searching for a spot to sit and rest. Mum found a patch of short grass in the shelter of a lichen-speckled dry stone wall. I kneeled a few feet away, extracting slices of warm cake wrapped in foil from my knapsack and pouring the tea. It had rained briefly while we were walking and Isaac was squatting in a puddle in his wellies, peering at a beetle with an irridescent shell.

Mum raised her eyebrows as she took her slab of cake. 'Smells delicious! And still warm… what a treat!' She lifted her plastic cup as if to drink my health. Behind her, the orange petals of a wild montbretia trembled in the breeze.

'It does smell good, doesn't it,' I replied. I'd taken cake-making more seriously since becoming a mum, and was pleased with the appearance of this loaf : golden brown, well risen in the middle and only very slightly burnt at the edges.

I zipped up the knapsack and settled on the grass. Mum put down her cup and gazed intently at Isaac, who'd lifted the beetle out of the puddle and was watching it walk, unsteadily, across his hand and onto the back of his wrist. I opened my mouth to speak, but Mum drew her index finger to her lips, raised her eyebrows and nodded in his direction.

After a few moments she picked up her cup and took a swig. 'Sorry, love. You were about to say something?'

By now I had a mouthful of cake. 'Nothing important'.

She returned her gaze to Isaac and murmured, more to herself than me, 'That child's a marvel! The look of concentration on his face!'

Isaac was standing remarkably still, unperturbed by the sensation of tiny feet advancing across his soft white skin. I wondered what the beetle would do when it reached the elasticated cuff of his waterproof. Would it climb onto the slippery fabric and continue towards his shoulder? I was about to get up and interfere when suddenly it sprouted wings and flew towards a clump of blond seed grass several feet away.

'Oh no!' I exclaimed, but again Sheila put her finger to her lips, as Isaac trotted after the beetle.

'He's having the whale of a time,' she whispered. 'Leave him to it. If he can't find the beetle, there'll be something else to catch his attention in a minute. This place is paradise for a child of his age.' She broke off a chunk of cake and popped it in her mouth.

To me, this bit of the Lizard, in summer, was paradise full stop. And to be here with the two people I loved most in the world, was perfection. I glanced at Isaac, now on his knees with his back to us.

'Looks like he's found it!' I took another swig of tea and raised my gaze to the horizon. It was partly the vivid natural colours that thrilled me. From where we were sitting, on the grassy verge of a farm lane, we looked out through the weathered bars of a wooden gate into a field. Here a herd of black and russet-coloured cows, heads down, were moving slowly, in unison, across the flank of a hill. In the bright, dancing light to which the shower had given way, the grass they grazed was a sharp viridian. And behind their angular rumps, the sea rose up on end like a theatre set, a cool, beautiful blue.

I reached for the flask and unscrewed the lid. 'More tea?'

'Thank you.' Mum held out her cup, smiling at me. 'I feel so lucky!'

'So do I. We *are* very lucky, aren't we?'

I knew she appreciated the beauty of the Lizard as much as I did, but I also knew that the main cause of her joy was Isaac. His arrival in our lives had been something of a miracle. I'd wanted a child since I was in my twenties, but it had taken me till I was 42 to manage it. Mum had never told me she was hankering for a grandchild; but once he'd arrived she hadn't tried to conceal her delight.

I gazed at her, sitting with her shoulders propped against the wall in her dark green Goretex jacket. The usual silk scarf was tied around her head, in a futile attempt to prevent the wind messing with her hair. The two days in bed had done her good, leaving her skin soft and supple and warm colour in her cheeks. Whoever would believe she was eighty two?

Having abandoned the hunt for the beetle, Isaac was splashing in the puddle. I thought Mum was watching him, but her thoughts were elsewhere.

'When I'm with you two,' she announced, 'I feel I have a family again!'

I was taken aback. 'Don't you feel that the rest of the time?' My sister didn't have children, but she and Mum saw a lot of each other. I knew Mum was lonely at times; but it hadn't occurred to me that she felt a lack of family.

Slightly uncomfortable, she pursed her lips. 'Not really, if I'm honest.'

'Oh, Mum!' I got up and squatted down beside her, throwing my arms around her shoulders and nestling my head into her neck. 'I don't want you to feel like that...'

She reached up a bony hand, took hold of a tuft of my hair and tugged at it gently. 'There's something special about being three generations, like this, don't you think?'

*

Sheila came with us three times to the Lizard, on three successive summers. We were very happy to have her join us. Tim enjoyed her company as much as I did, and he and I got on better as a couple when she was present. Sheila's love for Isaac was plain to see: she would sit at the kitchen table and chat with him about everything under the sun, while we cooked or took showers or packed up picnics. She couldn't walk long distances, but if we drove her to a beach she was happy to sit on the sand, observing the waves, watching Isaac play, collecting shells and eating home made scones with us when we came out of the sea.

In 2004, our last summer in Cornwall, Isaac was four and seemed to grasp that his beloved Granny Sheila was 'full of oldness', as he put it. One afternoon at Kennack Sands he went for a long walk up the beach with Tim to buy an ice cream, while I was in the water. When they returned and got close to Sheila, Isaac saw that she was struggling to get to her feet. He ran towards her and threw himself down on the sand beside her. 'Granny Sheila,' he said, his mouth close to her ear, 'If you ever need me, just call me and I'll help you'. She told me about it that evening, with tears in her eyes. Sheila wasn't good at letting people help her, but Isaac had cut right through her defences.

One day I walked with Dan to Kynance Cove, leaving Tim to drive Sheila over when she woke from her afternoon nap. He brought her down the cinder track to the beach on his arm, and when they arrived he must have popped into the public toilets. I looked up from exploring a rock pool with Isaac and there she was, twenty yards away, in her pale linen trousers and white anorak, standing alone, very tall, on the stone bridge over the stream. She hadn't spotted us yet and was gazing out over the beach, swaying slightly, as if she found the crowd of bathers and the rough terrain a little overwhelming. My heart somersaulted in my chest, for the sight of her standing there, dressed in white, so out of place, was like a premonition of her death. It was as if she'd already left us, and this was her ghost. I grabbed Isaac by the hand and scrambled up the beach towards her.

*

Sheila made her new home in Bradford on Avon as pleasant as she'd made the house in Chichester. It had a large, very light 'through lounge' which looked onto the street at the front and the garden at the back. She had the walls painted in restful tertiary colours and arranged her two white sofas to face each other across the coffee table, which, as in Chichester, was always laden with a stack of books and newspapers. The sofas were old and Sheila allowed Isaac to jump from the one in the window to the one in the middle of the room, where he would land on a heap of coloured cushions, giggling in triumph. When I visited alone, I would lie on the sofa under the window with a cushion beneath my head and we'd drink tea and talk and talk.

Much of our conversation centred on Isaac, for Sheila was interested in the minutiae of his development. She loved to hear what he was talking about at bed time – his favourite hour for deep conversation – and what he was designing in the spiral-bound drawing books he kept by his bed. Isaac was a natural inventor and produced detailed drawings of his schemes, which included a packaging machine for cat biscuits, an irrigation system for watering Granny Sheila's garden and numerous adventure playgrounds with water features.

By now Alan had left London for Gloucestershire and was living with the partner he'd met in 1990. From time to time my parents met up at an old hotel, equidistant from their two homes. They'd have lunch and sit in the lounge for a couple of hours, discussing life and art and anything else that was on their minds. Both still drove in their mid-eighties.

By her late eighties, Sheila was struggling with her domestic tasks. Veronica had bought her a dishwasher, but Sheila disliked 'gadgets' and left it to idle under a kitchen counter. I'd arrive to find several days' worth of dirty dishes sitting beside the sink and when I opened the ancient fridge, there was very little food on its rusting 1960s shelves. Sheila was resistant to the idea of help, but in 2008 she reluctantly agreed that I could advertise for a local person to work for her a couple of times a week. A few days after pinning up an ad in the local post office, I received a phone call from a woman whose warm, slightly musical accent was oddly familiar.

'My name's Rachel,' she said slowly. 'I saw your ad for a cook and cleaner.'

It was Rachel Williams, whom I'd met in a creative writing group in Bath in 1999. The last time I'd seen her, she'd been expecting her third baby and working on a macabre fairy story about a wicked witch called 'Bacteria' and a kind, sister witch called 'Sterilia'. Since then Rachel's marriage had ended and she now lived with her children, five minutes' walk from Sheila. She thought she could provide the support Sheila needed.

The arrival of Rachel in Sheila's life was probably the best thing that happened to her in her latter years. Rachel was a painter and a strong, intelligent woman. She'd trained at Central St Martins in the early 1980s and worked in oils and watercolour. Her father and grandfather, both artists, had been from a social background not dissimilar to Sheila's. After the shock of her divorce, Rachel had stopped painting for a while; but by now she was working again, in a studio at the bottom of her garden.

'When I met your mother for the first time,' Rachel told me when we met up some years after Sheila's death, 'I felt as if I already knew her. It was a soul meeting. I saw Sheila's lovely intelligence and I thought to myself "I know you, I get you". I understood that she was elderly and frail, but her mind was sharp.'

Sheila was eighty eight when Rachel came to her aid. Initially Rachel worked two or three hours a week, dividing the time between cleaning, shopping and cooking. Rachel was competent at all these tasks but her real *forte* was good food. Soon she was making delicious pies and bakes, which she delivered to Sheila, on foot, in a wicker basket.

'It took her a while to get the hang of having a cook,' Rachel went on. 'She had a strange relationship with food: she liked to be sure she wouldn't run out, and the ingredients *had* to be organic; but her fridge habits were war-time.'

'The fridge was usually empty?'

'Well, not quite empty, but she wouldn't waste *anything*. She'd insist on eating up the last morsels before I could cook her something new. And I mustn't bring too much at once, or she'd feel overwhelmed and worry that she wouldn't be able to eat it all.'

Sheila had shown a similar reluctance to have supplies of dried and tinned food in her cupboards. Anna and I had tried to build up her reserves, but she'd put up vigorous resistance. We'd wondered if she had a form of anorexia, but Rachel disagreed.

'No, no, Sheila liked to eat. I cooked her chicken pies and green veg soup, which she liked very much, and she got me to buy her ready-made fish pies from Sainsbury's. She wasn't anorexic, but she *was* a bit of a Spartan, was Sheila. And, of course, she was a *very* slow eater.'

Rachel worked for Sheila for seven years, right up to the last days of her life. When I visited, Sheila often told me how much she enjoyed Rachel's company. 'That woman's a scream!' she would say, 'so funny.' And sometimes, when we were sitting on the sofas, drinking tea and eating chocolate biscuits, Rachel would let herself in the back door with the wicker basket, its contents draped in a tea towel. She'd call out a friendly 'Hello!', go to the fridge and unload two or three dishes in foil baking trays, each with a cardboard lid carefully marked with the contents and the date. Then she'd leave a little note on the kitchen table and tiptoe out. But on occasions when I wasn't there, Sheila said, Rachel would come into the living room and let off steam about her family life.

There were also conversations about painting. Rachel brought work for Sheila to look at; and she studied the portraits on Sheila's walls, fascinated by the way she'd used her palette knife.

'I'd not seen much like it,' Rachel told me. 'Sheila would put on small ticks of paint with the knife, over-layering, gradually building it up. She was so good at modeling the face, wasn't she? She got the right colour and the right tone.'

To me it seemed ironic that Rachel held this view of Sheila's skills, given the way she'd been criticized at Camberwell. But Rachel was right: in most of her portraits, Sheila showed an absolute mastery of tone.

'D'you remember *Thoughts are Things*?' Rachel went on.

I did, of course. Written in the late nineteenth century by an American journalist named Prentice Mulford, it was a slender volume of spiritual wisdom to which Sheila had attached immense value. I'd never read it, but Sheila had often explained to me the central thesis, namely that we must take control of our thoughts, because they determine our reality. If we think negative thoughts, our lives will be full of negativity; whereas, if we think happy, positive thoughts, our lives will go well and we'll flourish. She used to talk about the book if she thought I was feeling low.

'Sheila swore by *Thoughts are Things*,' Rachel went on. 'She used to say "I've been reading it all these years, because it's *true!* It's so important to take responsibility for what we say and think".' She sighed. 'Sheila had times when she was very upbeat and philosophical, in our conversations. And her love of poetry! Once she gave me a poem about horses by Apollinaire and asked me what I got from it. She was a deep thinker, your mum.'

I pictured Sheila and Rachel sitting together in the living room, reading and re-reading the poem. I felt a twinge of envy, for I regretted not having spent more time with Mum during her last years. I'd been a lone parent by then, struggling to cope with a difficult job and the needs of my son and feeling helpless in the face of Sheila's increasing frailty. But I understood, now, that

Sheila's friendship with Rachel had been blessed by a special quality of freshness and simplicity *precisely because* Rachel wasn't her daughter. The practical transactions between them had centred around chicken pies and bags of shopping from Sainsburys; beyond that, they simply liked and understood each other.

'You were so good to her, Rachel. She'd have been terribly lonely during those years without you popping in and out.'

Rachel looked at me as if unsure what to say. 'I know.' She took a breath. 'One day, she told me that I was her best friend in Bradford on Avon.'

I winced. It still bothered me that Sheila had felt so isolated in Bradford. She'd moved there with the intention of being roughly mid-way between me in Bristol and Anna in Oxford, but neither of us had been close enough to provide the company she needed.

I changed the subject. 'Did Sheila ever speak about Joe?'

Rachel fixed her eyes on me. 'She did, from time to time; but not in detail.' She dropped her voice. 'I saw him, you know, in the house.'

'You *what*?' Rachel had often told me she was psychic, but I'd never understood what she meant.

'I saw him, in the house,' she repeated calmly. 'I told Sheila I thought I'd seen a figure in the hallway and described him to her: a tall, slim man in a suit. To which she replied, "Oh, I think I know who that is!"'

'Did Sheila see him, too?'

'No. And when I saw him the second time, I didn't mention it to her.'

Chapter 32
The Irish Nurse

Sail for the shore the tall white ships of summer
Folded now the blue bays and the ecstatic islands
Opening now the red rough trawlers of autumn
And the grey seabirds riding the roaring sea.
SD, 2002

ON SATURDAY 7 MARCH 2015, Rachel and I were sitting side by side on a sofa in the lobby of a nursing home in Gloucestershire. Sheila was upstairs, asleep in her room. We were chatting quietly, whiling away the time till Sheila woke up. She'd been admitted to the home the previous Saturday following an infection and a bout of bronchitis. I was spending as much time with her as I could and today I intended to remain until it was time to collect Isaac from the station. He was in Bristol with his schoolmates, celebrating his fifteenth birthday.

We were still chatting when a nurse I'd not seen before came up and took me aside. She was small and thin, aged about sixty and I took an instant liking to her careworn face. 'Your mum's breathing has changed,' she said in a soft Irish accent. 'I'd like you to come upstairs.'

'Is she going?' I whispered. Sheila was very weak and very frail, but no longer ill. I'd been entertaining thoughts of bringing her home to stay with me and Isaac, once she was strong enough to travel.

The nurse looked me in the eye. 'I think she might be.'

I turned back to Rachel and told her what the nurse had said. As I spoke I took out my phone and tried calling my sister, but there was no reply. Then I asked Rachel to come upstairs with me.

When we entered the warm, thickly carpeted room, Sheila was lying very still in the centre of the bed, her long, slim body pushing up the covers like a jagged mountain range. Her eyes were open but as I approached her pillow, I had the uneasy feeling that she wasn't aware of my presence. Rachel stood close beside me and the nurse took up position on the far side of the bed. 'How're you doing now, Shei-la?' she asked in her Dublin accent. 'I've brought these lovely women to see you. Your daughter,' – she nodded at me – 'and your good friend, Shei-la.'

There was no response. Sheila stared straight ahead of her, eye-lids lowered, her breathing slower and noisier than when I'd seen her an hour earlier. Rachel and I stood motionless, our eyes fixed on Sheila's face. When at last I glanced sideways, tears were trickling down Rachel's cheeks. Then a very strange thing happened. As if experiencing a sudden wave of energy, Sheila turned her head away from me and Rachel and fixed her gaze on the ceiling, at the point where it met the corner of the room. An expression close to rapture spread across her pale face.

'What is it, Sheila?' the nurse asked gently. 'You're seeing something up there, Sheila, aren't you?' She glanced at me and Rachel. 'Something beautiful, you're seeing.' We all three stood very still, our eyes switching from the animated look on Sheila's face to the spot on the ceiling and back again. Then I heard a sudden whooshing sound, like that of a big bird taking flight, and she was gone.

Epilogue

Alan died in March 2020, in his own bed at Ivy Cottage. In the five years that have elapsed since then, I've missed him much more than I expected to. In the first couple of years, while my sister and her partner obtained probate and found homes for his sculptures, I felt increasingly sad about how little time Dad and I had spent together, over the years. I dwelled on the memory of a couple of summer evenings in 1995 when we went out landscape painting together, in the fields near Avening. Why hadn't we done that more? I asked myself. Fraught though our relationship often was, we had a great deal in common: a shared passion for landscape, a love of painting, walking, travel; a talent for learning new languages. But I knew only too well what had kept us apart: bad feelings about the past and frequent rows. If I had a pound for every angry letter I'd written to Dad over the years, and another pound for every angry letter I'd received from him, I would be a wealthy woman.

Time is a healer, and so is loss. Today the walls of my house display many of Dad's landscapes as well as the exquisite portrait he made of Mum that day in 1983 when they met to paint each other. Two of Dad's portrait sculptures adorn the mantelpiece in my work room. A coiled clay lamp he made at Hawkley sits on one of my filing cabinets and a photo of him in his wartime officer's uniform perches on the plan chest. He's smiling, handsome, frighteningly young. And when I'm feeling tired or jaded, I remind myself of a conversation we had only two weeks before he died. One of the carers had advised me to raise with Dad the subject of his death, and to reassure him that we, his children, would be okay without him. So I did, over a cup of tea. 'We'll miss you, Dad,' I told him, 'but we'll be okay.' He was propped up on pillows and he looked at me, a little surprised, mumbling that it was good to talk about death. I sat holding my tea, ready to listen, but he said nothing more. Then, after a few minutes, he turned his big brown eyes on me and said, half in a whisper but with real force, 'You must keep going, keep going!'

As for Sheila, I miss her too, but I have the comfort of knowing that we shared a great deal and spoke about most of the things that mattered. In the ten years since her passing, Isaac has finished school, been to university, climbed a lot of rock and started his first serious job. I've packed in being a lawyer, moved away from Gloucestershire and established myself in a new life by the sea. Two of Sheila's self-portraits greet me when I climb the stairs of my new home, but I'm free to do as I please and no longer feel responsible for her wellbeing.

TT October 2025

Acknowledgements

I would like to thank the following people for the assistance and encouragement they gave me while I was writing Sheila:

Tomris Atabey, Jane Carey, Rob Collins, Patricia Digby, Penelope Dimond, Kylie Fitzpatrick, Rhiannon Flood McGaw, Claudia Lank, Rachel Lathan, Jaen Loftin, Janine Mather, Sara Robertson-Jonas, Anne Robin, Ian Sherwood, Nikki Siegen Smith, Joan Spiekermann, Sophie Temple Muir, Anna Thornhill, Chris Wheeler and Catherine Wilson.

Sheila: Portrait of an Unknown Artist
can be purchased via the QR code or by using this link:
tinyurl.com/Buy-Sheila

Sheila Denning's paintings can be seen at
www.sheiladenning.com

Information about Teresa Thornhill's
other books can be found at
www.teresathornhill.com